U31

BUSINESS PROCESSES

BUSINESS PROCESSES

MODELLING AND ANALYSIS FOR
RE-ENGINEERING AND IMPROVEMENT

Martyn A. Ould

Quality and Technical Director, Praxis plc, Bath, UK

JOHN WILEY & SONS

Chichester • New York • Brisbane • Toronto • Singapore

PO 6214

First published 1995 by John Wiley & Sons Ltd,
Baffins Lane, Chichester
West Sussex PO19 1UD, England

National   01243 779777
International   (+44) 1243 779777

Other Wiley Editorial Offices

John Wiley & Sons, Inc., 605 Third Avenue,
New York, NY 10158-0012, USA

Jacaranda Wiley Ltd, 33 Park Road, Milton,
Queensland 4064, Australia

John Wiley & Sons (Canada) Ltd, 22 Worcester Road,
Rexdale, Ontario M9W 1L1, Canada

John Wiley & Sons (SEA) Pte Ltd, 37 Jalan Pemimpin #05-04,
Block B, Union Industrial Building, Singapore 2057

Library of Congress Cataloging-in-Publication Data

Ould, M. A. (Martyn A.), 1948—
    Business processes : modelling and analysis for re-engineering and
    improvement / Martyn A. Ould
        p. cm.
    Includes index.
    ISBN 0-471-95352-0 (cloth)
    1. Reengineering (Management) 2. Systems analysis. I. Title
HD58.87.095 1995
658.4'063—dc20   95–3608
                                                          CIP

British Library Cataloguing in Publication Data

A catalogue record for this book is available from the British Library

ISBN 0-471-95352-0

The text is set in 10/12pt Palatino by the author.
Printed and bound in Great Britain by Bookcraft (Bath) Ltd.

CONTENTS

PREFACE   vii

1   THE PROCESS MODELLER'S NEEDS   1

2   BASIC CONCEPTS IN PROCESS MODELLING   29

3   MODELLING WITH RADS   42

4   ANIMATING A PROCESS MODEL   69

5   MICRO-MODELLING OF PROCESSES   75

6   MODELLING LARGE PROCESSES   93

7   PROCESS PATTERNS   124

8   MODELLING THE MATERIALS IN THE PROCESS   138

9   ANALYSING A PROCESS MODEL   150

10   MANAGING THE MODELLING   182

11   EPILOGUE   210

INDEX   212

PREFACE

This book arises from work done since 1986 at Praxis on the modelling and analysis of business processes, work that had its roots in research[1] undertaken into the modelling of the software development process. With the increased interest in the notion of *process* over recent years, we have developed the ideas, building on our experience with clients. The result is a method – STRIM® – for the elicitation, modelling, and analysis of business processes.

STRIM is about modelling organisational behaviour in a way that is revealing and communicative.

The sorts of process models that STRIM generates are designed to be of practical use in a number of situations, above all the re-engineering or re-design of business processes in a radical change or BPR context, and for improvement in an incremental change or TQM context. STRIM process models can also be used in ISO 9001 quality management systems as definitions of the way that a business wishes to do its business in order to deliver quality in its products or services. Finally they are the starting point for the development of process support systems based on workflow management and groupware products.

This book describes the method and gives examples of its use. It is intended for analysts who want to take a process-oriented view of a business or organisation, as well as people in an organisation wanting a way of thinking about how their business works. Those working in change management, information system strategy and implementation, process improvement, and quality management will derive benefit from using the method.

The method has now been used with a variety of organisations – amongst them financial institutions, leasing companies, computer manufacturers, government agencies, pharmaceutical companies, software product

---

[1] *Defining formal models of the software development process*, M A Ould & C Roberts, in *Software Engineering Environments*, ed P Brereton, Ellis Horwood, 1987

® STRIM is a registered mark of Praxis plc

manufacturers, and information service providers – for a variety of purposes, including the re-structuring of a business along process lines rather than functional lines, re-engineering of a sales and marketing function, assessment of the effect on a business of changes in regulatory requirements, analysis of usability problems of an installed IT system, and the evaluation of the "fit" of a proposed package with a business.

Experience with STRIM shows that its strength comes from several directions:

- Role Activity Diagrams – the principal notation of STRIM – are intuitively easy to read because they concentrate on people and on what people do, which makes them ideal for use by ordinary folk as well as analysts;

- STRIM allows the analyst to explore the relationship between the process and the organisation;

- Role Activity Diagrams (RADs) show the dynamics of a process – the responsibilities, the drivers and the parallelism that make it work – which makes them ideal for getting a real understanding of what goes on in the process;

- STRIM can be used at a variety of levels, from the way a business broadly conducts its business to how a small procedure operates, which makes it ideal for both broad-brush understanding and detailed work instructions;

- STRIM has sound theoretical underpinnings, which makes Role Activity Diagrams ideal for animation, analysis and execution.

In short, STRIM provides the analyst with the intellectual machinery for working with processes, as well as a nice way of drawing pictures.

As ever with a new area, many shoulders have been stood upon. My thanks go to Clive Roberts (once at Praxis and now running Co-Ordination Systems Limited) whose original idea it was to bring RADs and RML (Requirements Modeling Language) together to model the software engineering process, and who continues to provide insight into the topic; to Tim Huckvale with whom I have done a great deal of the process modelling consultancy and training that has contributed so much experience to this handbook; to other colleagues at Praxis including Ian Spalding and Barry Lupton; and perhaps most of all to the original creators of RADs and RML: Anatol Holt and Sol Greenspan respectively.

The story still unfolds: our own work with clients moves the theory and practice on a little further every day, particularly in the use of STRIM as a business analysis method that leads pretty much seamlessly into object-oriented approaches for computer system development, and as the analysis phase of a workflow system development method code-named *Basyl*. So this book is necessarily a snapshot. If you have any criticisms, comments, or contributions, please contact me at Praxis. My e-mail address is mao@praxis.co.uk.

Martyn Ould, Hinton Charterhouse, Bath, UK

1

THE PROCESS MODELLER'S NEEDS

THE NOTION OF "PROCESS"

Every organisation has a number of *processes* that it carries out in order to achieve its business objectives; for example

- handling orders for goods
- recruiting staff
- designing new products
- making investment decisions.

Each such process is some kind of activity within the organisation where people work together to achieve some desired outcome. For instance, in the above cases the outcomes might be

- to respond to a customer order by shipping the requested goods and invoicing the customer for payment
- to respond to the staffing needs of the organisation by engaging staff of the right type and capabilities on appropriate terms and conditions
- to answer a gap in the market place with a product that can be manufactured, marketed and sold profitably
- to decide how available funds will be allocated to financial instruments in order to realise gains of the right value at an acceptable level of risk.

We won't attempt a one-line definition of *process* straight off, but we will work around the concept a little first.

To start with, let me point out some of the essential features of a process as defined in this book. A process involves *activity*: people and/or machines *do* things. A process also generally involves more than one person or machine: a process is about *groups*; it concerns *collaborative* activity. And a process has a *goal*: it is intended to achieve something.

Organisations often have "procedures" which describe what is to be done in certain situations. For instance, there might be a procedure for claiming expenses, a procedure for claiming overtime, and a procedure for dealing with a customer complaint. We will see that such procedures might constitute processes: the purposeful activity of groups.

We can also characterise "process" by what it is not (in the context of this book at least). It is not the same as a "function", eg Personnel, Manufacturing, Finance, Goods Inwards, or Credit Control. These are parts of the organisation which have responsibilities, staff and resources; but they are not processes, though they might take part in processes. In fact, we shall see later that the relationship between processes and functions can be complex and indeed that the efficient operation of processes can be hindered by an organisation's structures. In a re-engineering context we will want to explore that relationship between the organisation and the process.

Types of processes

It is useful to divide business processes into the three broad types shown in figure 1-1:

— core processes

— support processes

— management processes.

(I've called these types "broad" because they are useful but not absolute: other categorisations are of course possible, but we shall see later that these allow us to work with business processes in a productive way.)

Figure 1-1 – The three types of business process

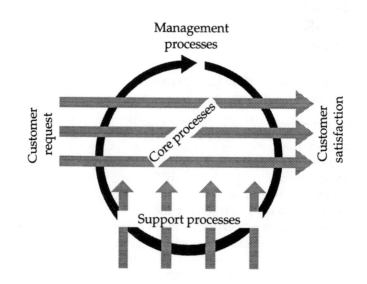

Core processes concentrate on satisfying external customers. They directly add value in a way perceived by the customer of the business. They respond to a customer request and generate customer satisfaction.

Support processes concentrate on satisfying internal customers. They might add value to the customer indirectly by supporting a core business process, or they might add value to the business directly by providing a suitable working environment.

Management processes concern themselves with managing the core processes or the support processes, or they concern themselves with planning at the business level.

WHY WORRY ABOUT PROCESSES?

There have been a number of "movements" in the 1980s and early 1990s that have made people recognise that they have processes, and that these processes are what the organisation is about. In each the central notion is that of *process* and consequently there is a need to be able to picture a process, through a *process model*. To understand the needs of the process modeller we must look at the various situations we might find ourselves in where process is important. We can readily identify the following six. They are not completely separate but it is useful to consider them separately for now. They are

- Situations where there is a need for a shared *understanding* of what the business does and how it does it.
- Situations where a *common approach* is to be adopted and perhaps mandated, for instance through a Quality Management System (QMS).
- *Incremental improvement* programmes, such as might be initiated under the banner of Total Quality Management (TQM).
- *Radical change* programmes, such as might be carried out using the principles and techniques of Business Process Re-engineering (BPR).
- Situations where the *alignment of information technology* (IT) systems with the needs of the business is being questioned.
- Situations where new forms of *process technology* such as workflow management systems and workgroup computing systems are to be applied to give active support to the business process.

Understanding your business

It has to be said that not every organisation recognises that it operates processes, even though it knows perfectly well how it is structured into functions and what each of those functions is responsible for. Whilst people might appreciate in some abstract way that the organisation can only work through their collaboration, they might individually have very little idea of how the collaboration actually works – they each do their bit, but how do the bits fit together? When we have modelled a process within an organisation, people will often remark "you know, I've never really thought of things in terms of a *process* that starts there and ends there". People know about what they do, who they depend on, and who they pass things on to. But they might well not be aware of the larger process in which they, along with many others, play a part.

Simply modelling the process can provide individuals and groups with a perspective on the organisation that transcends parochial views and, as a result, can promote a more collaborative spirit. "Now I know why you want that, I can make sure you get it reliably". We are interested in helping people to "get out of the functional silos".

A model that makes the process *visible* to the parties concerned can bring great value in itself.

Quality Management Systems

In Europe particularly, the emergence and development of the ISO 9000 series of standards has led to an increased concern with how an organisation goes about its business in a way that ensures quality in the products or services that it delivers to its customers. For instance, ISO 9001[1] sets a standard for a Quality Management System (QMS) used to support a design/development, production, installation, and servicing capability. Central to the standard is the notion that key processes should be defined in some way so that they are repeatable, measurable, and improvable. The details are unimportant here, but the message is: if you are concerned with ensuring the quality of your product or service, you must concern yourself with the processes that deliver that product or service.

Typically, therefore, an organisation will describe how its key processes are carried out in a way that

-   communicates the processes to those who must carry them out ("how should I do this piece of work?")

-   provides the opportunity for independent assessment of the organisation's conformance to the process it has laid down for itself ("are these people doing what they said they would do?")

-   acts as a basis for future improvement of the process ("we do this now, but how could we do it better?").

Such descriptions tend to be lodged in some form of Quality Manual and they can take many forms, typically some mixture of text and diagram. A good description – model – of a process will be one that *communicates* in sufficient detail to those that must carry it out, and that is *precise* enough to permit an assessment of conformance.

Incremental improvement

It has long been recognised in the disciplines of TQM that the cost-effectiveness and profitability of a process are determined by the quality of the goods or services it produces, and that quality is itself determined by the process as well

---

[1] ISO 9001: *Quality systems – assurance model for design/development, production, installation, and servicing capability*

as the inputs and the workers. In particular, if we want to reduce wastage (of materials, or resources, or time) we need to address the "common causes" (to use the jargon) of defects, and this means removing systemic errors, ie those introduced by the process itself.

To do this, we need a way of exploring at a detailed level just what happens between the customer making a request and the customer going away satisfied with the goods or services we have provided, and, within that flow, we need to understand where defects and/or unnecessary delays are introduced so that we can adjust the process to remove their cause. Central to that exploration is a model of the process.

The aim is that, bit by bit, we refine the process and gradually eradicate those systemic causes of poor quality: we are in the arena of incremental improvement.

Radical change

In the Business Process Re-engineering arena, incremental improvement is not enough. Here we are looking for major breakthroughs, an 80% reduction in cycle time not 10%, reducing staff levels to one-fifth not by one-fifth. And to do this we are prepared to make radical changes, not just tinkering with the fine detail of our processes but making major changes in our organisational structure, and questioning the very need for doing things the way we have done them for years, or even why we have those processes at all. We are prepared to ask questions like "can we operate without a central Purchasing Department?", or "is tendering the only way we can ensure the best price for bought-in goods and services?", or "what would happen if invoicing was done by the recipient of the goods rather than Accounts?".

In this context, detailed maps of our current processes are largely irrelevant. We've decided that we will only consider big changes – detail is simply not interesting. But broad-brush models of the way our business operates, of what processes we have and how they traverse the functional silos, could give us clues as to the sorts of radical change we might imagine.

And when we have decided how we want our new organisation to land when we have thrown the existing one in the air, we will need some way of designing the new processes, ensuring that they fit with those that survive and with each other, and that they make sense in our new flattened or process-oriented organisational structure.

Process design means, again, being able to model the process, this time the *new* process.

Alignment of IT systems with the business

I have worked with an IT department which had built a system designed to support the information needs of a particular group within the business. The system was designed to provide that group with a way of recording and tracking progress with the items they were processing in real-time. But at the time the system was designed no-one had recognised that the work of that function was inextricably linked with the work of another group who had their own IT system; the new system quite simply "clashed" with the process by which each work item was handled. As a result the users resorted to inputting information *once the process had finished*, and as a result the system failed to provide the real-time support which it had been intended to give.

Rightly or wrongly, past IT systems have often been considered to have been failures in that they have not brought the benefits to the business that were promised. I would assert that this has been for one simple reason: the starting assumption in the minds of those that build IT systems (and I have been amongst them) has been that data and information are central: that if we start with an analysis of the information needs of the individual in the business process we will build a system that supports the business effectively. Unfortunately, this ignores one important feature of businesses: they do not work simply by ensuring individuals have information at their finger-tips; they work by having processes in which groups collaborate effectively. I would assert that good IT follows firstly from an understanding of the way that the business does its business, and only then from an understanding of the information that the business needs because of the way it chooses to do its business. Process precedes information.

Once I have decided how I will do my business – my process – I can decide the information needs that are generated and hence the systems I need to support them.

Building process support systems

In recent years, a new class of software infrastructure products has emerged: *workflow management systems*. These provide active support to a business process by controlling the flow of work items around the organisation automatically, routing each work item and its supporting information and (electronic) documents and images from person to person in the process, from workstation to workstation.

Such systems clearly need some model of the process, a model that describes the flow from role to role, the decisions, the alternative paths, the concurrent activity on the work item, exception handling, escalation paths, and so on. We shall look at such systems in more detail later in this chapter, but suffice it to say here that, once again, we can see the need to be able to model a process in terms of roles, activities, decisions and flows from role to role (what we will generally refer to as *interactions*).

STRIM – A SYSTEMATIC TECHNIQUE FOR ROLE & INTERACTION MODELLING

For whatever reason we have started to take an interest in our processes, we will need some way to record and analyse them. And to discuss something, we must have a language with which to describe it and talk about it. This is where STRIM comes in.

STRIM is an approach to the elicitation, modelling and analysis of organisational processes. The *method* for modelling and analysis uses *three languages* with which a process is described. This book describes the method and the main notation.

Two diagrammatic languages are used to capture the results of the elicitation: one that concentrates on the process – *Role Activity Diagrams* (RADs) – and one that concentrates on the business entities involved – traditional entity models. The STRIM analyst might also use a textual language – *SPML* – to describe the organisation's process in a form that has well defined semantics that facilitate consistency checking and enactment.

The method includes techniques for both qualitative and quantitative analysis of the process once a model has been produced; this is an important feature when the technique is being used as part of a business process re-engineering or restructuring activity. In any process modelling method we will want to find more than a notation, more than a way of drawing pictures: we will want to find "intellectual machinery" that helps us to think about our processes.

But before we look at the method and notations themselves we need to examine in a little more detail our motivations in modelling processes, and in particular the sorts of things we will be interested in capturing in the model.

DESCRIBING, ANALYSING, ENACTING

A recurrent theme in this book is the idea that the way a process model looks will largely be determined by the perspectives we choose to take, which in turn are determined by the reasons we have for modelling in the first place. We have seen above that there are a number of reasons for taking a process-oriented view of our organisation, and that we have many reasons now for modelling the processes within it.

Taking a different perspective, Mark Greenwood[2] has a useful categorisation of reasons for modelling:

– to describe a process
– to analyse a process
– to enact a process.

I now outline these individually, leaving extended discussion to later chapters.

Modelling to describe a process

This is what we do when we want, amongst other things,

– to define a process ("this is how we shall together handle customer complaints"),
– to communicate it to others ("this is how your work contributes to the department's goals"),

---

[2] *Process terminology – a software engineering perspective*, R M Greenwood, in *IOPener*, **2**, 1, pp7-9, Praxis plc, Bath, UK, August 1993

- to share it across a group of people ("so, this is how we do things round here"),
- to negotiate around it ("if you could do this, my life would be made much easier; in return I can ...").

If, for example, a group is seeking ISO 9001 certification for its Quality Management System it will want to define its processes in its Quality Manual. A descriptive process model – in some form – will therefore be found in such a Manual. In a sense, it acts as a work instruction to people in the organisation. Text is very often used to describe how things are done, but it is hard in the serial nature of text to describe something that has possibly many threads, decisions, concurrent activities and so on. A diagram is a traditional way of dealing with this. In Praxis a number of our processes are described in our Quality Manual in the form of Role Activity Diagrams. Those diagrams tell people what is expected of them when carrying out the processes; in particular we specify in quite considerable detail the key business processes of planning and reporting projects, of bidding for new contracts, and purchasing – all processes which have an important and direct financial interest to the company and which we therefore want to ensure some degree of conformance to.

I have worked with one group of managers in a multinational product company who wanted to define a planning process that they would use, involving their management and other corporate functions such as "HQ", "Finance" and "Auditors". They already had a process in place but it was not well articulated and they were fairly certain that they did not all have the same view of the process. The process was that of deciding on the portfolio of products in which they would fund investment, and the process of developing a new product within that overall planning process. They already had a short verbal description of the proposed process and we used the methods described in this book to capture those processes completely. In addition to giving them greater understanding through the analysis, the method gave them a clear diagram of the two processes, a diagram which then went into their Procedures Manual. It also filled in many gaps in the textual description which only became apparent when the process was explored pictorially.

Modelling to analyse a process

Once we have a model of a process, we may well want to use the model to explore the properties of the process itself. Some of the questions we will want to ask will be quantitative: "what is the average cycle time?", "how much will the cycle time be affected by changing the process in such-and-such a way?", "where are the bottlenecks?", "can this process deadlock?". Other questions will be qualitative: "do we have the optimum division of tasks across the people involved?", "why does this paperwork flow back and forth?", "are the right decisions being made at the right level in the organisation?".

Such analysis is a common precursor to improving the organisation by:

- changing the ordering of activities
- changing responsibilities for activities or decisions

- changing scheduling mechanisms
- increasing or decreasing the amount of parallel activity
- removing (or inserting) buffers or stores for materials between steps in a process
- restructuring functions to align them better with the process
- and so on.

Any organisation involved in TQM or other process improvement activity will want to model its key processes and analyse them for weaknesses or inefficiencies on paper, before trying out improvements in real-life.

Modelling to enact a process

Traditionally, when computer support has been considered for supporting the activity of an organisation, some form of analysis of the organisation has been carried out in order to identify where automation could best be applied. Since the mid-1970s that analysis has concentrated on data, and into the 1990s data analysis has been the cornerstone of process modelling: data-flow analysis, entity modelling, and entity life-history modelling in particular have featured large. Not for nothing have we talked about *Information* Technology – IT.

Figure 1-2 – Data-oriented system architecture

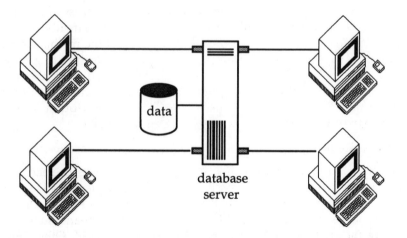

But the resulting information systems have for the most part had a very simple architecture, as suggested in figure 1-2. In essence, they simply provide the individual with a peek'n'poke facility into some central database – most importantly *they only give explicit support to the individual*. Each individual is connected to the data, as the figure suggests. But organisational processes are not just collections of individuals operating independently, as such an architecture might suggest. Organisational processes are carried out by groups of people acting collaboratively to achieve a goal. If our computer systems are to reflect this they must support groups more directly. In recent years, tools and packages have been appearing under the titles *workflow management* (WFM) and *workgroup computing* (WGC). Their architecture recognises that people who connect to the system are working together *and interacting*, and so that architecture must above all support interaction.

Now, traditional data-oriented systems analysis and design have served us perfectly well when we build data-oriented systems supporting individuals. But the new WFM products require new analysis and design methods. Data-oriented analysis methods provided us with various sorts of data model. WFM products need process-oriented methods providing us with process models. We might say that "as Yourdon is to data support systems, so STRIM is to process support systems".

STRIM is the new method in the world of PT: *Process* Technology.

We can go one step further. Given a data model, it is possible to store this in a database and use it directly to generate forms and reports that the individual can use to add, amend or present data. In essence, the data model can be "executed". This is the basis of automatic application generators. What is the analogue for process models? Clearly we would like to be able to give a computer system our process model and have it *enact* that model, ie "run" the model, supporting the participants in the process as the process proceeds, handling their agendas, supporting their interactions, and perhaps playing its own part in the process. Systems that provide this sort of support are termed *enactment systems* and they provide us with the third motive for process modelling: they require a process model whose "meaning" is sufficiently well defined to allow them to enact the process without further human intervention to define it. This use of process models has important implications for the process modelling method and its notations, and so I explore this further here, starting with a little history.

The original work on which STRIM was subsequently based was done as part of the *IPSE 2.5* project within the UK *Alvey Programme* in 1986. The task that Clive Roberts and I undertook for ICL (to whom Praxis were subcontracted) was to develop a language which, firstly, could be used to describe the software engineering process, and, secondly, was defined to a point where a process model written in that language could be given to a computer system which would the "enact" the process, thereby supporting the group who would collectively carry it out. The solution we developed[3] was a combination of Anatol Holt's Role Activity Diagrams[4] to which we made small adaptations,

---

[3] *Defining formal models of the software development process*, M A Ould & C Roberts, in *Software Engineering Environments*, ed P Brereton, Ellis Horwood, 1987

[4] *Coordination system technology as the basis for a programming environment*, A W Holt, H R Ramsey & J D Grimes, *Electrical Communication*, **57**, 4, pp307-314, 1983

and Sol Greenspan's Requirements Modeling Language[5] (RML) from which we developed the *STRIM Process Modelling Language* (SPML) essentially by adding the notion of *role*.

To the everyday user of STRIM, the presence of SPML is not important. But to the analyst and to those interested in building enactment systems, automatic generators, or simulation systems, the presence of a formal language with full semantics, underpinning RADs, is vital. Without those semantics we cannot say unambiguously what a given RAD means, and hence cannot "execute" it in any way. When Clive Roberts and I developed SPML we had to provide formal semantics for the language so that in principle at least it was executable. (There were other difficult technical problems such as the need to cater for on-the-fly changes of the process, but these do not concern us here.) We also defined a number of transformation rules which allowed one to write an SPML version of a RAD; this meant that a RAD had strong semantics itself – a powerful feature for a notation which is intended to be used in the analysis of processes to be supported with WFM or groupware architectures and toolsets, and it is this feature that is important in the area of modelling to enact a process. Holt himself describes the application of his Role/Activity Theory to *coordination systems* for software programming environments whose conceptual model is based around what programmers as a group *do*, rather than around the data they operate on.

Figure 1-3 – Process-oriented system architecture

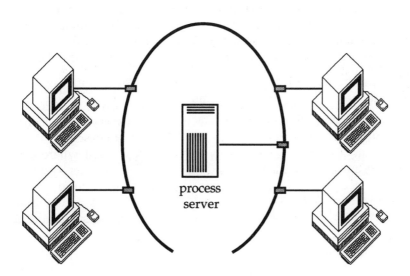

process
server

[5] *Requirements modeling: a knowledge representation approach to software requirements definition*, Sol Greenspan, Technical Report CSRG-15, Computer Systems Research Group, University of Toronto, 1985

These areas of workflow management and workgroup computing have a real need for some way of thinking about and describing a process. Whilst we might still have a system which physically consists of user workstations networked to some form of process server (figure 1-3), the logical architecture is radically different: rather than only providing peek'n'poke data access to each individual, the system now sees the individuals as collaborators in a process, a model of which sits in some form on the process server. As the individuals act and the system contributes, so individuals influence each other's activity as determined by the process model.

If we plan to implement a workflow system using a workflow management software product then we had better be confident that the workflow we plan to support with the system is a good one in the first place, and that, before we start to build it, we have a clear statement of what the process to be supported is. The first of these issues is the BPR or TQM issue: just what should the process be? If we simply automate the process as it currently stands – historical, encrusted with work-arounds, out of tune with best practice – we would be "paving cow paths", setting in concrete an inappropriate process. I address the area of the use of STRIM in a BPR context in chapter 9. The second issue is one of having the right languages with which to design the workflow system, and this is the subject matter of Praxis' approach to the development of workflow systems, *Basyl*, a brief outline of which is given in chapter 10.

In summary, in any given situation, the three motives of description, analysis and enactment can be mixed up in varying quantities, so we would like our modelling method and notations to give us a handle on all of them to some useful degree. STRIM and its notations give that handle.

WHAT HAPPENS IN REAL-WORLD PROCESSES?

To understand what STRIM does it is proper to start by asking "what sort of things happen in real-world processes?", ie "what sorts of things do we want to be able to model?". There are five key things:

1   What the organisation is trying to achieve with the process: the business *goals* for the process.

2   What constraints the organisation puts on what people can do and how they should operate: the business *rules*.

3   What individuals *do* to achieve the goals.

4   How processes are divided over *roles*.

5   How individuals within groups *interact* to work collaboratively in order to get the job done.

We now take each of these in turn.

The process has *goals*

For instance, the goal of a process might be to deliver computer systems, to maintain positive cash flow, to provide a medical care service to its customers, or to manage a research budget. It must be possible to see from our process models, how a process is achieving the goals set for it, and ideally to be able to identify the point(s) in the process where those goals can be said to have been achieved or maintained. We can identify two types of goal: steady-state and point-wise.

Steady-state goals

When I run my life in financial terms, one of my aims is to regulate my earning and spending so as to keep my bank balance in credit. At any time I want the bank to be looking after my money rather than the other way round.

The critical point is the "at any time". I want to see a steady state in which I am in credit.

This is a common type of goal in organisations. The process of managing cash flow in a company has the same goal: that of maintaining a steady state in which the company keeps a positive cash flow as expenditure and earnings rise and fall. If the process is successful we should be able to observe the company at any time and note a positive cash flow.

Point-wise goals

Perhaps more often a process *works towards* the achievement of an goal, rather than trying to maintain a certain state. The goal of an insurance company in its New Policy Applications Department might be to respond to a customer with a proposal within seven days of receipt of their application. Each step in the process can contribute to the successful achievement of that "point-wise" goal: there comes a point when we can say "here the goal of the process has been achieved". The goal of the process of carrying out a software development project for a client is to satisfy the client with a timely delivery of working software. The only point at which we can check whether we have been successful is the point of delivery: is it on time and does it work? Until that point we can only make predictions.

Any given process might have several goals: the New Policy Applications Department in a life insurance company wants to get a correct policy proposal out within seven days of receipt of the application; it might also want to ensure that the business it takes on is good business, ie that the premiums it charges adequately cover the risk (a steady-state goal); and it might also have the goal of making the terms offered available to those assessing the competitiveness of the company's products (another point-wise goal).

On the way towards achieving a "final" goal, we can often identify "sub-goals" which represent milestones of some sort. Issuing the proposal to the customer requires that, at some point en route, the risk be satisfactorily assessed and that approval be obtained for the final assessed premium.

In our process model we will want to be able to model goals and sub-goals.

The business runs according to *rules*

The *activities* in an organisational process are carried out according to a particular logic when the process "runs", that logic being what the "business rules" are all about. Business rules are the way that activity in the organisation is constrained. These rules can take a number of forms:

- *Policy*. A company might have a policy of out-sourcing the management of its computer facilities, or that nobody can approve their own work, or that all product tests must be carried out by someone independent of the production group.

- *Procedures*. Many organisational activities are regulated and defined in the form of procedures. For example, in Praxis there are closely defined procedures for planning projects, reporting project status, and purchasing. These procedures are there because the company wishes to control commitment – especially financial commitment – closely.

  Procedures can also exist to make interfaces efficient: all requests for training follow the same procedure so that people requesting training do not need to invent how to make a request, and the people handling requests know in what form they will arrive.

- *Standards*. Standards are often laid down to define a common appearance or layout for something produced during the process. In Praxis, project plans and reports conform to a standard layout. The reasons for such standardisation are again twofold: efficiency – everyone knows what a report looks like and where to find the information they are interested in – and control – we want to ensure that certain topics always get covered and certain information is always included.

- *Responsibility levels, authorisation and delegation mechanisms*. These prescribe who can do what and how they are empowered. Standard procedures will often involve such mechanisms: who can sign off purchases above what value, who can authorise a change in production schedules, who can cancel a project, who can delegate what to whom.

All these are rules that govern "how things get done around here", and we need to be able to capture them in our process models.

Individuals *do* things to achieve goals

When individuals do their work they carry out value-adding, productive activities. For instance, in the business of getting a book published, various people write the book, prepare the index, draw the diagrams, check the copy, set the type, print the book, and get it to the shops. Each of these activities does something in a way that we hope adds value and contributes to the business of achieving the goals of the process. We must be able to model this variety of activity.

Processes are divided over *roles*

A role involves a *set* of actions that are generally carried out by an individual or group within the organisation. Moreover, a role includes the logic that controls the actions. The actions are *all those necessary to carry out some area or areas of responsibility*. I say "or areas" because a role might be defined to have several areas of responsibility.

So, in the process of getting a book published, there are roles such as the author, the publisher's editor and the bookseller. Within the role, those activities are carried out according to a particular logic: we do things in certain orders, we decide to do this rather than that in certain situations, and sometimes we can do things in parallel. By predicting the target market place, the publisher will decide whether the book will come out first in hardback or paperback and the process thereafter will be different in the two cases. The designer will decide on typographical issues such as layout and typeface. The printer will print the pages and bind the books, ready for the retailer to sell to the public.

A whole set of roles are involved in the process, each carrying out its activities, making its decisions, and getting on with any number of streams of work at the same time, all in pursuit of carrying out its responsibility.

Within Praxis, an important role is that of *managing a project*. Within the role there are many activities that need to be done: planning, reporting, monitoring, managing staff, liaising with suppliers, working with the client, and so on. The role would be *acted* by one person at a time, a person who is given the title *Project Manager*. The role of managing project *P0289* could be acted by me today, and by another person tomorrow. The role is separate from the people who act it.

A role could be carried out by a group. The work of a whole Praxis Division for instance is concerned with the process of *doing projects*. If we were modelling how Praxis worked in a broad-brush way we might identify the Division as one role with that as its responsibility, even though a whole group of people were involved in acting the role and, indeed, that group changes in time as people come and go.

Finally, a role has resources necessary to do its activities. Those resources might reside permanently with the role (the Project Manager has a set of plans), or be passed into the "role body" (the Project Manager receives terms of reference for the project they are to manage).

The role is one of the most important concepts in STRIM process modelling, and it deserves a fuller analysis later. Roles are central to understanding a process, and especially its relationship to the organisation. Roles must feature strongly in our process models.

Individuals within a group *interact*

We have already observed that people do not only operate as independent individuals – they interact: project managers liaise with suppliers, manage staff, and report to senior management; authors and publishers agree on the contract, and the designer and editor agree on the layout.

Processes invariably involve the collaboration of a number of individuals or groups, and that collaboration takes place through many sorts of *interaction*, such as

- I pass you some information
- I delegate a task to you
- I give you authority to do something
- We agree on an action

- We jointly approve something
- You report your status to me
- You pass me the results of your work
- I wait for you to do something
- I chase the progress of your work.

All of these are just as vital to the smooth running of the process as the activities that individual roles carry out on their own. A process is the sum of the contributions of the individuals acting as individuals and collaborating as a group.

So individuals may wait, collect, check, organise, monitor, chase, interact, distribute, identify, re-organise, report, plan, create routines, and so on: a multiplicity of apparently "non-productive" activities which, it is to be hoped, further the process they are part of. Management activity is particularly composed of such activities carried out to organise or facilitate a process. For instance, in the business of getting a book published, my editor manages the process by agreeing production schedules, ensuring I deliver the copy on time, making sure that the marketing people have information with which to publicise the book, and so on – all interactions with other roles to facilitate the process. Meanwhile, the editor and I agree on the medium I will use to prepare the copy and this will subsequently determine the activities of the production department: re-keying from a printed typescript, translating from an obscure word-processing package, or printing bromides directly from the electronic form I provide. The book designer will agree the layout and typeface with the editor and house designer.

So, in summary, to model a process comprehensively we want be able to model goals, rules, activities, roles and interactions. These are the principal concepts in the modelling languages of STRIM.

THE PLACE OF INFORMATION AND ENTITIES IN PROCESS MODELLING

At this point, one might well ask "why is *data* or *information* not in this list of concepts?". The simple answer is that in our approach to process modelling we concentrate unashamedly on what people *do*, rather than on what people do it with. Once we have chosen an organisational structure and the processes it will operate, then we can decide on the information needed by individuals and groups to perform those processes in that organisational structure.

Process precedes information.

That said, it can be very useful during a process modelling exercise to examine what I shall call the "essential business entities". These are things that are the central subject matter of the business, irrespective almost of the way the business does business. To a car manufacturer, cars are essential business entities, but Invoice Forms are not – they can't get away from cars, but Invoice Forms are not essential, they are just an implementation mechanism for demanding money from customers. To an invoicing department, invoices are an essential business entity, but Leave Request Forms are not; the first are the central subject matter of that group, the second are not.

Given a process model – a description of how the business does its business or plans to do its business – we can start to investigate the information needs of the process: who needs what information to do that, or to make that decision? And how does that information get to that person?

WHEN IS A PROCESS MODEL "COMPLETE"?

If we examine an island such as Jersey or Manhattan to answer the apparently simple question "how long is its coastline?", we come up against a problem. If there is a road around the island we could measure its length and decide that that is the length of the coastline. But the road doesn't trace round each inlet (there might be a bridge over it), or round each promontory (it cuts across the base). To get a "more accurate" measurement we might decide to walk around the coastline with a pedometer, walking into each inlet and around each promontory along the coastal path. We will get a greater distance than we obtained from the length of the coastal road. To get a yet "more accurate" figure we might decide – having much spare time – to run a tape-measure along the edge of the water as we pace the coastal path. We will obtain a yet larger distance. And so on.

This is a good metaphor for processes. There is always more detail if you want to look for it. Whether the detail is useful and justifies the expense of collection, only the process modeller can determine – there is no simple rule that can tell you "you have finished!". Completeness is in the eye of the modeller.

The problem is highlighted when the process is being investigated, for instance through sessions with groups of "process actors". Just how much detail is it worth getting into with them? I address this important question in chapter 10.

WHEN IS A PROCESS MODEL "RIGHT"?

In fact things are worse. *There is no single viewpoint of a process.* In other words, *there is no single model of a process.* Our viewpoint will vary as our motives vary. If we are interested in why a process seems to bottleneck in certain areas we will want to model the process from the point of view of how work is allocated to individuals. If we are interested in how the functional subdivisions of the organisation impede or facilitate the flow of a transaction through a process that crosses the functional boundaries we will want to view the process in terms of those boundaries and the interactions across them, without worrying too much about *how* each function does its work.

There are as many models of a single process as there are viewpoints that we might want to take. The perspective taken, what is left in and what is not – all these decisions rest on the judgement of the modeller. Again, no simple rule will say what perspective should be taken in any given situation, though in chapter 10 I present some guidelines to the modeller. This is a point that I shall return to many times in the book. Relevance is in the eye of the modeller, too. A model is "right" if it helps. It helps if it *reveals* things we want to know, or can be analysed quantitatively to predict outcomes, or can be adjusted to test proposed changes, or simply aids understanding. We shall see in chapter 10 that the most important thing at the start of a modelling activity is to be clear about the *purpose* of the model. The model itself cannot do anything – it is a tool that will work well in the right hands in the right situation, and badly otherwise.

Indeed, we might take several perspectives corresponding to the different perceived purposes of the process we are looking at. In our work for a pharmaceutical company, Tim Huckvale and I initially prepared two models of the same process, essentially seeing the same process from two perspectives: one from that of the scientists doing the science necessary to take a new drug compound to market, another from that of the management pushing the development of the compound through the various stages of process scale-up and trials whilst weeding out those compounds that do not offer future success. In *Soft Systems* terms[6], these views could be considered to be *holons* which we "put against the world" in order to learn about it. Each corresponds to a different idea of the purpose of the process (/system). The Research Chemist might see the purpose of the process to be to produce a way of making the drug compound safely in the required quantities and to the required purity; the Regulatory Affairs Group might see its purpose to be the production of the information and audit trail of development which will satisfy the industry regulators; the Clinician will see its purpose to be the timely production of sufficient quantities of drug for the clinical trials they are planning; the senior management will see the purpose to be either to get a successful-looking compound to manufacturing as quickly as possible or to drop an unsuccessful-looking compound as early as possible; and so on.

If we think of a model as a sort of map which tells us about the terrain we are interested in we can see some useful parallels perhaps. If I walk into a map store and ask for a map, I'll probably be asked "what do you want the map for?". I could have a number of reasons:

1   To walk from Paddington railway station to Victoria railway station in London. I need a route map to help me find my way around. In particular, it will need to be a fairly detailed map as I am interested in being able to trace my steps through London's winding and narrow streets. I shall need street names but won't need to know if streets are one-way.

2   To drive from Bath to Birmingham. Again I am looking for help in finding my way around, but now I shall need a map on a different scale: one that shows me the broad shape of the country and the major roads will do. I won't need anything showing country lanes or small villages or the local topography of the countryside I shall be passing through.

[6] *Soft Systems Methodology in action*, P Checkland & J Scholes, Wiley, 1990; *Practical Soft Systems Analysis*, D Patching, Pitman Publishing, 1990

3   To allow me to agree with someone on a spot in London where we will meet. In this case my reason for needing a map involves someone else: we will use the map as an agreed definition of something, we can agree on where we will meet in a pre-defined surrounding.

4   To agree on a boundary to be drawn on the sale of some land. Here, we want to define something not already defined, and to place it in some larger context.

5   To decide where to move an existing footpath. In England, a footpath may well go back many centuries; its end-points and its route will have been determined by needs from the past. Changes in surroundings might make moving it sensible. We need to know what the options are.

6   To decide where to route a new road. If I am planning a completely new road from *A* to *B* I shall need to explore the options and the impact that each will have on things that I want untouched. I want a map that shows topography to a level of detail that allows exploration of impact.

7   To record the position of underground cables. Here, as a cable company say, I shall be maintaining my own maps of where my cables run relative to the infrastructure of the town. I need these maps to allow my staff to find the cables in the future.

The parallels between maps and process models are clear. Before we carry out some process modelling we will need to know quite clearly what sort of information we shall want from the model so that we can choose the scale it is at, and the sorts of detail it shows. In subsequent chapters we will explore the sorts of model that can be drawn and in chapter 10 we will relate those styles of model back to the different reasons we have for modelling.

EIGHT LAWS FOR PROCESS MODELLING[7]

To finish this chapter let me try to capture some general needs of the process modeller in eight laws:

1   If you must have abstractions, make them concrete abstractions. Any process modelling notation must deal in concepts that people relate to. Otherwise how can they tell if a model's right?

2   The real world is messy. The notation must be able to model mess when necessary. Muddle modelling is the norm, not the exception.

3   A model must mean something and only one thing. If your model is ambiguous, how can you tell what it is telling you?

4   Process models are about people, and for people. The notation must make sense to people. If you can't explain the model in ten minutes, it doesn't make sense.

---

[7] This section first appeared in a similar form in *IOPener*, **2**, 4, Praxis plc, July 1994

5   There's what people actually do. And there's what they effectively do. These are different and we must be able to model both.

6   People do processes, but they work in functions. These two mess each other up. A model must capture both – and the conflict.

7   It's what people do, not what they do it to, that counts. A process is about doing, deciding, and cooperating. Not about data.

8   There are some basic business patterns like the processing of a unit of work, plans, delegation, periodic activity, and contracts. We want to be able to capture them in our models.

Some words of explanation.

Law 1: If you must have abstractions, make them concrete abstractions

When we model something we describe it, and to describe something we need a language. A model uses a limited language – a limited number of concepts – that allows us to say the things we want to say, to describe the things we want to describe. Take the following example. If we want to model a nation's economy we might capture it in terms of the flow of money between the various places it can reside: the Treasury, people's savings, money in circulation, investment instruments of various sorts, and so on. We would be working with two abstract concepts: the "stock", of which each of those residences is an example; and a "flow" – the movement of money between two stocks. By varying the rates of flow we can investigate the behaviour of the model and perhaps deduce something about the behaviour of the real economy. (An early economic model used precisely these abstractions, and made them concrete by using plastic containers of water to represent stocks, and piping and pumps between containers to represent flows. The stocks and flows were represented as plumbing, and money by water.)

When we model processes – what people do – we will need a small number of abstractions that represent real-world things, but they must be concrete enough for someone looking at our model to readily understand the model and what it is telling them.

Law 2: The real world is messy

At a suitably high level of abstraction, any process can be made to look neat and tidy. Figure 1-4 summarises the process of collecting taxes from you and me and giving them to the government to spend. Tidy isn't it? So how is it that tax collection causes so much grief and there is so much money to be made out of helping people with their tax affairs? The fact is of course that the tax collection process is complex and involved. A summary diagram like the above hides all that – and can make it next to useless if we want to improve the process or support it with a workflow management system. On the plus side, it summarises what tax collection is about: namely that there is some relationship between The People and The Government that involves The Tax Collector.

So we'll decide to "decompose" this neat picture, but still keep it neat by ensuring that we restrict the number of boxes on the diagram to, say, no more than seven. After all, someone did once say that people have trouble with handling more than seven items of information at any one time. And, if we want to, we'll allow ourselves to "decompose" any one of those boxes in turn onto its own diagram with another seven-ish boxes to describe it; and so on. Standing back from this, we seem to be saying that our process model can take the form of a hierarchy, consisting of a set of diagrams, each of which (with the exception of the topmost one) expands a single box on its "parent" diagram.

Figure 1-4 – Tax collection: pure simplicity

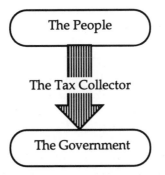

So the model has the sort of form shown in figure 1-5. A neat hierarchical model. Question: if this is a good model, then it must be "like" the real world it claims to model – is it? In particular, the structure of the process in the model must reflect the structure of the process in the real world. So when we look at the world, do we find neatly ordered processes, with each activity in a process neatly decomposable?

Figure 1-5 – Are the world's processes really this neat and tidy?

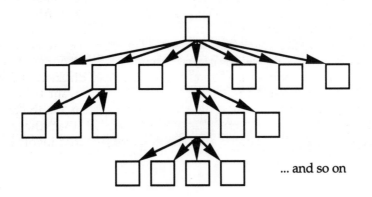

... and so on

Our experience says "no, we don't". Real real-world processes, as they happen, are complex, gangling, even muddled or messy (these are not my words – they are words frequently used by the people whose processes I model). They wander here, there and everywhere; the hierarchical picture fails to show that: it replaces convolution by neat (but irrelevant) hierarchy. Our processes might have been neat and tidy when they started life, but over time, what with one thing and another, they've become messy. In fact the whole reason we want to re-engineer them could be that they've become messy and inappropriate.

The message for our process modelling approach is that we cannot let the notation dictate to us that our models must be neat hierarchies (or indeed any other pre-defined structure). In a very few instances a process will indeed be a neat hierarchy, but more often than not we will be modelling muddle and our notation must give us the means of handling that. More: our approach must give us the means of "summarising" or "collapsing" a model in a way that hides detail but does not model what is not there.

Unfortunately the IT world has for years been using hierarchies as a way of designing synthetic things like computer programs, and software structures of all kinds. The great mistake has been to assume that we can use such hierarchic notions to describe *organic* things like businesses. But businesses are not the product of tidy design activities over which the designer has had full control. They are the product of time and many uncoordinated changes by many hands. Traditional structured approaches from the IT world just won't work.

Law 3: A model must mean something and only one thing

What does figure 1-4 mean to you? What do the two boxes mean? What does the arrow mean? And what do the names on the boxes and arrows add? "Money" doesn't appear anywhere in the picture but that probably didn't bother you; you took it as read and assumed it was what the arrow represented. But the arrow could mean "Paperwork". Suppose we accept that the arrow represents money flowing from The People to The Government. Can we assume from the single head on the arrow that the money only flows one way? In fact it doesn't. I recently got a tax rebate. Would having a two-headed arrow be more accurate? Let us assume that, because the arrow has the label "The Tax Collector", The Tax Collector is the agent for the flow, what makes it happen on behalf of The Government. Would that mean then that the Tax Collector sometimes makes the flow go from The Government to The People? Does the Tax Collector act as your agent for giving money to you?

It was such a simple diagram – two boxes and an arrow – but there seem to be a host of questions without definite answers. And the reason for that is that I have no clear meaning for the symbols I've used in the diagram. "A picture says a thousand words" – a different thousand words to each of us, unless we agree on the *semantics* of our notation. If I can't tell what my process model means, I can't tell what needs doing. When I choose a notation for my models, I need to be sure that I have clear semantics for them: I know what a box means, I know what a line means, I know what each little symbol means. The process is unambiguously defined.

Law 4: Process models are about people, and for people

When we model a process we are describing what people do. (Of course, machines of various sorts might play a part in a process, but they don't have to be asked their opinion so I can restrict my concerns to the people.) To find out what people do I'll need to ask them and watch them: "process elicitation". As a minimum I shall want to put my model of their process in front of them and have them discuss it, correct it and improve it. My preference will be to get them to do the modelling with my help. I'd like them to develop the model and to use the model themselves to re-engineer the process.

I can now put laws 2 and 3 together and define law 4: the concepts I use in my model must be concepts people relate to in daily life, and their meaning must be clearly defined. The notation must make sense to people. If you can't explain it in ten minutes, it doesn't make sense.

Of course, any well founded notation will have subtleties and potential complexities, and the use of these will only come with experience. But a newcomer to a model must be able to understand quickly what the model is saying. If the model needs extensive interpretation by a skilled analyst before it can be understood by the person on the shop-floor the battle is half-lost. People need to "own" the model of their process. The acid test is this: at their first modelling session, can an ordinary person go to the whiteboard and correct a mistake in the model so that it correctly describes what happens?

Law 5: There's what people actually do. And there's what they effectively do

When the Accounts Department raises an invoice against a customer's order, what they are *effectively* doing is extracting payment for the goods or services supplied. What they *actually* do is involve themselves and others in a paper-chase, in which the flow of paper is further embellished with activities of transcription, checking, updating, copying, chasing, phoning, ...

When we look at a process as-is, we see what people actually do, and one of our models might be of this as-is actual process. But, when we want to understand how the process might be re-engineered, or what the possibilities for technology support are, or how the organisation and roles and responsibilities might be changed to improve things, we will need to get to the bottom of the process, to understand what it is *effectively* about.

Our modelling method and notation must allow us to prepare both sorts of model, what we might call *concrete* (as-is) and *abstract* (effective) models. Or re-engineering won't be helped.

Law 6: People do processes, but they work in functions

Ask most people what they do in an organisation and they will tell you which department they work in. Ask some more questions and they will tell you how they contribute to the work of the department: where the work comes from and where they send their work to.

The lessons from TQM and BPR have been that what people really do is play a part in one or more *processes*, and that these processes invariably cut through the boundaries between departments. Getting the organisation to recognise the existence of these "cross-functional" processes and to deal with the conflict that occurs at the boundaries between the "functional silos" is a major part of re-engineering.

This leads to an implication for our modelling approach: do I have ways of modelling the process from a functional point of view and from a non-functional, responsibility point of view? Can I separate out responsibilities from functions? This must be possible if I am considering re-engineering through change in the functional structure or in the responsibilities of functions.

Law 7: It's what people do, not what they do it to, that counts

What do people do? By way of example, what do I do?

I carry out activities: I write an article; I facilitate a workshop for a client; I elicit a client's process; I give a training course.

I often have a number of activities going on in parallel: I start a new piece of work for a client; I put one activity down to do another; I stop everything to fill in my timesheet; I resume one of the activities I put down; I finish an activity.

I make decisions: I decide that the text for the brochure need not go for another formal review but can go straight to the graphic artist; I decide that a request for new computer hardware is acceptable; I decide that an invoice is correct and can be sent to the client.

And I interact with other people: the graphic artist and I agree on the final layout of the brochure; I send the manuscript of my book to the publisher; I delegate responsibility for hardware procurement to my facilities manager.

In all these things that occupy my day, I am doing things, sometimes on my own, sometimes with others. I'm playing a part in a number of different processes at any one time, and in each I may have a number of actions in progress. It's reasonable then to expect that any notation I use to model those processes should allow me to capture: activities, concurrent activities, decision making and cooperative activities.

Of course, I don't always want to model what each and every individual does in a process. Sometimes I might want to work at a higher level and to model what the various groups or people do – teams, projects, task forces, departments, companies, even entire nations – treating each as an "individual".

Here again there has been an unfortunate influence from the IT world on our process modelling (and I speak as a software engineer of many years). The IT world concentrates almost exclusively on *data*. On what people do things to. This is not surprising. Computers gave up computing pretty soon after their invention to concentrate on looking after people's data: memory became a cheap, voluminous commodity and that memory was as good as permanent. We've exploited that. When IT people build information systems they principally design databases and ways of getting the data in and out. Their methods (SSADM, IE, Yourdon, Jackson, SADT, Merise, and so on) rightly concentrate on the data aspects of the business being supported, and the notations are about data: Data Flow Diagrams, Entity Models, Entity Life Histories etc. But we should not expect their hammers to be good for driving home our screws. We are in the process business not the data business.

Law 8: There are some basic business patterns; let's see them

Life is not totally unstructured. When we look at how any business works we can see a number of common patterns in its processes.

The work of many people or groups revolves around handling a stream of "work items". A department deals with loan applications; or develops new cars; or makes televisions; or audits projects. Each loan application, car, television or audit is a "work item", and the department will have a process for dealing with their type of work item. "When the loan application first arrives, X calls the customer to acknowledge receipt and at the same time ...". "Development of a new car starts with the market research department carrying out a QFD activity and doing customer surveys, ...". If we want to model what an organisation does, identifying the work items and the processes in place for handling them is good first step.

Given that a department will often have many work items in progress at any one time, a further process is generally overlaid: a management process. This concerns itself with ensuring a smooth flow of work items, good resource allocation, proper handling of priorities, resolution of priority clashes, customer satisfaction, and so on. Separating the work item process from its management process is a good second step.

A work item process is generally started up by some external trigger: a customer request the need for a new model. Other processes start up on a regular, cyclical basis: the annual staff appraisal, the monthly progress review, the half-yearly budget planning. We need to be able to separate and model these.

Much process activity is done in the context of some sort of "contract", minimally a matching request-response pair perhaps with negotiation about the requirement and the delivery. If I delegate a task to you, I expect a subsequent report back. When the Loan Request Processing Department asks the Underwriting Department for an assessment of the premium required, they expect to receive that assessment subsequently. I need to be able to represent this common pattern in my process model.

All these patterns underlie processes, and whether the process works well or not, and how we might re-engineer it, will often depend on whether the right pattern is in the right place: should this process be cycle-driven or event-driven? Should this delegation be extended or reduced? Is the "contract" between these two departments appropriate for making the overall process flow smoothly.

Another call on our process modelling method and notation.

THE "SO WHAT?" TEST

We will see, as the chapters pass, that we are building up what we might call "intellectual machinery", machinery which we can use to analyse our processes and hence our organisations. Drawing diagrams is of itself a therapeutic activity with its own rewards, but the real test must be the "so what?" test: "just what is this modelling doing for us?".

What the process analyst will look for in a process modelling and analysis method is machinery that makes analysis possible.

The key features of STRIM that give us that machinery are

−   the completeness with which it can accurately specify business activity, and the business rules that control it

−   the way that the relationship between the process and the organisation can be explored, in particular through the notion of "role" and through the notion of "abstract" and "concrete" process models

−   the way that different patterns of organisational behaviour can be recognised and modelled

−   the way that the relationships between processes or views of processes can be properly defined.

In the following chapters we will build that machinery. It is then the analyst's job ... to use it!

WHAT IS A "PROCESS"?

We are at the end of chapter 1 and I have still not attempted a definition of the term *process*. This is intentional of course, as I mentioned earlier. But let me recap the key features of the thing that we call "process":

−   it contains purposeful activity (ie things are done for a reason)

−   it is carried out collaboratively by a group (ie we are concerned with more than the work of the individual)

−   it often crosses functional boundaries (ie the organisation is not the process)

−   it is invariably driven by the outside world (ie our processes generally have "customers" in some shape or form).

This list of features can of course be expanded on ... and this book is simply that expansion.

THE STRUCTURE OF THIS BOOK

It has a simple plan:

−   Chapter 2 takes the needs we have of our process models and explores the basic concepts that will be used in STRIM to satisfy those needs.

−   Chapter 3 introduces the main diagrammatic notation of STRIM and shows how it can be used to capture the real-world aspects of processes in terms of a few basic intuitive concepts.

−   Chapter 4 describes how a process model can be animated to illustrate the behaviour described.

- Chapter 5 explores "modelling-in-the-small" to show how a variety of common small-scale situations – *clichés* – can be handled in STRIM.
- Chapter 6 covers the modelling of large processes, and the connections between processes.
- Chapter 7 discusses what might be called "modelling-in-the-large", covering the larger, macro-scale *patterns* of organisational behaviour that are often encountered, and how they can be modelled.
- Chapter 8 looks at how the business entities involved in a process can be modelled, given the process model as the starting point.
- Chapter 9 pulls together all the machinery so far developed to show how STRIM models can be analysed and used for improvement and re-engineering.
- Chapter 10 describes how a modelling project itself should be conducted: what steps should be followed, how the picture should be built up, and how specific situations lead to specific perspectives.
- Chapter 11 offers the shortest of summaries as an epilogue.

WARNINGS

Some warnings are in order.

STRIM is a method for the analyst. This being so, we will not be afraid of using precise and specialised terminology between us as analysts. This book introduces a number of detailed technical ideas and terms, essential to the analyst for real understanding of a process, and for the accurate capture of a process in a process model. But one person's terminology is of course another's jargon, and the analyst needs to be careful when working with "ordinary" people. My (good) experience is that, whilst I have these ideas and terms in my head, ordinary people can work with one of our process models happily and productively without them. My (bitter) experience is that the effect on an ordinary person of hearing the word "instantiate" for example is akin to a sharp blow between the eyes with a heavy club: it switches them off. Exercise caution.

Like all methods STRIM does some things and not others. It is designed primarily for *qualitative* analysis; quantitative analysis requires different and complementary methods. Because it is about *modelling* STRIM is most useful in situations where models are useful; if you are a BPR "purist" you will probably eschew anything that considers the current process and STRIM will not be of interest. But if you are in the vast mid-ground between totally radical business change and incremental, fine-grained improvement with TQM, then STRIM will provide you with insights.

STRIM is a set of ideas. There are many ideas for different situations. There is no obligation to use all of them at the same time, only to pick the ones that you need. You can use STRIM in a rough and ready fashion or you can exploit all the subtleties of representation that it offers.

STRIM is not a cook-book. There is no recipe and no cooking instructions. There are concepts to be used. Take your pick.

2

BASIC CONCEPTS IN PROCESS MODELLING

INTRODUCTION

Our analysis of the needs of the process modeller leads us naturally to the key concepts that we will be looking for in our process modelling language. It will come as no surprise that when we model a process using STRIM we use the concepts of *roles* which are composed of *activities* which produce and operate on *entities*, and which communicate, coordinate and collaborate through *interactions*.

I now examine each of these notions in more detail.

ROLES AND ACTORS

A role involves a set of activities which, taken together, carry out a particular responsibility or set of responsibilities. If our business were that of a publisher and we were interested in the process of publishing a book we might identify roles such as *Authoring, Copy Editing, Designing, Editing, Planning, Producing, Marketing*, and so on. Roles that come quickly to mind in software development include *Project Managing, Configuration Controlling, Programming, Quality Assuring*, and *Designing*. In a retail store we might find roles such as *Buyer, Shop Floor Assistant, Customer, Store Manager, Check-out Assistant*, and *Security*.

Note how in the first two sets of examples I have named the roles with gerunds, ie -ing words used as nouns. Our first inclination when naming roles might be to use names like *Store Manager*, but this can make it too seductive to identify roles solely with post or job titles, forgetting that job titles are invariably made up of activities that often contribute to a number of different processes. For instance, the post "Managing Director" could be treated as a role, but it is clearly a post that has a part to play in many processes in the company's activity: as authoriser of large purchase orders, as setter of the company's strategy, and as an important part of maintaining the company's relationship with its clients. The post frequently combines a number of areas of responsibility in the organisation.

Equally, it is tempting to identify parts of the organisation as roles: departments, divisions, sections, or whatever. For instance, Reception at Praxis could be thought of as a role, but we can also view Reception as a group of people who contribute to several processes in the company: they act as our Goods Inwards and hence contribute to the purchasing process; as the people who answer telephone calls and greet guests they are part of our Marketing process. Similarly, a Finance Department, though forming a readily identifiable group of people, might actually participate in a number of separate though related processes including remunerating staff (by paying people), purchasing (by paying suppliers), and handling the company's cash-flow (by invoicing clients, chasing bad debts, and negotiating with banks).

Roles can in fact take many forms, viz

- a unique functional group: eg *Documentation Department, Accounts*

- a unique functional position or post: eg *Head of Analysis Department, Managing Director*

- a rank or job title: eg *Principal Analyst, Senior Engineer Grade 5*

- a replicated functional group: eg *Department, Branch*

- a replicated functional position or post: eg *Head of Department, Divisional Manager*

- a class of person: eg *Trade Union member, Customer, Expense Claiming*

- an abstraction: eg *Progress Chasing.*

Whether or not we associate posts or job titles or parts of the organisation with roles will, like so many similar decisions, depend on why we are modelling the process, and later in the book I cover the various situations in which different approaches are appropriate. Some process models that we have prepared for clients have had, on a single page, roles from each of the different forms.

Roles are types; role instances are acted

In the world of cars, there are many different types, for instance a Rover 214, or a Saab 900S. Given any type of car we will find on the roads a number of cars of that type. I have a car of the Rover 214 type; a colleague has a car of the same type; our two cars are both *instances* of the Rover 214 type.

These notions of a *type* and the *instances* of the type are important in the STRIM method. In fact, a role in STRIM is actually a *type*. That is, in principle there can be a number of different *instances* or *occurrences* of a role type active at any one time within an organisation. In this book I shall use the word *instance* in this sense of "occurrence". (Software engineers will recognise the terminology of object-orientation; not for nothing was SPML object-oriented.)

As an example, *Prime Minister* is a role type. I can point to several instances of this role around the world: "Prime Minister of the UK", "Prime

Minister of Australia", and "Prime Minister of Canada" to name three. These role instances exist independently of who is acting them at any one time. As I write, a man called John Major is acting the instance "Prime Minister of the UK". This instance was formerly acted by Margaret Thatcher. In fact, John Major acts a number of other role instances concurrently, one being that of "Member of Parliament for Huntingdon", itself an instance of the role type *Member of Parliament*.

As a further example, in Praxis we have a number of projects running at any one time. Each project has its own Project Manager who is at some stage in the role of *Project Managing*. We express this technically by saying "that person is acting an instance of the role type *Project Managing*". Associated with each project is an instance of the role *Project Managing* and that instance will (generally) have an actor.

An actor can take many forms. It might be a single person, a group of people, a computer, a person or group assisted by computers, a machine tool, a company – indeed, any agent in the real-world capable of carrying out the work in the role. In a RAD we are generally concerned with showing what is *done*: whether an individual activity in a role is done by people or by a computer is implementation detail.

We need to be careful to distinguish between the role instance – which has its own existence – and its current actor. Suppose we are looking at the process of Staff Development in an organisation. We might identify the role *Managing Staff Training*, and once the organisation has got to a certain point there will be an instance of that role. But if the person acting that role instance (probably someone in the post of Staff Training Manager) resigns, the instance does not disappear: it is still there, and the organisation will try to "fill" that role instance by recruiting someone to take it over; in the meantime it might get someone else to act that role instance until a full-time replacement is found – a deputy will carry out the role until a permanent actor can be found.

No mapping between role instances and actors

This separation between role instance and actor goes further. In fact, we can summarise it by saying that there is no implied mapping between the two. Let us explore the possible combinations.

In the case of Praxis projects, we would expect to see only one instance of the role *Project Managing* being acted on a given development project, ie within one "running" of the process of "Develop Software for a Client"; though there would be a number of instances of the role across the company, one per active project. This is a case where at most one instance of the role will exist when a process runs.

The single instance of *Project Managing* could be acted by different people at different times during the life-time of its project: Jack might be acting as project manager until March 19th, when he hands over the role (instance) to Jill. In a well-organised company we would not expect to discover that at some moment both Jack *and* Jill were acting the role, or a moment when nobody was acting it. So here is a case where we expect to find a one-to-one mapping between role instance and actor at any one time (though that mapping might change over time).

Within a given project, there could be several instances of the role of *Designing*, each being acted by a designer person, and, in a large project, perhaps hundreds of instances of *Programming*, each being acted by a programmer person. So, when the Develop Software for a Client process is running, we would find one *Project Managing* instance, a number of *Designing* instances, and many *Programming* instances. When we draw the model of the Develop Software for a Client process we only describe the role types, and hence imply that all programmers follow the same procedure. If, in the real-life process, some programmers follow one procedure and others follow another, we would expect to see two different role types in our process model. For instance, novice programmers might be constrained by a detailed procedure to ensure that they do not do anything that threatens the project (and incidentally to train them in good practice), whilst experienced programmers might follow a less rigorously defined procedure which recognises their expertise. Our process model might therefore contain two role types that have the same goal but operate different procedures: *Experienced Programming* and *Novice Programming*.

In our Develop Software for a Client process, we might well have somewhere a role with responsibility for controlling change to specifications, designs, code and so on: let us call it the *Controlling Changes* role. The *Controlling Changes* role will probably only have one instance on a project and that single instance might be acted by a whole team of people. Conversely, one (physical) actor might be acting several role instances simultaneously – for instance, on a small project, one person, Jill, might be acting both the single instance of *Project Managing*, the single instance of *Controlling Changes*, and perhaps one of two instances of *Programming*. Here is a case where the mapping from actors to role instances might be one-to-many.

To repeat, there is no one-to-one mapping implied by the idea of role instances and actors, and in our process models we will not necessarily show the business of allocating real actors to role instances – this is a scheduling issue which might not concern us when we are modelling.

The dynamics of roles, role instances, and actors

To emphasise this important distinction between role type, role instance and role instance actor, let's revisit the different forms that a role can take and look at how the number of instances and actors can change over time for each form.

– A unique functional group: eg *Documentation Department, Accounts*.

Within a given organisation we would expect to find only one instance of a named functional group such as these. In other words the role type (eg *Accounts*) has only one instance and that instance is effectively permanent; that is, we can take it as permanent for the purposes of the process model in which the role appears[1]. The actors of the role instance are of course the people (and computers!) who make up the Accounts Department, and, while the instance has a "permanent" existence (with the same qualification as above), the people will change. Today I might be a member of Accounts, helping act the role; tomorrow I might have resigned and someone else will have taken my place.

Summarising, there will be a single permanent instance of such a role, with variable actor(s).

- A unique functional position or post: eg *Head of Analysis Department, Managing Director.*

The situation here is similar to the functional group case above. There is only one instance of the type: there is only one Analysis Department and it has only one Head post; similarly there is only one Managing Director post. The holder of those posts can change of course, but the post (role instance) is permanent for the purpose of the model.

Summarising, there will be a single permanent instance of such a role, with variable actor.

- A rank or job title: eg *Principal Analyst, Senior Engineer Grade 5.*

The situation here is quite different. In an organisation, a certain number of people will have a given job title – say *Senior Engineer*– at any one time. Putting that another way, there will be a certain number of instances of the role *Senior Engineer*, and each of those instances is acted by one fixed person. The organisation might decide to promote someone in status from *Junior Engineer* to *Senior Engineer*. The result is that an instance of *Junior Engineer* will cease to exist and a new instance of *Senior Engineer* will come into being. The person involved will move from acting the *Junior Engineer* instance to acting the *Senior Engineer* instance. However, when we label a role with such a "badge" we are saying "anyone acting this role must have this badge".

Summarising, there may be a flux of instances of such a role and there is a one-to-one relationship between the role instance and the actor.

- A replicated functional group: eg *Department, Branch*

Such a group will appear in a process model when we want to refer to *any* Department, Branch etc and do not want to be specific about *which* Department we are concerned with, or we want to allow *any* department to play a particular part in the process. When the process runs, there may be any number of instances of the role – the branch in Oxford, the branch in Bath, the branch in Leicester, etc. These instances will generally be permanent for the duration of the process. The actors of this sort of role can of course change: staff at a given branch come and go.

---

[1] We can always think of a larger process in which the instance would be transient, for example the process of organisational change itself

- A replicated functional position or post: eg *Head of Department, Divisional Manager.*

  The situation here is slightly different. At any one time, there will, according to the organisational structure, be a fixed number of such posts: Head of Research Department, Head of Marketing Department, Head of Production Department, and so on. Each of these is an instance of the role *Head of Department.* And each role instance – each Department Head post – will have an actor: the current holder of that post.

  Summarising, in general the set of instances remains fixed for a given process, but there will be a change in actors as people are put in those posts and leave them.

- A class of person: eg *Trade Union member, Customer, Expense Claimant*

  This is like the replicated functional group: when a process runs, one or more instances will be created, but each will be identifiable with an individual, and the role instance is in a one-to-one relationship with that individual. If an instance of *Customer* comes into being it will be associated with and acted by a single person; the actor will not change – during the handling of a complaint from Mr Bloggs we do not expect to see Mrs Featherstonehaugh take over at some point: the instance's actor remains constant. The *Expense Claimant* role is what we do when we want to claim expenses; it is the role we act to claim expenses. Our main role might be *Supervisor,* but once a month we "slip into" the role of *Expense Claimant.*

- An abstraction: eg *Progress Chasing*

  This is a case where a gerund makes a good name for the role. It can be particularly useful to name an area of responsibility, rather than something that exists on the organogram for the organisation, such as a post or a department. I might start *Progress Chasing* an invoice but someone else might take over at some point if I ask them to; and there could be any number of us progress chasing various items at any one time.

The key characteristics of each of these forms of role are summarised in figure 2-1. We need to separate these out for three reasons. Firstly, it is useful to think about each role we plan to model and to ask which category it falls into as part of checking our understanding of the dynamics of the role. Secondly, we will need to know in particular whether a given role is transient or permanent when we come to animate a process model to see what sort of behaviour it defines for the organisation – this is covered in chapter 4. Thirdly, the relationship between actor and role instance is what the scheduling of staff and resources is all about, and this itself can be part of the process or indeed another process altogether.

Of the role forms in figure 2-1 we can expect some to appear on the organisation chart, namely the unique functional group and the unique post. Replicated functional groups and posts might appear if the chart shows things like "branches" and "regional offices" as classes of bodies that form the organisation, without naming specific ones such as "the northern regional office".

Figure 2-1 – Characteristics of role forms

Role form	Number of instances	Permanent instances?	Can actor change?
Unique functional group	one	✔	✔
Unique post	one	✔	✔
Job title	>one	✘	✘
Replicated functional group	>one	✘	✔
Replicated post	>one	✔	✔
Class of person	>one	✘	✘
Abstract role	>one	✘	✔

In summary, in general a role can have a number of instances at any one moment, and a role instance generally exists independently of the existence of an actor to act it. The actor can change and at a given instant no-one and nothing might be acting a given role instance.

It is also important to remember that role instances are concurrent things, with their own lives to lead. We will see, later in this chapter, that they operate independently except where they collaborate through interactions.

From now on, I shall take care to differentiate between a *role type*, a *role instance* and the *actor* of a role instance, unless the sense is clear from the context.

Roles start other roles

One role instance can cause the creation of new role instances to do new tasks. For instance, a *Project Managing* role instance will want to create instances of other roles (such as *Designing* and *Programming*) for the rest of the project once the (actual) project manager has determined how big the project is and what tasks have to be undertaken. Those roles will do the designing and programming on the project. In the pharmaceutical industry, when a chemical compound looks as though it has promising efficacy and safety properties, a team is set up to champion that compound through the long process of getting it to market. That team has responsibility for managing the compound's life thereafter: that *Compound Management Team* role is instantiated to carry out that responsibility. During the compound's development, many batches of raw drug material will be made for formulation for various trials. The role of *Making a Batch* is instantiated every time a batch has to be made; in fact there may be any number of instances of the role, depending on how many batches are somewhere in the process of being made at any given time.

Any role which is not permanent as far as the process is concerned will have to be instantiated at some point – we call these *transient roles*.

Note that creating a new role instance does not imply any allocation of real people or machines to act the role instance, as far as a RAD is concerned. The *actual* team of people who manage the life of a candidate compound may well change over the many years during which the compound is developed, but the role instance – the compound team – remains. When a batch of compound is to be made, the role instance is started and a process research chemist is allocated to actually make the batch, ie to act the role instance – it could be John or it could be Jill. Again we are being careful to separate role instance from its actor.

In Praxis, when we win a contract to do some work for a client, the Divisional Director responsible completes a *Project Inception Memo*. This actually has two effects: firstly to create the project by notifying its number to our Quality Assurance team, thereby creating an instance of the role *Project Manager*, and secondly to nominate the initial actor of that role instance. We could separate these two activities but for convenience do it with the same form. When the project manager changes – Jill takes over from John – the Divisional Director uses a *Change of Project Manager* form; this has the effect of changing the actor but otherwise leaving the role instance unchanged.

Committees and meetings as roles

It can often be the case that a corporate body such as "The Board" sometimes acts as a single role that performs various activities, monitoring, acting as an approval authority, planning, etc, whilst at other points in the process the individual members act in their own right: CEO, Finance Director, Chairman, etc; or the Divisional Directors might act collectively in one role – *Divisional Management Committee* – and individually in their own right in the role *Divisional Director*. In the latter case we might expect a Divisional Director to have an interaction with the Divisional Management Committee in order to submit a divisional plan as input to the corporate plan. If Shirley is a Divisional Director she will act each of the roles in that process, putting on the right hat at the right moment.

In summary, it is not unusual to see a committee on a RAD standing as a single role, and the component members as separate roles.

Equally, it is sometimes useful to regard a regular meeting as playing a role in a process, particularly if it has some executive responsibility. A meeting might be ordained to happen, say, monthly in order to agree the priorities of the coming month's activity, or to approve the expenditure of a department, or simply to exchange information between the attendees.

Computer systems as roles

We saw earlier that a computer can be an actor of a role (instance): in the work of *Accounts* we will find people doing things (handling purchases, invoices, orders, cash advances etc), but we might also find computers doing things such as automatically preparing lists of aged debtors each Monday. It may be that a large information system (running on a computer) plays such a large part in a process that we could consider it as having a role of its own. There would be one instance of that role and, trivially, one actor. Other people-acted roles would of course have interactions with it, either to put data in or get data out.

ACTIVITIES

Activities are what actors do as "individuals" in their roles.

In the process of developing new pharmaceutical drugs, activities might include *Prepare potential drug compound, Carry out clinical trial, Prepare submission to Regulatory Authority,* and *Check drug stability.*

In the process of buying a house we might find activities such as *Contact estate agents (realtors), Obtain finance, Obtain planning permission,* and *Negotiate the price.*

In the software development process, activities might include *Prepare project plan, Draw up data dictionary, Carry out proof obligation, Transform algorithm, Verify code against specification, Build system* and *Add component to library.*

Note how we name activities with verbs: "prepare", "draw up", "verify", etc. An activity needs to be well defined, in particular we need to know what makes it start and what makes it stop, what state the world is in when it starts and what state the world is in when it stops, ie when and why an activity is done. Let us look at this in more detail.

Like roles, activities are defined in STRIM as types that have instances. If we are speaking informally about a process we would say "activity A starts"; speaking formally we would say "an instance of activity type A is created". An instance of an activity type is created when the organisation's process is in a particular condition – we call this the *activating* or *triggering condition* for the activity. This is a sufficient condition for the activity instance to start. For example, in an organisation that has a policy of paying invoices three months after receiving them, the activity *Pay Invoiced Amount* would have as a triggering condition the fact that payment of an invoice has been due for three months. The *stopping condition* of an activity is the condition of the world that causes an instance to cease to exist, ie that "stops the activity". *Pay Invoiced Amount* would probably have as its stopping condition the fact that a cheque for the invoiced amount had been sent to the supplier.

There may be other conditions that are also true when an activity is started and which we want to note (though they are not what makes the activity start); these are collectively referred to as the activity's *pre-condition.* Thus, in the late-paying organisation, the activity *Pay Invoiced Amount* might have as a pre-condition the fact that payment has been authorised. Similarly, each activity will have some *post-condition* which describes the state of the world at the time that the activity stops. A post-condition of the activity *Pay Invoiced Amount* might be that appropriate ledger entries have been made. A post-condition is an outcome.

As an example in the software development process, take a hypothetical activity type called *Compile Source Code*. The activating condition for this could be *source code successfully syntax-checked*; a pre-condition could be *access available to validated library*; the stopping condition could be *successful compilation*; and a post-condition could be *corresponding object file available in the object directory*.

An important part of defining an activity is to do with the materials involved in it. We say that an activity uses (and possibly consumes) its *inputs*, and produces *outputs*. Those inputs and outputs we will refer to as *entities*. We examine entities in their own right in a moment.

Activities not only have important properties of their own, they also relate to each other in different ways. There are three ways:

- Activity *A* might always follow activity *B*: a cheque cannot be sent until the expense claim has been approved. So activities may be *ordered* and follow a particular sequence.

- Either activity *A* is carried out or activity *B* is carried out depending on whether some condition *C* holds: if the expense claim is over £1,000 it is paid by electronic transfer through the bank, otherwise by cheque. So activities may be *conditional*.

- At some point both activity *A* and activity *B* can proceed in parallel: once the expense claim has been approved, the money can be paid to the claimant and the relevant department budget can be debited. So activities may be *concurrent*.

In our process model we will want to be able to show where activities are sequential, conditional or concurrent. These will be one way in which some business rules will be represented.

INTERACTIONS

We have seen how one of the most important things that happens in a process, especially in terms of "moving the process on" or "making progress", is the interactions that take place between roles, such as when a manager delegates a task to a subordinate, or a report is handed over.

In the process of Develop Software for a Client, the role *Project Managing* will want to interact with the roles *Designing* and *Programming* to obtain status reports on work completed, and the *Designing* role will want to pass specifications of programs to be written to the *Programming* role. In the process of Developing a Portfolio of Products, the *Board of Directors* will want to pass a statement of direction to the *Product Strategy Board* along with a budget level and targets. In return the *Product Strategy Board* will present the *Board of Directors* with information on the chosen portfolio, and progress reports against budget and targets.

In STRIM terms, an interaction is neutral and has no implied direction – it is just some coordination between roles. But an interaction might involve the transfer of something, some entity (see below) – what we call a *gram* – from the sphere of concern of one role to that of the other. For example, the *Managing a*

Division role will interact with the *Project Managing* role so that the Divisional Manager can pass the Project Manager some terms of reference for the project they are to manage. In some cases there will be an exchange of grams: I give you money in return for goods. But an interaction need not involve the transfer of a gram: for instance, you and I might interact simply to agree on something – "nothing changes hands". For instance, the Sales Team, the Marketing Team and the Production Group of a product company might agree that a new product should go to market: that interaction might consist of a discussion around the table and an agreed launch date.

An interaction can be two-party – involving two roles – or multi-party, involving a number of roles. However many parties are involved, interactions are always *synchronous*; that is, both role instances must be ready for the interaction to take place before it can start, it starts at the same moment for each party, and it completes at the same moment for each party at which point they enter their respective new states. In some cases an interaction might physically take a few seconds (I give you a memo containing some terms of reference), in others months (a vendor and purchaser agree on the contractual terms of a sale). As elsewhere in our modelling notation we do not capture absolute time. One way of thinking about an interaction is as *an alignment of states*. This is in part what I mean when, above, I say that "both role instances must be ready for the interaction to take place before it can start, it starts at the same moment for each party, and it completes at the same moment for each party at which point they enter their respective new states". For you and me to interact, we must both be in the required state beforehand, we go through the interaction together, and then we go to our respective after-states.

This deserves closer examination, but we must leave further detail until chapter 5.

PROCESS GOALS

We saw in chapter 1 how there are two sorts of goals that a process might have: point-wise goals and steady-state goals. We can now flesh these ideas out a little more.

In our process model we will want to identify the point (or points) where the goal of the process has been achieved. In the simplest case we will be able to identify some point in the activity of a particular role where the state of the process is "goal achieved". After a particular activity or interaction has completed we can recognise that the goal has been achieved. For instance, in a process for handling reported credit card losses, we might say that, once there has been an interaction with the customer in which the latter has been sent a new credit card, the goal "client has been sent replacement credit card" has been achieved. We can identify the role in which, at some point, that state has been achieved, ie the state at that point *is* the goal. Reaching that state is reaching the goal.

In some situations the goal might be more complex and equivalent not to one state in one role, but to a combination of states in a number of roles. For instance, the real goal of the Handle Reported Credit Card Loss process might actually be not only that a new card is sent to the customer, but also that the credit card fraud bureau is informed, and that the card number has been entered on the list of lost cards that is circulated to retailers. The goal is a composite goal but can be recognised simply as that combination of a number of roles' states across the process.

This indicates, I hope, how important it is to see process models as descriptions of *the way that organisations change state*, from their initial state (someone wanting a service or whatever) to their final state (service delivered).

Another way of seeing processes that is sometimes proposed is to think of them taking inputs and producing outputs. This has a certain appeal, especially to those brought up in the information processing world. In STRIM we tend away from this view. Whilst we can make liberal interpretations as to what might constitute an "input" or an "output", things need to be stretched somewhat to make them work convincingly. In particular, inputs and outputs smack of things physical, as one would have in a manufacturing process: raw materials go in as inputs and finished products come out as outputs. Many processes, however, have goals which are not tangible in this way: a process that uses a lot of interaction in order to inform people could be said to produce as output "informed people". I would rather say that its *goal* is to inform people and we can recognise the *state* where the right people have been informed. In a process to deal with a customer complaint one of the goals might be to ensure that the customer feels they have achieved some satisfaction by making the complaint. I could try and re-phrase this to say "the output of the process is a person who is satisfied", or "the output of the process is the satisfaction felt by the customer". But I don't think it is helpful in modelling terms to think of the process having as input "customer needing to be satisfied" and producing as output "satisfied customer". Better surely to say "our goal is to reach the state where the customer is satisfied" and to identify the point in the process where the assertion "the customer is satisfied" can be made. Similarly, very often we put in place reporting lines so that, frankly, managers can have a warm feeling that things are happening. For me, the goal is to leave managers with a warm feeling, rather than "to produce as output warm managers". I shall want to identify the point in the process where we can agree that the managers feel warm.

The steady-state goal is more complicated. By definition it says that something is true at all times, or – softening this a little – that it is true at a number of points in the process (the times when we choose to look for instance). I might want to be sure that at all times everyone has the latest information on product changes, or that expenditure is always kept within budget levels set at the start of the year. (In the case of such steady-state goals it is even less intuitive to think in terms of "inputs" and "outputs".)

In summary, a goal is simply a desired state.

ENTITIES

"Entity" is the name we give to anything which is the subject matter of an activity. For instance, a manager will prepare a *plan*, write a *report*, draw up *terms of reference*, or approve a *document*. *Plan, Report, Terms of Reference*, and *Document* are entities.

Entities can be the inputs and outputs of an activity: a programmer uses a *specification* as an input to the programming activity and produces a *program* as an output; or a warehouse person uses a *picking list* as input to the packing activity. Entities can also be the subject of interactions: if I delegate a task to you I will pass the information necessary as some *Terms of Reference*; when you have finished the work you will pass me the *Results*. The grams of an interaction are entities.

Like roles and activities, entities come as types or classes which can be instantiated. In fact when an activity instance produces one of its outputs we consider it to be *instantiating* the relevant entity type.

When we define an entity, we will want to ascribe properties to it. Amongst those that are covered by STRIM are the parts from which a compound entity is composed if it is a composite thing, and "invariants", ie things that are always true about the entity. For example, a *technical specification* might be defined to be made up of a *contents list, document control information*, a *scope section*, a *control flow section*, and a *data flow section*, followed by *performance details*. A *production plan* might be made up of a *list of input resources*, a *timetable*, and a *definition* of the process to be used. An invariant of the entity *production lathe* is that it is *up to date in its maintenance schedule*.

3

MODELLING WITH RADs

INTRODUCTION

We have now looked at the variety of needs of the process modeller and at the aspects of the real-world that we will want to see in our models if we are going to satisfy those needs.

In this chapter I concentrate on modelling with RADs, in particular introducing the notation and how it can be used to model simple everyday situations. Chapter 4 describes how we can animate a process model in the form of a RAD in order to explore the possible behaviour of an organisation following that process; chapter 5 looks at more complex micro-modelling issues in detail, while chapters 6 and 7 cover macro-modelling and the issues around working with large and connected processes; chapter 8 looks at how the information needs of a process are handled in STRIM; chapter 9 goes on to look at the different ways in which one can analyse a process described as a RAD.

REPRESENTING THE PROCESS

The process model is recorded in the form of a *Role Activity Diagram* (RAD). A RAD shows the roles, their component activities and their interactions, together with external events and the logic that determines what activities are carried out when.

The notation for RADs is summarised in figure 3-1. Figure 3-2 shows a RAD for a simple process, to give a feel for what a complete RAD looks like. A RAD represents the whole of a process as far as we wish to capture it. Somewhere on the RAD we name the process it is modelling. This might be "Develop Software for a Client", "Develop a Portfolio of Products", "Arrange Payment of Benefits", "Manage Cash Flow", or "Provide First-line Support to Customers".

We now look in detail at the notation and how it is used to capture the concepts covered in chapter 2.

Figure 3-1 – The RAD notation

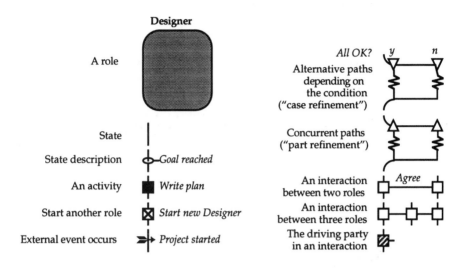

(Computer tools that support the preparation of RADs may use slightly different symbols but the shape is of no importance. It is the *meaning* we attach to those symbols that is important, and it is that meaning which this chapter addresses.)

REPRESENTING ROLES AND ACTIVITIES

Each role in the process is represented by the contents of a shaded block. (For convenience we sometimes draw a single role as a number of separate shaded blocks if there are indeed separate parts of the role and it makes the RAD easier to draw.) In figure 3-2, there are three roles with the names *Divisional Director*, *Project Manager* and *Designer*. All activities and interactions take place within those three roles, as far as this model of this process is concerned.

Within each role there are a number of *activities* indicated by black boxes, the annotation against each black box describing the activity succinctly using a verb (such as "write" or "prepare"). In figure 3-2 for example, the *Project Manager* role carries out an activity to *Write TOR for Designer* in order to prepare some terms of reference.

The fact that an activity is shown as a black box is significant: it says that, as far as we are concerned *in this model*, we do not care how this activity is carried out, so long as the requisite outputs are produced. (The question naturally arises as to whether one can "decompose" or "open up" a black box. This is an important issue which is covered in chapter 6.)

Figure 3-2 – The RAD for a simple process

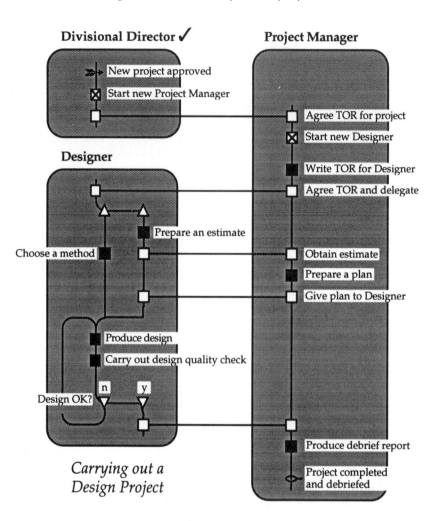

*Carrying out a
Design Project*

Although each of the roles in figure 3-2 consists of just one "thread" starting at the top of the grey box, there is no reason why a given role need not consist of a number of separate threads. For instance in the process in figure 3-3, the *Divisional Director* role has two threads: one which apparently is concerned with taking part in the annual budget setting cycle and the other with the monthly reporting cycle. Those threads can start and then operate quite independently. (The little spring-shaped symbol in this and subsequent RADs indicates that the RAD continues but that we are not concerned with how.)

Figure 3-3 – A role with two separate threads

Divisional Director

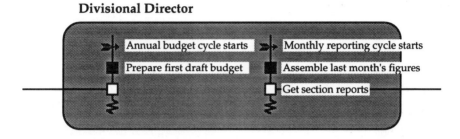

REPRESENTING ROLES BEING STARTED – ROLE INSTANTIATION

One role can *instantiate* another role, ie start a new instance of that role: this is indicated by a square with a cross inside it. In figure 3-2, the *Project Manager* role instantiates the *Designer* role. The annotation against the crossed box identifies the role being instantiated.

In a RAD we have no separate symbol to represent the "ending" of a role instance once its work is done. If we need to show this explicitly we simply use an activity labelled something like *Close down the Task Force*.

REPRESENTING INTERACTIONS

An *interaction* between roles is shown as a white box in one role connected by a horizontal line to a white box in another role. An interaction can involve any number of roles and signifies that the roles involved must pass through it together – they synchronise. In figure 3-2, the *Project Manager* role interacts with the *Designer* role in order to *Agree TOR and delegate*. We always annotate an interaction in a way that makes clear what is happening, and that might indicate whether any grams (entities) pass during the interaction. Interaction lines do not carry arrows to indicate the "flow" of any gram: we simply place appropriate annotation at the appropriate end. For example, in figure 3-2 the *Project Manager* role receives an estimate from the *Designer* role, and this is indicated by placing the annotation *Obtain estimate* at the *Project Manager* role end of the interaction line.

An interaction can involve any number of parties; as an example figure 3-4 shows an interaction involving four roles. We refer to the white box in each role as a *part-interaction*. If it is useful, we can add further annotation to the interaction, perhaps naming each part-interaction with a label that expresses how it appears to the role that carries out that part-interaction, and even a further label for the entire interaction. An example is give in figure 3-5.

The synchronisation aspect of an interaction is important: if I reach my side and you are not ready, I must wait until you are; as soon as we are both ready the interaction can take place. (I deal with this idea in more detail in chapter 5.) As with an activity, an interaction has a *triggering condition*, which is the condition corresponding to each participating role being in the state before its part-interaction. So the overall triggering condition is effectively the state reached when all the participating roles are ready for the interaction.

Figure 3-4 – A four-party interaction

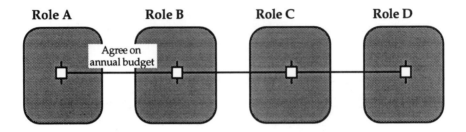

An interaction can be very simple (eg "I give you some terms of reference"), or very complex (eg "the three parties meet to negotiate and agree the price of a piece of work, drawing up the agreement as a legal document and obtaining financial securities from a bank"). As ever, what we regard as "atomic" in our RAD depends on why we are drawing the RAD. We always show whatever detail is appropriate to *that* model for *that* purpose. An interaction that is shown as a single line on a RAD might, if "opened up", show the involvement of other roles not otherwise mentioned in this RAD, new interactions between them and other roles, and all the richness of organisational behaviour.

Figure 3-5 – Labelling the components of an interaction

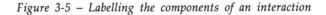
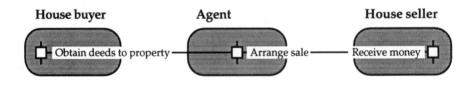

When we label an interaction we can choose whether to describe it in terms of its purpose or the mechanism used, or both. For instance, in figure 3-6 we have modelled an interaction in terms of the mechanism (what physically happens) in the upper fragment and its purpose (what we are trying to achieve) in the lower fragment.

In some situations it is useful to show which party to an interaction takes the lead or is responsible for making it happen. We do this simply by shading in the part-interaction in the "driving role". In figure 3-6 we have used this notation to indicate that the *Widget Making Supervisor* takes the initiative in the interaction.

In chapter 9 we will see how, by "abstracting" from a concrete description of a process to an abstract form, we can start to look for improvement through changes in either the organisation or the process. When we want to design a process we might start with an abstract view of it and then design an organisation and other mechanisms to make it concrete. But more of this later.

Figure 3-6 – Mechanism vs purpose in an interaction

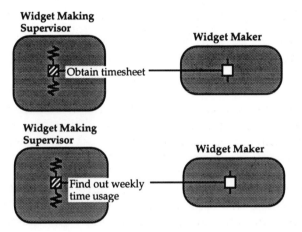

REPRESENTING ROLES AND STATES

The vertical lines between activities *within* a role are more than just ways of connecting the various boxes. They represent *states* or *conditions* which the role can be in. Understanding of a RAD is greatly enhanced if lines are seen as *states* rather than just representing "flow" from one activity or interaction to another. This will become more and more apparent as we look more carefully at RADs and the way processes work. Sometimes on a RAD we wish to say what state the world is in at a particular part of the process; in other words we wish to label the state. We do this by simply putting a magnifying glass on the state line and annotating it; thus, in figure 3-2, the final state of the *Project Manager* role is *Project completed and debriefed* (which is probably the goal of the whole process).

In real life we are quite used to the notion of state, even though we might not recognise it: "how are you getting on with my expense claim?" is another way of saying "what state have you got to with processing my expense claim?". We happily ask "has authorisation to proceed been given yet?", or "has the Finance Director given his approval yet?". In these too, we are asking about the state the process has reached.

A RAD shows a number of role *types* each composed of a number of activity *types*. When a role type is instantiated we can think of the new instance starting with a token sitting on the "opening state", or "when a role instance instantiates another role, the new role instance starts at the 'top' of its activities". As the process unfolds and the role instance proceeds through its activities and interactions, the changes of state are marked by changes in the positions of tokens on the permissible states (the so-called "marking" of the model). For instance, suppose a role instance is in the state shown in figure 3-7.

Figure 3-7 – A role instance ready to do an activity

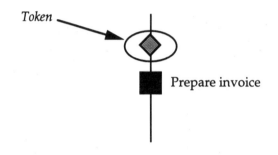

The token shown as a grey lozenge sitting on the state line before the activity *Prepare invoice* indicates that the next thing that the role can do is carry out that activity. Nothing else is needed for the activity to start. To capture this idea we say that the state in front of the activity represents its *triggering condition*, that is, the condition of the role instance which will cause the activity to start (strictly, to be instantiated). A token sitting on a particular state can be thought of as representing the potential future behaviour of the role instance.

When the activity does start, the role instance is in the state of carrying it out (and the token essentially disappears, though you might think of a token sitting in the activity box). When the activity has finished (figure 3-8), a token appears on the state immediately following the activity to indicate that the role instance is now in that state.[1] We define that state as the *post-condition* of the activity.

It is important to understand just what happens when a RAD "runs" so that you can make correct interpretations of the model for comparison with what happens when the real-life process runs, or to see how a proposed process would

---

[1] If you are familiar with the notion of a *Petri Net*, you will recognise the RAD as a Petri Net with the activities, external events (see below) and interactions as transitions, and the state lines as places. Tokens then "flow" around the net, with the transitions (process elements) taking the net from one marking to another in the traditional way.

look when it does run. This animation of a RAD is dealt with in detail in chapter 4.

Figure 3-8 – A role instance just after an activity

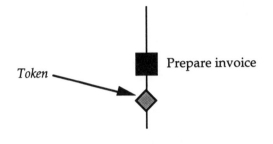

REPRESENTING ALTERNATIVE COURSES OF ACTION

At some points in the process, what happens next might depend on some condition or state. For example, the way a clerk deals with an application for overtime might depend on the salary band of the claimant; how a chemist will make a batch of drug compound for a clinical trial will depend on which pilot plant has been allocated for the production; the way an order for a shrub is dealt with by a horticulturist depends on the time of year the order is received and when the shrub concerned is best shipped.

We represent such alternative courses of action with the notation shown in figure 3-1 for *case refinement*. Essentially, we are refining the state of the process according to different predicates or "cases". An example in figure 3-2 is the *Design OK?* predicate in the *Designer* role. Using our token scheme, we can think of a token passing down the leg of the case refinement that corresponds to the predicate that is true; the role goes in different directions depending on the state of things. Figures 3-9 and 3-10 illustrate this.

Figure 3-9 – The state before a case refinement

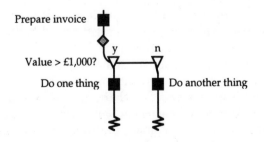

Immediately after the activity *Prepare invoice* we can imagine a token on the state line leading out of *Prepare invoice*'s black box as shown in figure 3-9. The case refinement says that, if the predicate *Value > £1,000* is true, this is equivalent to figure 3-10 with the token on the corresponding state line; whilst, if *Value > £1,000* is not true it is equivalent to figure 3-11 with the token on the other state line.

Figure 3-10 – The state after a case refinement in one case

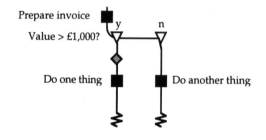

Figure 3-11 – The state after a case refinement in the other case

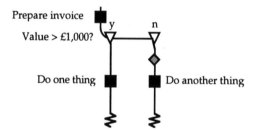

The two-way case refinement generalises quite naturally to *N*-way case refinements. The way an organisation carries out a particular part of the process might, for instance, depend on which of its offices it is carried out in. We would show this with an *N*-way case refinement such as that in figure 3-12. Here, the process proceeds differently according to whether the location is London, New York, Paris, or Stykkisholmur.

You could think of case refinement as a *case* statement in a programming language or as a decision box in a conventional flowchart. But it is important to note that, unlike a decision box on a flowchart, there is no activity going on "in" the symbol for case refinement – no person or machine is doing anything to *make* the decision: the process is simply going in different directions depending on the state it is in. So, the value of the *Design OK?* predicate must be determined as a result of some prior activity in the process, such as the preceding quality control activity *Carry out design quality check* in this case; the case refinement does not itself "contain" any activity to check the design. Figure 3-13 would therefore be wrong: the annotation is a description of an activity and not a predicate (question) about the state.

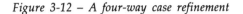

Figure 3-12 – A four-way case refinement

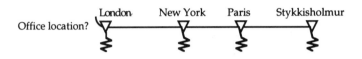

Case refinement naturally allows us to represent conditional iteration within a role, as in the example in figure 3-2 where the designer repeatedly produces and checks a design until it is OK. Anywhere on a single state line is the same, so the three role instance states shown in figure 3-14 are equivalent in that in all three cases the next possible activity of the role is *Produce design*. One might object that the first and third states in the figure are quite different since in the first state you don't have a design whilst in the third state you do. True, but, the RAD is telling us that, as far as this process is concerned, having a design that has failed its quality check is no different from having no design at all: in each case you have to produce a new design. The states are equivalent in that *they define the same future behaviour*. If this is not what we wanted to model then we have the wrong model.

Figure 3-13 – An incorrect case refinement

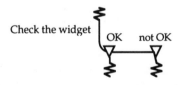

In some situations, whichever of the alternative threads of activity is followed, we finally want to "return" to some "main" thread of activity. In this case we use the representation in figure 3-1, with the threads joining up again when they have finished (ie the case states are recombined). We can best visualise what this means by looking at it using tokens. In figure 3-15, whichever of the four case threads is followed we require the main thread to be picked up finally. Thus any of the token placings shown in figure 3-16 is equivalent to that in figure 3-17.

Figure 3-14 – Three equivalent role instance states

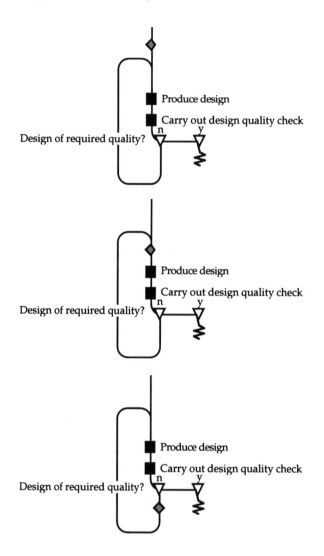

Figure 3-15 – Four case refinement threads finally return to a common thread

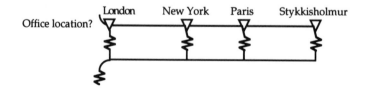

Figure 3-16 – Three alternative "final" token placings in a case refinement

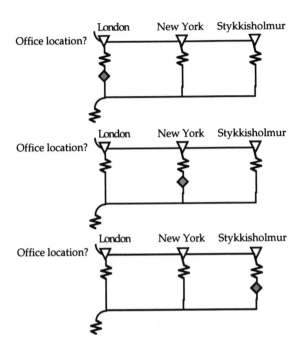

Figure 3-17 – The equivalent token placing

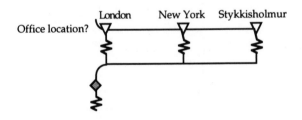

In other situations, a process does not operate this way. The example in figure 3-2 is a case in point: if the design is OK, completion can be reported back to the project manager, but, if the design is not OK, a rework cycle is required – the two alternative threads do not recombine. And in some situations a mixture of the two is possible, as shown in the four-way case refinement of figure 3-18.

Figure 3-18 – A hybrid four-way case refinement

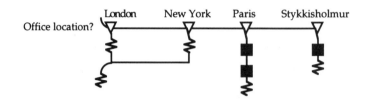

Since we like our RADs to be revealing, we sometimes adopt an abbreviation for simple case refinements in order to reduce the "clutter" on the diagram. Figure 3-19 shows, on the left-hand side the full case refinement with a single activity only being done if there is an R in the month, whilst on the right-hand side we capture the conditionality in the name of the activity. Words like "if appropriate" or "as necessary" might be useful. This can also be done with conditional interactions but greater care is needed.

Figure 3-19 – Abbreviating a simple case refinement

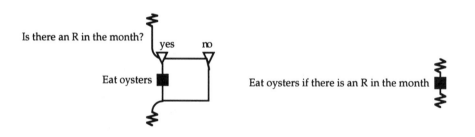

(The less technically minded can skip the remainder of this section and resume at the next section. For the more technically minded, the following observation might be useful.)

The term "case refinement" is carefully chosen: the construct does indeed show how the state of the role is refined depending on the different cases. Strictly we could redraw figure 3-18 as figure 3-20, with the four threads each labelled with the state which causes it to be followed, rather than showing some question and the possible answers at the heads of the threads.

Figure 3-20 – Explicit naming of case refinement threads

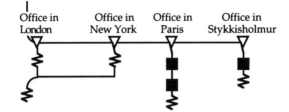

In the general case we could consider the case refinement shown in figure 3-21. If the state in front of the refinement is *S1*, and the states following it are *S2* through *S5* as shown then the case refinement construct tells us that

S2 = S1 & "Location=London"

S3 = S1 & "Location=New York"

S4 = S1 & "Location=Paris"

S5 = S1 & "Location=Stykkisholmur"

In other words, the refinement sets up a set of equations between the states.

Figure 3-21 – Case refinement in general

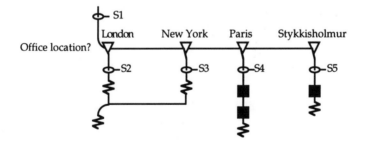

We could go further and simply label the individual threads with the conditions that cause them to be followed, *but without requiring that as a set they should be mutually exclusive.* In other words, any thread whose condition is true will start (strictly, the first process element in such a thread – interaction or activity, or whatever – will have its triggering condition satisfied). However, in our RADs we generally expect the conditions on a case refinement to be mutually exclusive.

Going one step further we can say that there is no requirement that at least one thread must be activated. In other words, in the example in figure 3-18, it might be the case that we also have an office in Tokyo for which the case refinement has nothing to say, in which case the RAD "peters out" (in this area at least – other parts might still be active).

REPRESENTING CONCURRENT THREADS OF ACTION

There might be a point at which a role can start a number of separate threads of activity that can be carried out concurrently. This is represented in a RAD by the symbol shown in figure 3-1 for *part refinement*. The state of the role is being refined (divided) into a number of separate parts. An example of part refinement is the early split in the *Designer* role in figure 3-2 where a designer carries out two concurrent threads of activity. On one thread the designer chooses a method; on the other they first prepare an estimate, then interact with the project manager to pass over the estimate; and finally wait for a second interaction to receive a plan back from the project manager. Part refinement can involve any number of threads of concurrent activity, depending on just how much concurrency is possible in the work of the role.

Figure 3-22 – The state before a three-way part refinement

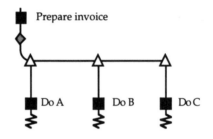

Figure 3-23 – The equivalent state at the start of a three-way part refinement

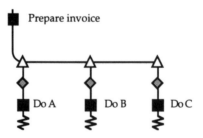

Using tokens again, we can think of the single token that reaches the part refinement becoming a number of tokens, each of which passes down one thread of the part refinement. In figure 3-22, the activity *Prepare invoice* has completed and there is a state token on the state line coming out of *Prepare invoice* and before the part refinement. This state is entirely equivalent to that shown in figure 3-23 where the token before the part refinement has "turned into" one on each of the separate part threads.

This state is entirely equivalent to that shown in figure 3-23 where the token before the part refinement has "turned into" one on each of the separate part threads.

It is sometimes the case that all the concurrent threads must complete before the role can proceed to further activity; in this case we use the representation in figure 3-24, with the threads being joined once they have finished (ie the part states are recombined). We can expect that at some point after the part threads have gone their separate ways, they will all have finished and hence there will be a token sitting on the state at the end of each thread, as shown in the example in figure 3-24. This is precisely the same state as that shown in figure 3-25 where the part thread tokens have all been replaced by a single token on the state line immediately after the closure of the part refinement.

Figure 3-24 – The state at the end of a three-way part refinement

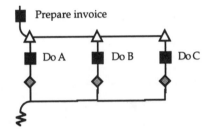

Figure 3-25 – The equivalent state after a three-way part refinement

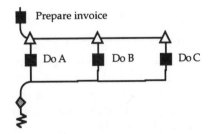

In some cases however, a process does not operate this way. A project manager's activity might be considered as two quite separate areas of responsibility or "sub-roles": keeping staff occupied with work and liaising with the client. These might be the two threads of an early part refinement of the role, which need never recombine. In figure 3-26 we show a RAD in which the part refinements all recombine; on the other hand, in figure 3-27 two of the four threads recombine, whilst two others never do, one endlessly looping on itself and the other diving off to somewhere else in the process.

Figure 3-26 – A four-way part refinement where all threads recombine at closure

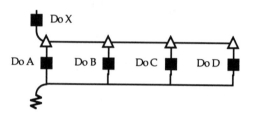

Figure 3-27 – A four-way part refinement where only two threads recombine

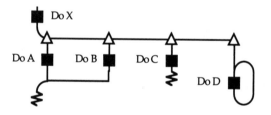

It is important to note that whenever two or more threads recombine at the refinement's closure the role cannot proceed in that "area" until all those threads have completed.

Replicated part refinement

In some situations, a thread of activity might be started up a number of times simultaneously, once for each of a number of cases. For instance, when a Line Manager wants to find out the state of each of the projects currently active, they will have an interaction with each of the current Project Managers. The number of projects active at any one moment may be variable so we need a way of representing this. Figure 3-28 shows how we do it. The single thread that is to be replicated is shown within the usual case refinement structure, and the replication is indicated with an asterisk. The number of times the thread is replicated is captured in some annotation, in this case *For each active project.* (If the sense is clear the asterisk is not shown.)

As in a usual part refinement, the replicated threads might or might not recombine.

Figure 3-28 – A replicated part refinement

Line Manager

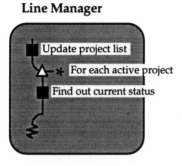

Combining threads in a role's action

It is quite often the case that we want two or more parts of the action of a role to come together, even though they did not originate as separate threads from a part refinement. For instance, the payroll department will prepare a cheque for an employee and get it authorised at the end of a number of different procedures, all of which start from different triggering points:

– at the end of the month when the salary payment is due and the timesheet has been checked

– whenever a cash advance has been approved

– whenever the reimbursement of expenses has been approved.

To show these different parts of the role coming together to a single thread we simply combine the state lines at the appropriate point as in figure 3-29. This says simply that whichever of those states the role is in, its future behaviour is the same, viz it makes payment.

The threads can come from anywhere within the role.[2] Organisational activity often ambles around from role to role, dividing and recombining, ducking and weaving, jumping off at tangents, sometimes coming back. Our notation must allow us to model the "untidiness" of the real world. Within a

---

[2] A note for those with a software engineering background. I often say that in RADs "gotos are considered normal". The reason is simple: we are modelling the real world, and the real world is not Dijkstra-structured, no matter how much we might prefer it to be!

role, threads of activity can divide, recombine, and switch to other threads without constraint – simply because that is the way the real world operates: as a network rather than a hierarchy. And roles can operate in a similar way using interactions as the mechanism for "jumping".

Figure 3-29 – Three threads combine to form one

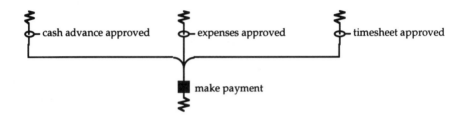

(The remainder of this section is again for the more technically minded. Skip to the start of the next section if you are not.)

Putting this in state terms, the fragment in figure 3-30 tells us that if state S1 is the post-condition of A1, state S2 is the post-condition of A2, and state S3 is the triggering condition of A3, then S1⇒S3 and S2⇒S3 (this is the minimal condition; it is often the case that we can assume that S1=S2=S3).

Figure 3-30 – Thread combination in state terms

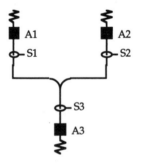

An obvious situation where we want to have threads leading to the same thread is the case of a loop. Suppose that once I have done activity X I can carry out activity Y as often as I like: as soon as I have finished Y I can do it again. Figure 3-31 models this situation. Of course, any amount of process can form the body of a loop – it need not be a single activity. More complicated issues to do with repeated behaviour are dealt with in chapter 5.

Figure 3-31 – Looping for ever on an activity

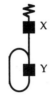

REPRESENTING EXTERNAL EVENTS

As with any modelling scheme we must decide what is in the model and what is outside; and once we have made that decision we have to represent the boundary between what we have chosen to include and what we have excluded. In a process model, we define the boundary in terms of black box activities, interactions (one side of which we do not explore), and – of interest here – those points in the process at which *events* occur outside the process we are modelling and impinge on our process. (The question of the *boundary* of a process model is dealt with in more detail in chapter 5.)

We show an event by an arrow placed on the state line – see figure 3-1 – and annotated with a brief description of the event concerned. In figure 3-2 we see that the single thread of the *Divisional Director* role "gets going" as soon as the external event *New project approved* has occurred. In strict terms, an external event moves the role concerned from the state preceding the little arrow to the state just after it – imagine this in terms of the movement of a token. In figure 3-32 we see a role waiting for someone to resign. We have labelled the states before and after to emphasise the way the event changes the state.

Figure 3-32 – The before and after states of an event

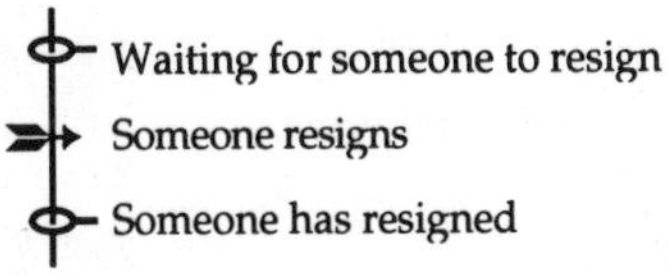

          Waiting for someone to resign

          Someone resigns

          Someone has resigned

In figure 3-2 the RAD is telling us that a *Divisional Director* role instance must wait until a new project has been approved – somewhere outside this process – before it can proceed. (Of course, Divisional Directors can be expected to do more than wait around like this; but in this process model we are only concerned with this "contribution" made by the role to this process.)

The event arrow is a commonly used notation, as we often want to show external events triggering activity in a role in the process we are modelling, as well as allowing the role to "move on". Such events can take a number of forms.

Calendar time and clock time

End of month might be an absolute time event that causes the start of month-end paperwork (figure 3-33). *1800hrs Thursday* might signal the start of work on the weekly wages cycle. *1st May* might signal the start of the annual budget round.

Figure 3-33 – An event marking calendar or clock time

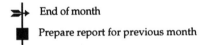

End of month

Prepare report for previous month

The passage of time

Sometimes work has to be suspended until a certain period of time has passed since the completion of a prior activity. Our little arrow symbol allows us to represent this. *Thirty days later* could be used to define a "relative" time event: thirty days after an invoice has been sent out we might check that payment has been received. Figure 3-34 shows a situation where a letter is sent to a customer and the role waits two weeks before making a phone call to follow up the letter.

Figure 3-34 – An event marking the passage of time

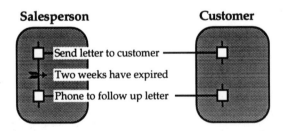

An external event

We might want to capture the fact that something has happened outside our process which has an impact on it and is purposely communicated to it. For instance, suppose we are modelling the recruitment process in a company. The resignation of a member of staff will cause a thread of activity to start in the *Human Resources* role in our process, preparing job specifications, contacting recruitment agencies and so on. The person resigning would communicate their resignation to the Human Resources role in some way. We might not be concerned in our model to know the detail of the resignation, or how it was communicated or any more details, other than that it has occurred and that a certain post is to become vacant. We would represent this using something like figure 3-35.

Figure 3-35 – An external event

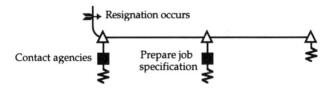

We could on the other hand take the view that the resignation is in some way an interaction between the *Human Resources* role in our process and some role in the other process, and we would end up with something like figure 3-36. But this adds little and only moves the boundary of our process out to some portion of the role *Resigning*, leading us firstly to think (perhaps unnecessarily) about the identity of that external role, and secondly what led up to that interaction in the *Resigning* role! As it stands, figure 3-36 shows a process which depends on the role *Resigning* deciding to have the *Notify resignation* interaction for anything to happen.

However if we are concerned, for instance, to check the way we deal with someone who has resigned it is obviously important that this interaction should appear, and, indeed, we might decide we want to capture precisely *how* that interaction takes place.

Figure 3-36 – Treating an external event as an interaction

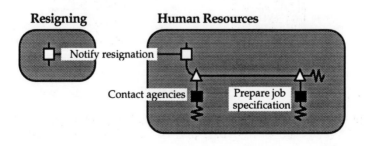

The external event might be more "distant". In our *Human Resources* role we might have a mechanism for handling changes in the legislation to do with employment terms and conditions. We might prepare for anticipated changes and then, at the moment that the legislation passes into law, swing into action with those changes. We can regard this as an external event and represent it straightforwardly as in figure 3-37.

Figure 3-37 – A "distant" external event

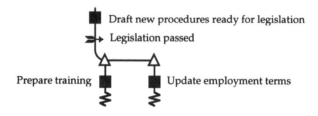

Once again, we could feel – perhaps with less justification this time – that this is really an interaction, and should be shown differently as in figure 3-38. The interaction is of course rather tenuous: something along the lines of "Human Resources hears about new legislation passed by the Legislature"; the Legislature probably doesn't feel it is interacting directly with our HR people – they simply publish new legislation in a well known place and our HR people read about it there. Which representation we choose will depend, as ever, on why we are modelling.

Figure 3-38 – An external event modelled as an interaction

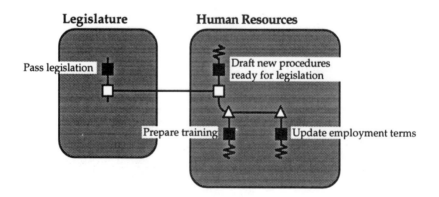

An internal event

It is not uncommon for certain parts of the process to be started off according to the dictates of a plan which is prepared *during* the process we are modelling. In other words, the *threads* of activity that will be carried out are known, but exactly which threads will be done and which order they will be done might be decided on-the-fly, as the process proceeds. Those decisions – what and when – are what plans are all about. Our plan will tell us that, when a certain condition is right, a certain thread of activity should be started, but we cannot tell which or when until we are into the process.

Figure 3-39 – Internal events

Suppose our business is developing new electrical goods. At various points in the design and development of a new product we will need to carry out various tests and obtain certificates of compliance with certain regulations. Which tests and which regulations will vary from product to product, and they will be different for a toaster and a hand-dryer. To model such a general Develop New Electrical Product process we will therefore need to show threads of activity to do with carrying out tests and obtaining certificates, with those threads being activated according to "internal events" – effectively "the plan says the moment is right". Figure 3-39 gives an example.

Figure 3-40 – Waiting for set of (variable) activities to complete

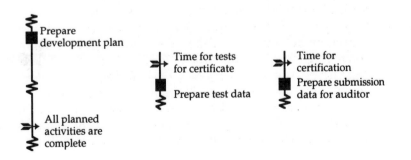

Equally we might want to wait at some point in the process for a set of planned activity (threads) to have completed before continuing. For instance we might plan a set of certification tests and then wait for them all to be completed before proceeding; we cannot explicitly show a part refinement for the tests as we do not know at modelling time which tests will be carried out. Our RAD might then look as in figure 3-40.

As-and-when events

Finally there is the situation where a thread of activity can be triggered at any time. It might be on a whim – "let's carry out an audit of the retail side of the business". If we are not concerned with modelling the lead-up to that event we can show it quite simply on a RAD, as in figure 3-41.

Figure 3-41 – An as-and-when event

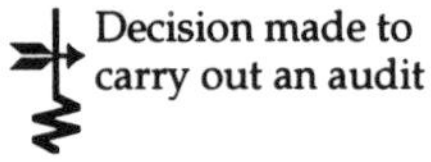

Decision made to
carry out an audit

In some situations we might not even feel the need to model the event so explicitly, especially where the activity that is carried out on triggering is an interaction. This is dealt with further in chapter 5.

Some examples

Figure 3-42 shows some typical situations modelled in different ways. The first pair of RAD fragments shows a manager who has to prepare a report at the end of the month *and* whenever the Board requests a report. The second pair shows the manager writing the report at the end of the month or the end of the accounting period, whichever comes first. The third shows the manager writing the report at the end of the month or the end of the accounting period whichever is the later.

Events can perform magic

An event is a way of defining part of the boundary of our model. We are recognising that something happens "out there" that affects "in here". The actual effect can include a little magic: the event might cause the importation of something into the process (strictly, into the role body), or it might change the state of something already in the process (strictly, inside the role body).

Figure 3-43 shows an event – *Application form arrives from customer* – that imports something into the role: the application form from the customer. The fact that we have shown its arrival as an external event says that we don't care (for the purposes of this model at least) how this happens. It just does. The role now has that application form in its possession, in its role body.

Figure 3-42 – Some sample events modelled

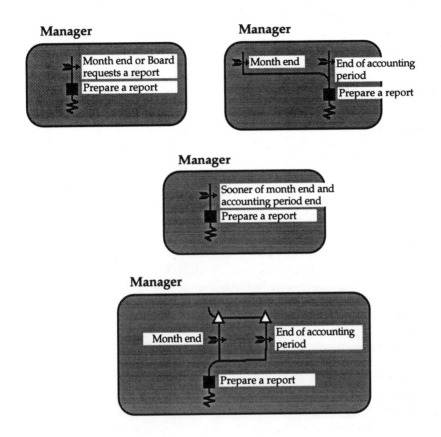

Figure 3-43 – An event importing something into the role body

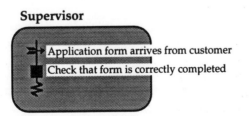

Figure 3-44 shows an external event changing the state of something already in the role body: the sales predictions in the possession of the Chief Accountant have, somehow (and we're not saying how), been changed.

Figure 3-44 – An event changing the state of something in the role body

Chief Accountant

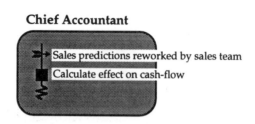

TERMINOLOGY

It is worth checking at this point on the terminology that we have used. Coming from a software engineering background, it is not surprising that our terminology aligns more or less with that adopted in the software engineering process world where a great deal of research work has been done into the modelling of processes. Humphrey and Feiler[3] define a *process* as "a set of partially ordered steps intended to reach a goal" – a RAD is clearly about such a process, with the partial ordering being captured in terms of strict ordering (*A* follows *B*) and case and part refinement. A process is composed of *process elements* – in a RAD the process elements are activities, interactions, and instantiations. Curtis *et al* have given other definitions[4]:

- *agent* – a human or machine who performs a process element: what we call an *actor*

- *role* – a coherent set of process elements to be assigned to an agent as a unit of functional responsibility

- *artefact* – a product created or modified by the enactment of a process element: what we call *entity*.

---

[3] *Software process development and enactment: concepts and definitions*, W S Humphrey & P H Feiler, Technical Report SEI-92-TR-4, Software Engineering Institute, Carnegie Mellon University, Pittsburgh, 1992

[4] *Process modelling*, W Curtis, M I Kellner & J Over, *Communications of the ACM*, **35**, 9, pp75-90, September 1992 (a paper well worth reading even though it is specifically about the software development process)

4

ANIMATING A PROCESS MODEL

INTRODUCTION

When we draw a RAD we are essentially drawing a static model, but one that describes the potential behaviour of an organisation when it carries out the process that we have modelled. As we looked at each concept in the notation in chapter 3 – case refinement, part refinement etc – we found it useful to animate the fragments of RAD in order to understand the sorts of behaviour that we had effectively defined. In this chapter we will look at the business of animation on a larger scale: that of the entire RAD. How do we look at a RAD and animate it to see what the process *does*?

A RAD describes a process in terms of the relationships between *types* of roles, types of activities, types of interaction, and types of events. When we animate a RAD we will look at *instances* of roles, activities, interactions and events, and we will be interested in the actual *states* of role instances.

A REMINDER ABOUT STATE

Each line (other than that indicating an interaction) represents a potential state of a role instance. Because a role instance can have more than one thread of work active at any one moment we can be stricter and say that each line represents a potential *sub-state* of a role instance. For instance, when a role instance enters a part refinement with three threads, its state becomes composed of the "sum" of the states on each of those three threads. We showed the state of an instance by placing tokens on the appropriate state lines. We will refer to the position of those tokens as the "marking" of the role instance (to borrow some terminology from Petri Net theory). As the role instance does work – carrying out activities, taking part in interactions, responding to external events – so the position of the tokens will vary: the marking will vary to reflect the change of state of the role instance. We can imagine a software tool on our workstation that shows us our role instance as a RAD with tokens on the state lines to tell us where we have got in carrying out that role. As we do items of work so the marking will change to reflect the way we are moving through the process.

If we stood back and looked at a running process we would see a set of role instances, each in its current state. If we asked the question "what is the state of the process?" we could answer by saying that it is the "sum" of the states of all those separate role instances. This matches real life: "how far have we got with dealing with that insurance claim?", "well, the loss adjuster is currently waiting to arrange a meeting at the claimant's house, the clerk dealing with it has checked with the police and we're sorting out liability with the lawyers right now".

We will be able to tell when the process has reached its goal when the desired states are reached in certain of the role instances.

HOW ROLE INSTANCES "START"

Suppose that a role has just been instantiated in a running process (eg a Task Force has been set up), or a process has just started and there is a pre-existing role instance for one of the roles. What happens to that role instance? To answer this, let's step back for a moment.

Figure 4-1 – "After doing A we can do B"

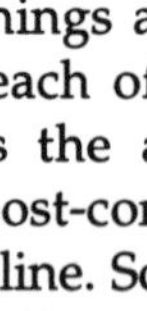

Inside a role we draw all the things a role does or responds to: activities, part-interactions, and events. For each of these we can define the triggering condition: the state which allows the activity, or whatever, to start. We define those states by making the post-condition of one thing the triggering of the next: by connecting them with a line. So, in figure 4-1, when we have done A we can do B: or, in our jargon, the post-condition of A is the triggering condition of B.

Suppose now that we have a thread of activity whose beginning is as shown in figure 4-2. What is the triggering condition of activity A? The rule is that, at the head of a thread, it is the condition "true", and since the value of this condition is always "true" we can deduce that activity A is always ready to run. In other words, for any instance of the role, there is always a token sitting on the state preceding A, as shown in figure 4-3.

This generalises of course to each such thread in the role. Let's revisit the fragment of a process in figure 3-3. When the *Divisional Director* role instance in that process starts there will be a token at the top of each thread, as shown in figure 4-4.

Figure 4-2 – The start of a thread in a role

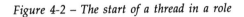

Figure 4-3 – A role instance thread starts

Figure 4-4 – A multi-thread role instance has started

Divisional Director

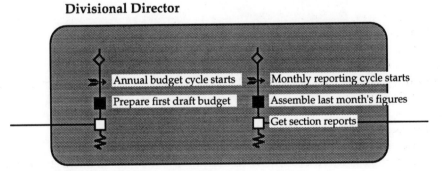

In general, what we will then find is that when a role instance starts it will do one of the following:

– wait in front of an activity, in which case it is up to the actor to decide whether and when to start the activity

– wait to take part in an interaction (see chapter 5 for more on this)

– wait for an event to happen, as in figure 4-4.

Suppose we have a process in which an *Admissions Clerk* role is always waiting for applications and refusals to be received and will start work on each one as it arrives, and on request will provide the *Personnel Director* with monthly statistics. An Admissions Clerk (instance) who is currently not working on any one of these three areas will be in the state shown in figure 4-5. If the Admissions Clerk then receives a refusal and has reviewed it, they will be in the state shown in figure 4-6. Note the token just after the *Review refusal* activity on the lower thread and the tokens still sitting at the start of all three threads.

Figure 4-5 – An idle Admissions Clerk

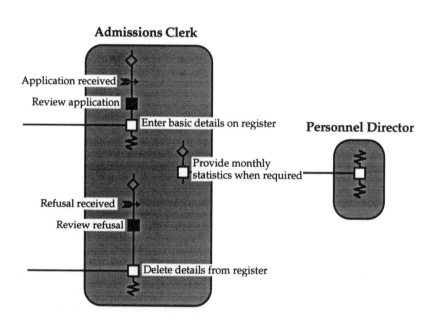

So, the rule is as follows: to animate a role instance we simply place a token at the head of each free thread and see what happens from there. As a thread starts so tokens will "move" through it, but there will always be a token at the head of each thread indicating that the thread can start again at any time.

Figure 4-6 – An Admissions Clerk working and waiting

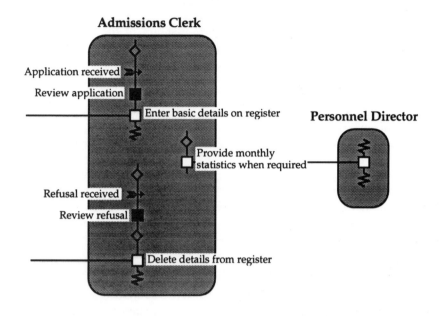

THE "INITIAL" STATE OF A PROCESS

A process might be one of two types:

- the sort that starts when necessary and, perhaps, completes at some time in the future; for instance, the process of running a project in Praxis starts when we win a contract for a client, and ends when that contract has been successfully completed.

- the sort that is constantly running; for instance, if we examine Praxis at any time we will find the process of, say, Managing Cash running constantly. Indeed it would be hard to define the moment it started other than the moment when the company was formed; and we hope the process – albeit in a changing shape – does not stop.

In the case of the constantly running process we need some extra notation. We want to be able to say "when you come to look at this process running, roles *A*, *B*, ..., and *Z* all have existing instances, and moreover, role *A* has two instances, and role *B* has 72 instances". Then, when we read the RAD, we can see what role instances already exist and hence can be assumed to be "running".

We indicate that a given role has an existing instance by following its name with a tick: ✓. If a role has 16 existing instances we follow its name with "16✓". If it has an indeterminate number of instances we mark it with "n✓". In the RAD in figure 3-2 we are showing one instance of the *Divisional Director* role in existence, and we can see that it is waiting for an external event before it gets the process going. There are no instances of *Project Manager* or of *Designer*; these will have to be created when the process runs, which is of course what the crossed box symbol is for.

In chapter 2 we saw that there are two sorts of role that typically have as-good-as permanent instances: the functional position or *post* (eg *Divisional Director*) and the functional group (eg *Accounts*). These will be the sorts of role that will have ticks against them on a RAD.

This is also a useful convention in those situations where we do not wish to model how a role gets started, eg by being started by yet another role (and what started that one? ...); we simply want it to exist in (at least one) instance. This is another way in which we mark the boundary of the process as we are modelling it, as with external events.

HOW ROLE INSTANCES "END"

We have no special notation in STRIM and RADs to mark the "death" of a role instance, no symbol that says "delete this role instance". When we want to show this we simply use a black-box activity with an appropriate label: eg *Close down the Task Force, Finish as Project Manager*, or *End role of Expense Claimant*.

5

MICRO-MODELLING OF PROCESSES

INTRODUCTION

So far, we have looked at the RAD notation and the basic principles of its use. In this chapter we look closely at some of the different detailed process situations that can be found and how they can be modelled in a RAD. We call these *clichés* – they are part of the stock-in-trade of the analyst. (I use the term in its neutral sense of "stereotyped expression" and attach no pejorative meaning to it.) In chapter 7 we look at the large-scale clichés, what we call *patterns*.

CLICHÉS INVOLVING INTERACTIONS

There are a number of "flavours" of interaction that we need to distinguish if we are to model adequately the subtleties in real-life. In this section I examine some of the issues. But first, let us look at what an interaction is in a bit more detail.

Let's look at a fragment of a process as shown in figure 5-1. There are two roles *A* and *B* which are going to interact. At some point *A* is going to send *B* some goods. *B* is only prepared to receive the goods after *Do this* and before *Do that*.

The rules for an interaction say that an interaction cannot start until the participating roles are in their respective pre-states, and that when the interaction finishes they both move into new respective post-states. Either role might get to the interaction before the other. If one is not ready, the "early" one must wait. The top part of figure 5-2 shows *A* waiting for *B* – note the position of the token. The bottom part of figure 5-2 shows *B* waiting for *A*.

Figure 5-1 – A basic interaction

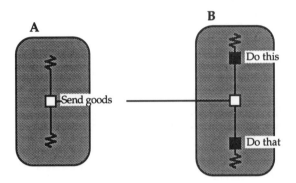

Figure 5-2 – Participating role instances must wait until all are ready

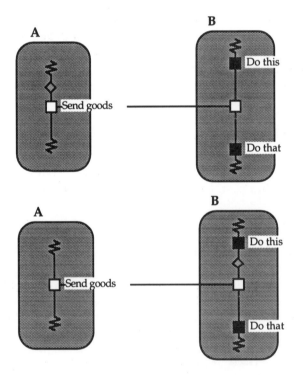

At some point they will both be in their respective pre-states for the interaction – figure 5-3 – and the interaction can start. When it has finished they move to their respective post-states – figure 5-4.

Figure 5-3 – The interaction can start

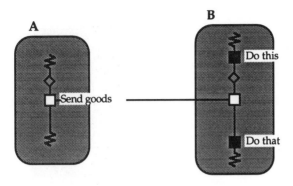

Figure 5-4 – The interaction has completed

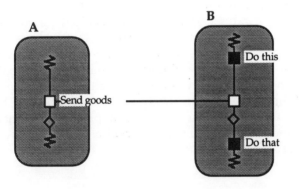

Loose ordering

Remember that a RAD shows strict ordering. It is very easy to draw strict ordering when it is not actually required or present in reality. For instance, if it is the case that *B* must have got to a certain point but then can accept the goods any time after then, *and* must have them before certain other activities can continue, then we render this as shown in figure 5-5. This figure says that once *B* has completed the activity *Do this* it can receive the goods while getting on with other tasks – shown by the part refinement – and once it has received the goods *and* completed those other tasks (indicated by the spring on the right-hand thread of the part refinement) it can *Do that*.

Figure 5-5 – Getting the strictness right

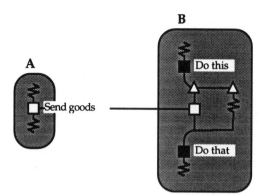

Service interactions

Let's take this a bit further. We have seen how roles interact through interactions, and that interactions can be said to "align" the states of participating role instances: that is, the participating role instances "go through" the interaction together. As far as the RAD is concerned the interaction is atomic; once it has started we know nothing except when it has finished. But of course many things happen between parties without apparently any need to synchronise so explicitly. For instance, some roles provide some form of on-demand service: a Line Manager will authorise leave requests at any time, rather than only at some prescribed point in *their* work. So some part of the Line Manager's work must involve "waiting around" in case such a demand arises.

Figure 5-6 – A role ready to have an interaction at any time

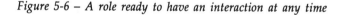

This cliché is modelled quite straightforwardly in a RAD by having a separate (ie concurrent) fragment in the service role "hanging free" – see figure 5-6. By definition, the triggering condition for such a part-interaction on the server's side is "true", ie that role is ready to undertake such an interaction on demand, at any time. Indeed, that fragment can be started/instantiated an indefinite number of times as requests for service come in, since the triggering condition remains "true". This is often what we want. Not all activity is strictly sequenced in the sense of "when *x* has finished do *y*"; often the logic is more catch-all: "whenever necessary do *y*". The interaction with a hanging fragment is a special case of this.

Primed service interactions

In some situations we might wish to have an activity thread hanging free, ready to respond, but only after some prior activity has been completed. For instance, once a business has acquired its VAT registration it can process any number of orders arriving asynchronously. We would show this cliché in a RAD as in figure 5-7. The VAT registration activity takes place and the role then enters a state where it is able to accept an interaction (a purchase order). That interaction causes two threads to start: one to process the order, and another to wait for another interaction (another purchase order). While the first order is being processed, a second can arrive which again causes the two threads to start: one to process the second order and another to wait for the third; and so on.

Figure 5-7 – Many-at-a-time processing after initialisation

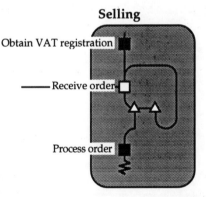

We can see this more easily by looking at it in terms of tokens. Figure 5-8 shows the states through which the RAD fragment passes:

1   Registration for VAT has been completed; waiting for the first order.

2   The first order has arrived via the interaction.

3   An equivalent state to state 2, using the definition of a part refinement.

4   An equivalent state to state 3, remembering that a state line shows a single state. The role is now ready to process the first order and also ready to accept the second.

Figure 5-8 – The successive states of figure 5-7

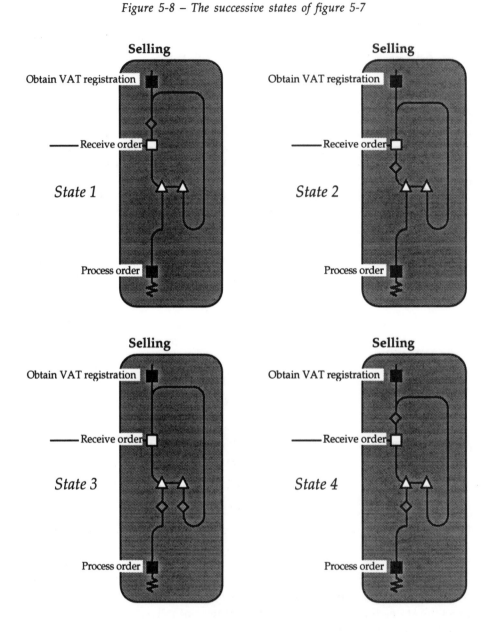

The thread to process an order is successively started as each order arrives. In fact, strictly, the activities on that thread are instantiated as and when their triggering condition becomes true. We can imagine that the activities on the thread are being instantiated as many times as there are orders. Certainly each "thread instance" proceeds independently, at its own pace. There is no implication that orders "queue" to follow the thread. In fact, it is quite possible for orders to be processed at different speeds – the RAD says nothing about which order is finished first.

Strictly sequenced service

In some cases it might not be desirable to have an activity thread hanging free in such a way that it can be activated at any time or indefinitely many times: we might wish to handle requests just one at a time in strict sequence. In this case a hanging interaction is clearly not what is wanted, and in order to serialise the processing of requests we put that processing in a loop with the interaction at its head. The processing can no longer take place asynchronously: it can only occur when the server has finished serving the previous request. This cliché is shown in figure 5-9.

Figure 5-9 – One-at-a-time processing

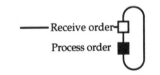

(A reasonable question is "how does this fragment start?". The answer is that we suppose that, when an instance of the role is started, a token is placed on the loop so that that side of the interaction is primed. But we do not need to show this.)

Sweeping interactions

Suppose that a process involves a role *A* of which there is only ever one instance (eg *Managing Director*), and that we want to represent the fact that, at month end, that role instance interacts with *all* instances of role *B* (eg *Project Manager*) to obtain status reports. How should we represent this cliché? This takes us back to the replicated part refinement described in chapter 3. We saw there how we could represent a single thread of activity being started (instantiated) many times concurrently, as in figure 5-10. If that thread contains an interaction with some other role, we are representing the situation where, in this case, the Line Manager goes off to all the Project Managers to find out their status, or, in our jargon, the instance of *Line Manager* interacts with all *Project Manager* instances concurrently.

As a convenient abbreviation for this we sometimes use the notation shown in figure 5-11 with exactly the same meaning as that of figure 5-10. Note the use of the "crow's foot" at the *Project Manager* end of the interaction; this means "all current instances of".

Figure 5-10 – A sweeping interaction

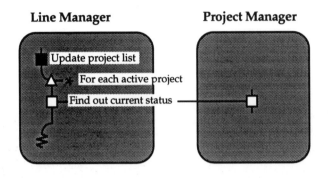

Figure 5-11 – A sweeping interaction abbreviated

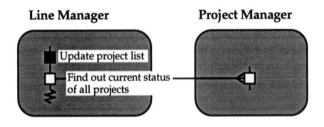

Conditional interactions

It is not uncommon for an interaction to take place only under certain conditions. For instance, suppose that you (a buyer) order some goods from me (a seller). When you receive the goods from me, you check that they are OK, and, if they are not, you send them back to me. The interaction for returning the goods to me only takes place *if* they are not OK. How should we model this? Our first thought might be to draw a process as shown in figure 5-12. Follow it through.

This would be wrong. Firstly, remember that a case refinement does not involve any action: it simply divides the state. So, the figure says that, in the *Selling* role, immediately after the goods have been shipped, we can refine the state marked *Goods sent* either into the state *OK goods sent* or into the state *Faulty goods sent*, and hence the token for the role instance can be immediately placed on one of the two arms of the case refinement. But if this really were the case it would mean that the seller knew immediately after shipment whether the goods were faulty or not and got ready to respond appropriately! If we assume that the seller is not so underhand we have modelled the wrong process. The problem is that the condition *Goods OK?* cannot be ascertained at that point within the body of the *Selling* role. Only the *Buying* role has the resources within its body to ascertain the value of the condition.

A correct model for this cliché would therefore be that shown in figure 5-13.

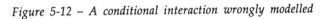

Figure 5-12 – A conditional interaction wrongly modelled

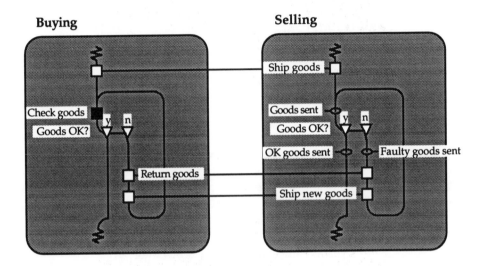

Figure 5-13 – A conditional interaction correctly modelled

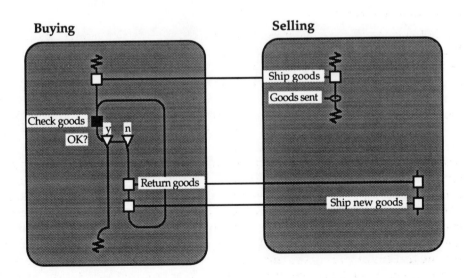

Here, we show the case refinement only in the *Buying* role and a second interaction with the *Selling* role only taking place if the goods are not OK. The *Selling* end of that interaction takes the form of a "hanging" fragment: it takes place whenever necessary, and we do not need to tie it into the rest of the role. Only if the *Buying* role takes the initiative and "forces" the interaction will the *Selling* role need to do anything about it. Presumably the seller doesn't ship goods and then start waiting for faulty returned goods before proceeding; the handling of faulty goods is a separate activity dealt with as and when – which is precisely what the hanging fragment says.

If the seller had a standard practice of always checking with the buyer that the goods delivered were satisfactory then we would explicitly model this of course.

Interacting with systems

We know that computer systems can sometimes play a role in a process and we might want to express this explicitly. Figure 5-14 captures this cliché in the situation where data is being put into a database; other interactions could show data being accessed.

It should not be regarded as a rule that computer systems should always be shown or should always be shown in this way. But we might well do this sort of modelling if we were modelling an as-is process and were particularly keen on understanding the ordering of interactions with a computer database.

Figure 5-14 – Interacting with a computer system

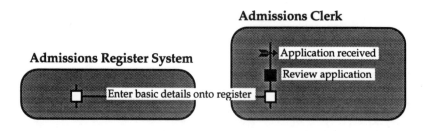

The simple contract

By now the modelling of the simple cliché of someone asking for and receiving a service should be child's play – see figure 5-15. This shows the basic elements. I have not connected *Request service* and *Pay for service*: in fact it makes no difference to the logic (try it with tokens), though it might look slightly odd not to have it. We can extend this cliché to the Winograd idiom described in chapter 7 and draw figure 5-16.

Figure 5-15 – Contracting for a service

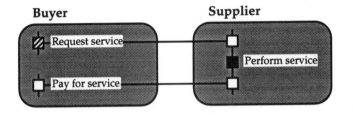

Figure 5-16 – A full contractual cycle initiated by a Buyer

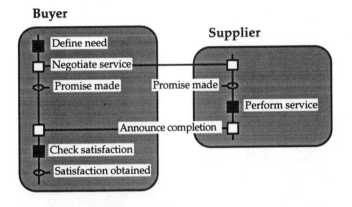

If the *Supplier* initiates the deal by making an offer we have the process shown in figure 5-17.

Figure 5-17 – A full contractual cycle initiated by a Supplier

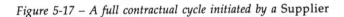

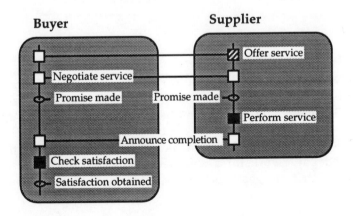

TIMING OUT AN ACTIVITY

What if a role wishes to "time-out" an activity it is carrying out? For instance, suppose a help-desk takes calls from users of a software product. If the help-desk person cannot answer the question there and then on the telephone they tell the caller that they will go away and investigate the enquiry and call back with an answer within the hour. If at the end of the hour, they don't have an answer to give the caller, they need to give an interim report on things and perhaps give a new deadline by which they will get back. We want to show both the intended process – immediate answer or call back within the hour – but also the process if an hour passes without an answer emerging from the investigation.

To do this we show the handling of a late activity as a response to the event which is the timing out of the activity. And when the activity does finish (or gets aborted perhaps) we take an appropriate course of action depending on whether it has timed out – see figure 5-18.

Figure 5-18 – An activity times out

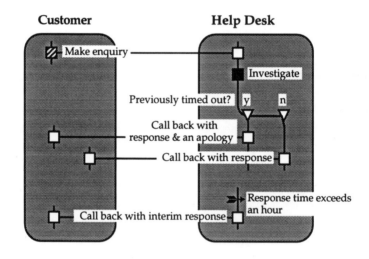

TIMING OUT AN INTERACTION

It is very common for people to wait for just so long for someone else to do something before they switch to "plan B" and take some other action. They "time out" the interaction. If it doesn't happen soon enough they cannot wait and must take some other action.

Figure 5-19 models a process in which a *Section Manager* waits until they have received paperwork for a shipment from *QA* and notification from *Manufacturing* that the goods are ready before authorising shipment of the goods by *Shipping*. There is an element of optimism about the world in this process: apparently the paperwork always arrives in a reasonable timeframe.

Figure 5-19 – An optimistic process

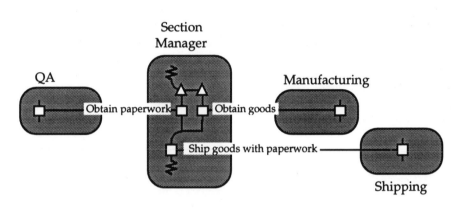

If we were modelling the process and did not press our questions very hard this is the story we might hear. But of course we might guess that the *Section Manager* won't wait for ever for the paperwork to turn up. Further questioning might reveal that the process as actually implemented takes a rather more pessimistic view of the world and has a work-around for when the paperwork is late, in other words, for when the *Obtain paperwork* interaction times out as perceived by the *Section Manager*.

That pessimistic process is shown in figure 5-20. The *Section Manager* starts the two interactions with *QA* and *Manufacturing* as before, but now, having received the goods from *Manufacturing*, has two possible courses of action: one in the case where the paperwork arrives on time (on the other thread of the part refinement), and another in the case where that interaction with *QA* times out. In the first case, the *Section Manager* proceeds as normal, shipping the goods with the paperwork. In the second case, they ship the goods with temporary paperwork and, at the same time, wait (even longer, in fact indefinitely) for the real paperwork to turn up. When it does, the follow-up paperwork can be sent off and the process resumes its "normal" course, with an invoice being sent to the consignee.

More complicated mechanisms can be modelled using a ➤ to pick up time-outs and respond to them. Note how two are used in figure 5-20: one to detect the possible initial time-out of the paperwork and another to detect the eventual arrival of the paperwork.

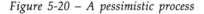

Figure 5-20 – A pessimistic process

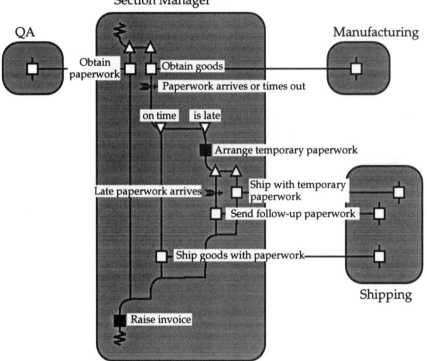

DRAWING THE BOUNDARY OF THE PROCESS

When we draw a RAD, no matter how much detail we put in it, or how "big" it is, we are always drawing a boundary somewhere, a boundary that says "for this model I'm not interested in what happens beyond here". It is useful to understand the different ways in which we can "cut" through the world to divide it into those bits we are interested in and those bits we are not.

The black box activity as a boundary

The first and obvious boundary in a RAD is the black box activity. By representing an activity as a black box we are treating it as an atom and saying that we are not concerned here with the detail of what goes on in that activity. The black box is a sort of lower boundary to the detail of activity that we want to capture. We might wish at some point to examine what happens "inside" the box – we deal with this in chapter 6. Of course, we might describe the activity to some level of detail via the name that we give it on the RAD. That name can be detailed and explicit, or as vague as we choose it to be.

Figure 5-21 gives examples of the sorts of things we might say when describing a single activity. Note how they might describe a small, short-lived action or something very large and very long-lasting.

Figure 5-21 – Varieties of activity "sizes"

Prepare production line for new car design

Complete hand-over form for production line

Agree pricing with dealerships

Issue Press Release

The interaction as a boundary

Similarly, an interaction is an atomic thing: we cannot tell what in detail goes on when the interaction takes place. It just happens at the appointed states in the participating roles and that's an end to it as far as the model is concerned. Another lower boundary of detail. Again, we shall deal with "decomposing" interactions in chapter 6.

As with an activity, the "size" and typical duration of an interaction can vary enormously and in figure 5-22 we can see some examples.

Figure 5-22 – Varieties of interaction "sizes"

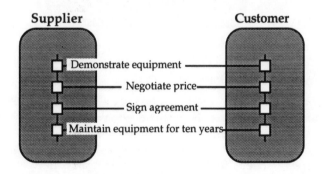

The external event as a boundary

The external event is clearly a boundary too. In figure 5-23, the event *Decision made to carry out an audit* says that the process moves forward when this event occurs, and that we are not interested in where or why or how it occurs, only that it occurs.

Figure 5-23 The external event as a boundary

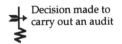

Decision made to
carry out an audit

Pre-existing roles as a boundary

We can consider pre-existing role instances as a form of boundary to our process. In figure 5-24 we are saying "however it came about, there is a single instance of the role *Task Force* when we come to look at this process". An instance might be there because it is, say, a fixed post in an organisation such as *Managing Director*, or because some other role in some other process – we care not what – has created the instance in order, say, to get this process going.

Figure 5-24 – The pre-existing role instance as boundary

Task Force ✓

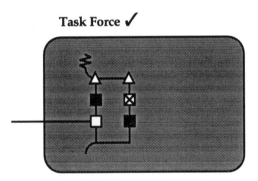

Boundary definition by omission

Finally, we sometimes show the boundary of a process simply by omitting things. The most common example of this is where we only draw those parts of a real-world role that are relevant to the process we are looking at. Figure 5-25 shows how we might wish to indicate that, for certain items of expenditure, the Finance Director needs to be told, and to that end there is an interaction with the *Finance Director* role. But we have chosen *not* to show just what the Finance Director does with the information – this is outside our interest perhaps. Clearly, the Finance Director does more in life than is suggested by this RAD, but everything else besides accepting notification of major expenditures is outside the boundary chosen for this perspective.

Figure 5-25 – Omission as boundary

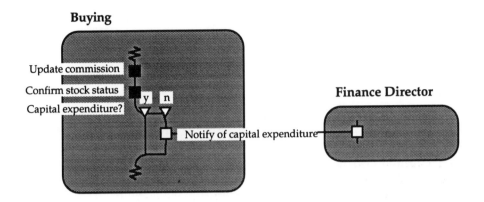

ADDING DETAILS ABOUT ACTIVITIES AND INTERACTIONS

Finally in this chapter we look at some of the details about the process that we might want to store on the RAD, details which concern the individual activities and interactions, and which could be of use during the analysis phase covered in chapter 9.

Most of the details can be stored against the individual process elements via the computer tool being used to store the RADs, so we do not have a separate notation for the RADs themselves. However, for the purposes of this chapter we will augment the basic notation to help us out.

Resources

Almost every activity will involve resources in some form. Those resources could be information, raw materials, intermediate product components, paperwork, computers, tools, equipment, ... in fact anything in the physical environment. The activity might both consume and produce resources: taking in raw materials, expending the effort of people, using machinery, and passing on finished goods, for instance.

In some cases, especially information, we might be particularly concerned with the *flow* of the resource around the process: one activity produces information used by another further down the process. So we annotate each activity with the resources it requires and produces. During drafting this can simply be done as shown in figure 5-26.

In chapter 8 we will look in a lot more detail at the part played by entities in the process and how we can complement the RAD with models of entities, their relationships, and their life histories.

Figure 5-26 – Modelling the resource usage and production of an activity

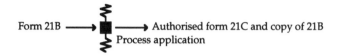

Form 21B ⟶ ■ ⟶ Authorised form 21C and copy of 21B
                    Process application

Duration and resource consumption

When we want to take a quantitative view of the process in chapter 9 we will probably need details about the duration of the individual activities and interactions and also on the amounts of resource they use: people and people's time, quantities of input materials and any other resources needed.

In some cases this information might already be known from measurement, or can be estimated, or might actually need measuring. If there is a significant spread in the figures, it can be useful to record that spread in some way: perhaps a sketch graph of the probability, or something along the lines of "it normally takes 2-3 days, never less than one, and in rare circumstances up to six". Once again we simply annotate the activity or interaction on the RAD with whatever information we wish to keep.

Case refinement frequencies

Case refinements represent alternative courses of action, and when we come to analyse the process it might well be important to know how often the different alternatives are followed. In figure 5-27, how often does the *Widget Maker* have to rework the design? We simply annotate the RAD in an appropriate way. Figure 5-27 shows a simple percentage, but there might be seasonal variation or it might depend on some other characteristic of the process (the depth of the items in the in-tray, the rate at which work is being done, etc).

Figure 5-27 – An annotated case refinement

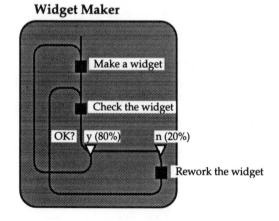

Widget Maker

Make a widget

Check the widget

OK?   y (80%)   n (20%)

Rework the widget

6

MODELLING LARGE PROCESSES

INTRODUCTION

We have now looked at the RAD notation, its basic principles, and how a RAD can be used to capture details of a business process in terms of a variety of clichés. In this chapter I take a first look at "modelling-in-the-large", in particular at how large processes can be handled with RADs. In the next chapter I look at the different perspectives that the modeller can take of a single process, and at the different large-scale clichés – what we refer to as *process patterns* – that are encountered.

There are times when the process being modelled is relatively small, that is, it can be drawn to the level of detail required on a single sheet of paper. This is the case where a simple procedure is being set down in a Procedures Manual or a Quality Manual: there are a few roles, a few activities each (say up to a dozen) and a few interactions. But in many cases, especially where a entire business is being modelled from several viewpoints, or a very large process (eg "product development") is to be considered, a number of issues arise as to how such large processes should be captured. Can we look at the process from different "levels" of detail? Can we show how a business is composed of a number of connected processes, that intersect and overlap in possibly complicated ways?

In this chapter we look at the answers to these questions as part of building the "machinery" we need. We start by considering just what we mean by "levels" and "abstractions" in a process model, and in a RAD in particular.

ABSTRACTIONS, DETAIL AND LEVELS

Intuitively we know we will want to be able to view a process from different levels, perhaps ranging from a high level, where we see the broad brush perspective with detail removed, to a low level, where we can inspect the minutiae of the process. In the high-level view we want to pull out the main features of the process, to see the wood rather than the trees.

A feature of the RAD notation is that we can of course model a process from any perspective we choose; we can put in what we like and leave out what we like, and we can draw the boundary of what we model where we like. In particular we can model the process at the broad-brush level, or the minutiae (and we can even mix the two levels on the same picture if that helps us). For instance, we might model the overall process by which a pharmaceutical company develops a new drug product for the marketplace as in figure 6-1. Once a promising molecule has been discovered by *Discovery*, three main roles develop the technology necessary for its production (*Process Scale-up*), ensure its safety and efficacy (*Clinical*), and determine the right delivery mechanism (*Formulation*), so that *Regulatory Affairs* can prepare the submission document that will be presented to the regulatory body (which we have chosen not to show) in order to get approval for the drug to be manufactured and sold. The RAD takes a very high-level view. The roles equate to entire departments or possibly separate companies, each involving thousands of people. The process itself can take a dozen years from start to end.

Figure 6-1 – A high-level process model of the development of a new drug

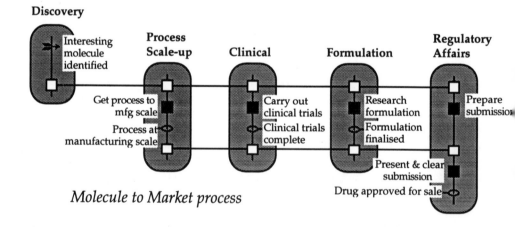

At this level our purpose is probably to provide context for some thinking about the way the process fits across our organisation. The model, to serve that purpose, omits a mass of detail. For instance, we have shown only the main roles, and we have shown them, through black-box activities, carrying out their work ignoring the fact that at some level those black boxes represent collaborative activity across the roles, albeit led by one role in each case. We might alternatively recognise the constant and detailed interactions they have with each other in carrying out their own work by replacing these black boxes with interactions.

At the other end of the spectrum, we might use a RAD to specify or describe the detailed procedure used in the Pharmacy to pack dosage forms for clinical trials. The roles would now be at a level where each is acted by an individual, with each activity taking a few hours. Such a model captures part of the process at a micro-level.

Extending this, should we expect to be able to take a high-level RAD of a process and decompose it into a set of RADs at "the next level" down, and then to decompose each of those in their turn?

To answer this we first need to understand the relationship between a high-level RAD and a low-level RAD. What connects the two? In what sense is the low-level RAD "part of" the high-level RAD? How do the roles, activities and interactions in the low-level RAD "map into" those in the high-level RAD? Indeed, is it in general possible or even sensible to construct a hierarchical decomposition of a process into a set of RADs at varying levels of detail?

Traditionally, information systems analysts have used data-oriented techniques to model the activity of a business. Data flow diagrams (DFDs), entity life histories (ELHs), entity-relationship-attribute (ERA) models, and Jackson structure charts are among the notations employed in the techniques, and they all centre around the concept of data. This has of course been a reasonable approach. The final target of the systems analyst has been some form of IT system which would probably be built around some sort of data store: a file system, relational database, or whatever. The storage and retrieval of data were the primitives of the machine and hence became the primitives of the business model. If we are going to build a database system then we had better analyse the process being automated from the point of view of the data it uses (or the entities it is concerned with).

Models like DFDs, ELHs and Jackson structure charts are the products of software engineering minds, and software engineers are very fond of *hierarchically* structured things – they are amenable to elegant, simple and well understood handling. As a result the models themselves take the form of hierarchies. And they work pretty well, in that the hierarchical structures that the notations impose are more or less present in the real world of computer systems and software.

I say "more or less" since the correspondence is not always as close as one would want it. Let me look at DFDs in particular.

A single level of a DFD shows a network of activities and datastores connected by data flows. A DFD recognises that a process/activity is not neatly structured at any given level and can be as involved as the people operating it wish to make it. But a DFD has a number of levels. An activity *A* in a level *N* DFD can be decomposed into its own level *N*+1 DFD, showing the sub-activities and data flows between them. The "external" data flows in and out of *A* at level *N* also become decomposed at level *N*+1. To make this work we invent various abstractions of activities and data flows at the higher levels. These might or might have analogues in the real system; in other words the abstractions might or might not correspond to real-world features. And throughout the levels, the decomposition is strict: an activity at one level must be "part of" an activity at a higher level – new activities cannot suddenly appear as we go down the decomposition.[1]

Generalising, I would say that hierarchical structures work well when we are dealing with synthetic objects, ie objects which we create as designers of systems. We can reason about hierarchies; they are easily drawn; they have a natural simplicity; and they allow us to design top-down, by a series of successive decompositions (although it is worth bearing in mind Michael Jackson's observation that though we might present our design in a neat hierarchical form, the design process itself is rarely top-down, being normally some combination of top-down, bottom-up and middle-out). But when we deal with real-world activity we are not dealing with purely synthetic objects, designed once for cleanliness and simplicity and remaining so. We are dealing with things which have evolved, possibly over decades. And as that evolution has continued so the process has lost any simplicity or cleanliness it might have started out with when we first set it up as a synthetic object. Entropy has increased: bits have been tacked on or chopped off to accommodate changes in the goals of the business or other forces; interfaces with newer processes have been created at the edges; and interfaces with old processes that have been stopped have been (partially) hacked off the edges. The result is rarely tidy, and invariably not a neat hierarchy of activity.

So, should RADs be levelled like DFDs? Strictly, our answer to this is "not unless the real world is". Organisational processes do not necessarily fit into a nice structured decomposition. In fact, rather than being hierarchical, processes tend to be multi-dimensional networks. For this reason, using techniques such as IDEF0[2] or any DFD-like notation where a hierarchical decomposition is *imposed* is, in my opinion, very dangerous. We should not assume our processes are structured in this way, and if they are not we should not force our models into such a straitjacket. I believe this danger can outweigh the advantage that such approaches can offer of providing "simple" high-level views of the process for those with little time to spend looking at them.

Having seen that processes have richer and more complex structures than just hierarchical decompositions, we now go on to look at the three different

---

[1] One of the reasons for such levelling of diagrams is the 7±2 "rule". This is a good rule for synthetic objects like programs. But we can hardly dare to suppose that the world at large has applied it when constructing its processes. When we build a model of a real-world artefact like a business we must decide how we will balance the accuracy of our model against the need to use our model as a means of communication and understanding. I tend to take the view that if a RAD turns out to be large and complex it is probably because it is modelling a large and complex process.

[2] Federal Information Processing Standards Publication 183, *Integration Definition for Function Modeling (IDEF0)*, National Institute of Standards and Technology, Washington DC, USA

relationships that a number of processes or process perspectives can have. They are:

1 *composition*: the processes operate largely independently but mesh at various points

2 *encapsulation*: one process is in some way an "expansion" of an element in the other

3 *activation*: one process starts another which then operates independently, possibly meshing subsequently.

Here an important point must be made. In each case what we want to do is recognise that we will be drawing more than one RAD. It may be that, in analysing the organisation, we choose to divide its activity into several processes, each described on its own RAD. We will want each of those RADs to be free-standing and "readable" on its own. But processes cannot be separated so easily and cleanly; if we cut an arm off a living body we chop through nerves and blood vessels, and to get a true picture we need to show where they came from or were heading. So we want a way of producing free-standing RADs yet showing where they are connected.

Similarly, if we have one RAD that shows a process and another RAD that "expands" on one part of the first RAD, we will want them to be free-standing and readable separately, but we want also to show that "upper-lower" relationship which connects them.

Our goal? Free-standing RADs whose inter-relationships are accurately portrayed.

We take the three types of relationship in turn.

COMPOSITION OF PROCESSES

When we look at an organisation we know we will see many processes operating: core processes, support processes and management processes. We also know that these processes do not operate entirely separately from one another, in particular two processes will often "mesh together" – there are points at which they intersect or synchronise in some way. For instance, a company might have an annual budget-setting process in which it reviews the portfolio of projects it wants to undertake in the coming year. This might mean that some new projects are started, some are told to adjust their rate of development, other told to close down. At the same time, each project will follow a project life-time process that might take several years (ie several rounds of budget setting). At points during that lifetime, the project will clearly need to mesh with the budget-setting process. We might draw these as separate processes on separate RADs. But we know that the processes mesh at various points, so we will want to show that meshing on the RADs whilst allowing each RAD to be free-standing.

What precisely do we mean by "process *A* meshes with process *B*"? In STRIM we mean firstly that there is a role that the two processes have in common, in other words at least one role has a responsibility in each process.

Secondly, we can expect to find a state of that role which appears in both processes; such a state represents some sort of synchronisation between the two processes. It is as if the person carrying out the common role can say "when I'm here in this process, I'm there in that process" – the common role has a common state too.

Figure 6-2 – Equivalent states in two processes

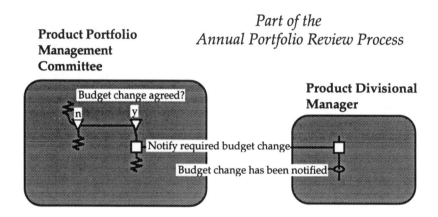

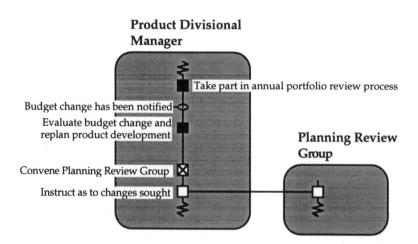

Let's take the example in figure 6-2. In an Annual Portfolio Review Process, the *Product Divisional Manager* is told of a change in their budget as decided by the *Product Portfolio Management Committee*. As far as that process (or our mapping of it is concerned) we are not interested in how the *Product Divisional Manager* responds to that: their response is the subject of another process, the Product Lifecycle Process. The *Product Divisional Manager* plays a part in that too and it is in the model of that process that we map their response.

So the *Product Divisional Manager* is the role that is common to the two processes. The common state is shown here as *Budget change has been notified*. In the Portfolio process the *Product Divisional Manager* is in that state after the interaction with the *Product Portfolio Management Committee*; in the Product process the *Product Divisional Manager* is in that state after the activity *Take part in annual portfolio review process*. We have used that activity to "summarise" what might be a number of interactions that the *Product Divisional Manager* has in the Portfolio process.

The important thing is that we show the meshing of the processes explicitly by showing where the state of the *Product Divisional Manager* role is the same in the two processes, namely where the *Budget change has been notified*. This completely defines the meshing of the two processes. Clearly, in some instances the meshing could be much more complex with a number of state equivalences defined to tie them together. But note that we always do it by giving the same name to states in the *same* role in the processes that are meshing.

As a further example, figure 6-3 shows an adaptation of part of the Monitor a Project process from Praxis' Quality Manual.

We can read from this that, during a project, the *Project Manager* has three concurrent threads of work. On one they undergo a quarterly review with the *Board*. On the third they continually hand out packages of work (WPs) to *Work Package Owners*, using a form called a *WPCC* to transfer the terms of reference. The *Work Package Owner* does the work and, on completion, reports to the *Project Manager* who, if the completion of the work package marks a contract milestone, prepares an Invoice Request and gets an approved invoice from *Accounts*. In the second thread of work, the *Project Manager* cycles on a monthly basis: at the middle of the month they have an interim progress review with the *Line Manager*, and at the end of the month they find out the status of each active work package by interrogating the respective *Work Package Owner*, and, once all the figures are in, update a Work Package Analysis (WPA), update the project activity network and pass a Charges Summary to *Accounts*. *Accounts* then prepare an invoice for the *Project Manager* to approve if the contract is a Time & Materials (T&M) contract.

Clearly, at two points we are straying into a different process altogether, namely that to do with the financial side of the company, and we might regard this as a separate process which we want to model separately. So let us cut the finance-related parts of the Monitor a Project process out and put them, together with other related action, into a separate process. Figure 6-4 shows one way we might do this (and remember that there are many ways in which we could make this cut). Note how just after the interactions with *Accounts*, the RAD "stops", leaving only a description of the states that this process leaves

Accounts in: *Charges Summary in hand* and *Invoice Request in hand*. Then in figure 6-5 we capture the financial side of things in a separate RAD of the Handle Invoices process. We show *Accounts* interacting with an abstract role *Anyone*, entering the states *Charges Summary in hand* and *Invoice Request in hand,* and then getting on with the job of dealing with those states: placing invoices, etc. We've cut the two processes apart but shown their connections through, in particular, the common states in the shared role *Accounts.*

Figure 6-3 – The Monitor a Project *process*

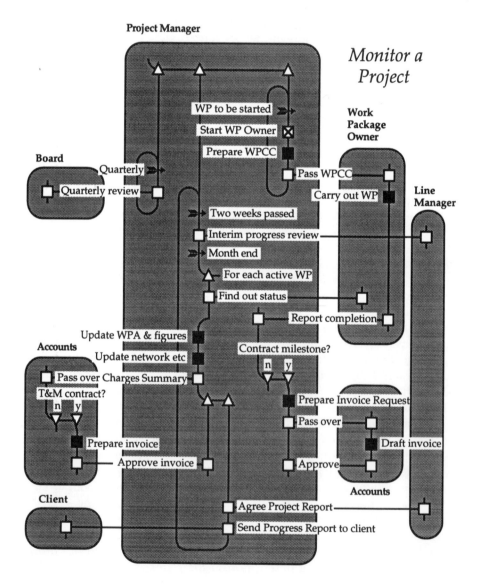

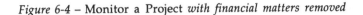

Figure 6-4 – Monitor a Project *with financial matters removed*

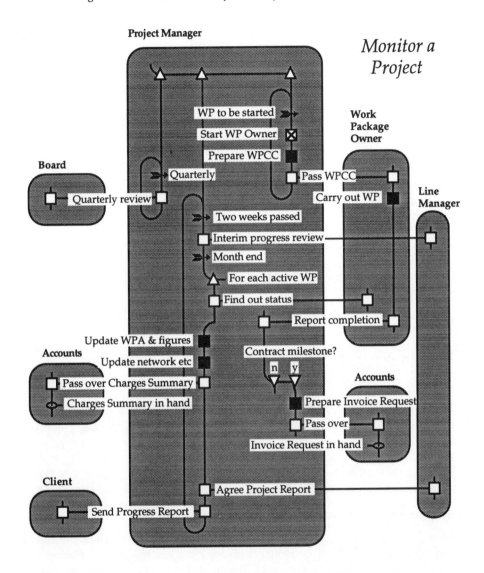

We can of course cut the boundary between two intersecting or meshing processes anywhere we like and there are many ways of representing the boundary. Which we choose depends on what we find useful for our purpose.

Figure 6-5 – A separate model of the Handle Invoices *process*

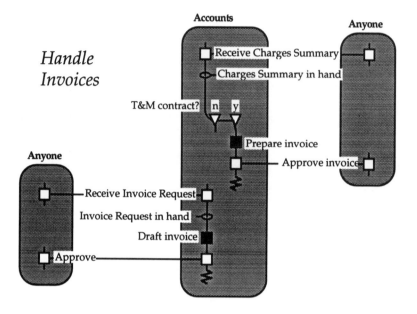

ENCAPSULATION OF PROCESSES

In a RAD we might well wish to "summarise" a whole mass of activity in a single black-box activity, not wishing – in this perspective – to get into the detail of how it is done. Similarly we might wish to summarise a complex interaction as a simple interaction, not wishing – in this perspective – to worry about the detail.

We noted above how simple decomposition such as is required in a DFD is rarely meaningful in a RAD, and in this section I look at this topic in detail.

Opening up a black-box activity

The question is "what happens if we 'open' a black box on a RAD"? What we see and what we model depends again on why we are modelling. Rather than seeing a "decomposition" of the black-box activity, I prefer to say that we are looking through a window and seeing part of the process from another perspective. We need to understand how that detailed perspective relates to the black box. In particular, we must remember that an activity (like an interaction) takes place over some period of time and at a particular place in the process, and so we need especially to understand the temporal relationships between the two perspectives, the "upper" and the "lower".

For instance, take the activity *Produce design* in figure 3-2. Suppose we open this black box. When we look through it we may find a whole world of process involving, in particular, new roles such as *Client, User, Quality*

Assurance, and *Chief Engineer.* These do not appear on the first RAD, nor are they "part of" either the role *Designing* or the role *Project Managing.* In taking *Produce design* as a process in its own right, we are starting to look at new parts of the world, parts that we were not interested in when we were drawing up the model of figure 3-2. So we are now going to draw two free-standing RADs whilst showing the relationship between them.

To understand how we open up a black box on a RAD, let us look at an example. Suppose we are a life insurance company and that the way an Underwriting Manager handles an application for an insurance policy depends on the office where the application is received; each office has its own procedure for carrying out part of the role *Underwriting Manager.* If we were not concerned with the detail of each office's procedure but did want to identify which procedure they used, then we might draw the relevant part of the process as in figure 6-6, showing the *Underwriting Manager* using procedure *P12* in the London office, procedure *P13a* at the New York office, and so on, with each shown as a black-box activity.

Figure 6-6 – Summarising processing styles at different offices

Underwriting Manager

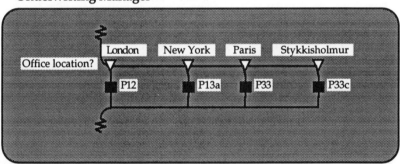

Suppose now that we want to go into detail about the different office procedures, but to do it separately so as not to clutter this RAD. How would we do this? Basically, we draw a new RAD for each office procedure's black box. In other words we treat each black box as a complete process and give it a RAD of its own; for instance "activity *P12*" on the main RAD becomes "process *P12*" on its own RAD. This feels right, but we have to ask what precisely we mean by saying "activity *P12* has its own RAD: process *P12*".

Firstly, what "starts" process *P12*? In process *P12* we will naturally expect to see as one of the roles the role *Underwriting Manager* from the "upper" process that carries out activity *P12*; and, moreover, we can assume that one instance of *Underwriting Manager* exists when process *P12* runs. We call this the "lead role" of the process: it is the one that pre-exists and that starts the whole thing going. So, the triggering condition of activity *P12* is also the state at the start of the lead role in process *P12*. We will show this by labelling the states accordingly.

Secondly, when we say "activity *P12* has its own RAD: process *P12*" we need to ask if we require that *all* of process *P12* should be completed before the black box for activity *P12* is deemed complete and the main process can proceed. If the answer were "yes" it would be like treating process *P12* as a "subroutine" which must "complete" before "control passes back to" the main process, to use software jargon. Again, there is a temptation (especially for the software engineer) to impose a tidy structural simplicity on the world; but the world is rarely so clean.

Instead, we recognise that there will be some state reached during process *P12* which is the same as the stopping condition of activity *P12*.

Representing all this is quite straightforward:

− We label the state *in front* of activity *P12* in some way, call it *A*. We then label the state at the top of role *R* in process *P12* as *A*. (Alternatively, we could show an external event *A reached* on process *P12*'s RAD, that event "firing" the lead role *Underwriting Manager* in process *P12* appropriately. But the state immediately after that is obviously *A*, so little is gained.)

− We label the state *after* activity *P12* in some way, call it *B*. We then show the same state *B* at the appropriate place on process *P12*'s RAD, thereby tying together the process containing activity *P12* and the process *P12* through their states. One important implication of this is that process *P12* does not have to complete entirely, ie it does not have to reach a state where no further activity takes place, before Activity *P12* is deemed complete. Instead we are saying that process *P12* must reach a *specified* state before activity *P12* is complete.

As an example of this, consider figure 6-7, continuing our example of the processing of insurance policy claim processing. In the London office they carry out procedure *P12* to obtain partner approval. On the first RAD fragment in figure 6-7, we show this simply as a black box, but before the black box (in fact, before the case refinement) we label the state as *Partner approval required;* and after the black box we have labelled the state to indicate that partner approval has been obtained for the resolution of the claim. In the second RAD fragment in figure 6-7, we show part of the RAD for the process of P12-style processing: the process might be quite complicated (we have shown just part of the full RAD in the figure), but at some point that same state − *Partner approval obtained* − is reached, at which the "main" RAD thread in Insurance Policy Claim Processing can proceed, even though there is clearly further procedural activity in process *P12* before it finishes. (Process elements have not been labelled in figure 6-7 where they are not pertinent to the example.)

Figure 6-7 – Activity P12 *and process* P12

Part of Insurance Policy Claim Processing

Underwriting Manager

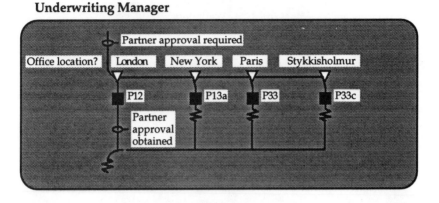

Part of Process P12

Underwriting Manager ✓

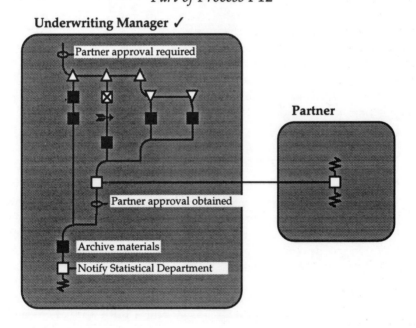

The state that marks the end of activity *P12* might be quite complex and correspond to the union of states in several roles in process *P12*. We would show that in the obvious way, with each sub-state individually identified somewhere in the lower process.

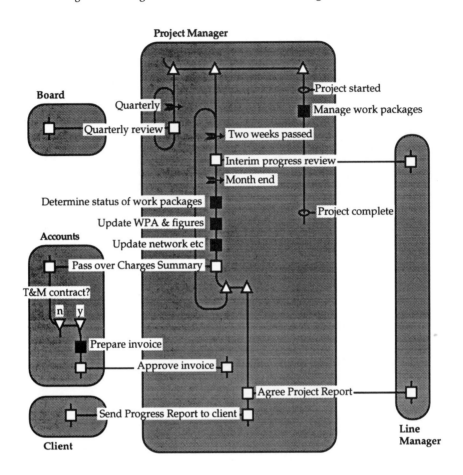

Figure 6-8 – Figure 6-4 without the Work Package Owner *role*

Let's look at a further example. Suppose that, in the process shown in figure 6-4 we wanted to take the right-most thread of activity in the *Project Manager* role and encapsulate that in a separate Manage Work Packages process. We might do this as in figure 6-8. On the part refinement in the original RAD we simply note the pre-state – *Project started* – and replace the whole area of activity by a single activity *Manage work packages*. Figure 6-9 expands that activity. In particular, note how, having delegated the task to the *Work Package Owner*, the *Project Manager* starts three threads of activity:

1   By "looping back to the top", the manager goes and waits (if necessary) for the next work package to need starting.

2   The manager sits in a loop finding out the status of the work package whenever they feel like it; this could be as part of the monthly status gathering. Note how this is now shown as a black box in the original, "main" RAD – *Determine status of work packages*.

3   The manager waits for completion of the work package and deals with any resulting contract milestone completion.

The main RAD now makes no mention of *Work Package Owners*.

Figure 6-9 – Manage Work Packages *expanded to its own RAD*

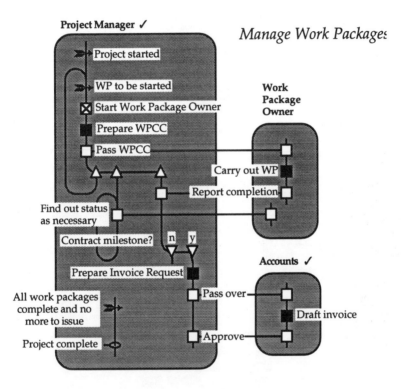

The question arises "how do we tie the completion of the *Manage Work Packages* activity in the main RAD to the completion of the Manage Work Packages process?". We need to ask what we mean by completion of the process: clearly it means that there are no more work packages to be handed out and all work packages that have been handed out have been finished. Since we do not know how many work packages will be dealt with when we draw the RAD we need to use an internal event to detect the state we are looking for in the Manage Work Packages process: *All work packages complete and no more to issue*. When this event occurs we are in the state *Project complete* which we can tie back to the main RAD.

Summary of encapsulation

Let's pull this together with a two-step procedure for opening a black-box activity:

1   In the "upper" process (figure 6-10) show the black-box activity to be
    opened in an appropriate role, label the state preceding it (its triggering
    condition), and label the state following it (its post-condition):

Figure 6-10

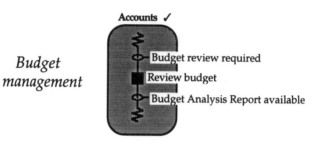

2   In the "lower" process (figure 6-11), give the state at the head of the
    thread the same label as the triggering condition of the activity in the
    upper process being expanded; and label the state marking "completion" of
    the activity being expanded with post-condition of the latter activity as
    shown in the upper process, thus tying the two processes together:

Figure 6-11

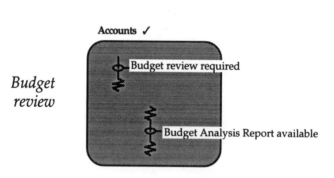

When we move from the upper process to the lower process we might find it
useful to work with a sub-role of the role in the upper process. So, in figure 6-12,
although we show *Accounts* as carrying out the activity *Review Budget* in the
Budget Management process, when we look into this we show the *Chief
Accountant* starting it off in the lower process. Since we want the RADs to be
free-standing we tie them together with some extra annotation on the activity
in the upper process.

It might also be the case that the post-condition we seek for the activity in the upper process is compound, in that it is composed of smaller goals achieved at different places – perhaps in different roles – in the lower process. Figure 6-12 gives an example of this too.

Figure 6-12 – Decomposing a role and compound goals

Budget Management

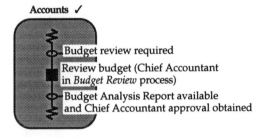

Budget Review

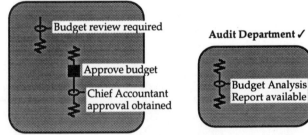

Opening up an interaction

In a high-level RAD we might summarise a complicated interaction in a single element. As an example, take a simplification of the interaction I used earlier: "two parties meet to discuss, negotiate and agree the price of a piece of work, drawing up the agreement as legal document and obtaining financial securities from a bank". On a RAD we might choose to represent this as an atomic interaction between roles *A* and *B* because we are not interested in that model in any further "detail" – we simply want to say that *A* and *B* have that interaction with that result, and we don't mind how they do it.

Suppose we now choose to "open up" this interaction. Rather than showing just more detail of what happens between *A* and *B*, we might find other roles involved, roles which perhaps did not appear on the first RAD: *Bank Manager Lawyer*, *Auditor* for example. We have not decomposed the atomic interaction in the DFD sense: we have opened it up like a window and looked at the process from a new angle, an angle which introduces new roles and activities and perhaps new entities, all of which were of no interest to the first RAD.

As with the way we opened black-box activities we need to understand the relationship between the high-level interaction and its "expansion". Not surprisingly, we do it by equating the triggering condition of the two part-interactions with corresponding starting states in the roles in the expanded process. The post-conditions of the part-interactions are similarly dealt with. See figure 6-13. In the expanded Finalising a Sale process, much can happen between the initial and final states.

Figure 6-13 – Expanding an interaction

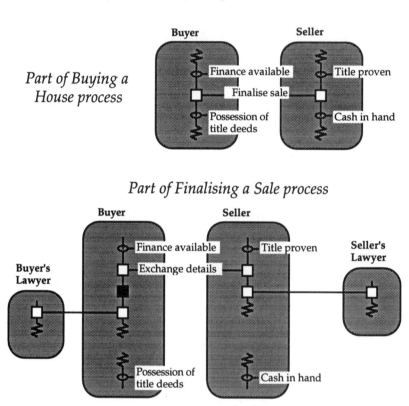

ACTIVATION OF PROCESSES

The final relationship between processes that we address is that where one process is able in some way to "activate" another, in other words to set it going in some fashion. The assumption is that if "process A 'activates' process B", then process B can in fact then go its own way independently of process A. The two might subsequently want to synchronise or connect up again in some way.

As an example, we might model the Strategic Review process of a company. As the mission, critical success factors, and future strategic goals are examined, change targets might be set for different parts of the company, and those targets in turn will lead to tactical Task Forces being "spun off" to implement them. When we model the Strategic Review process we will only want to show the tactical processes being activated; we won't want to get into detail about them. Figure 6-14 shows how we do this. In the activating process – in this case, Strategic Review – we show an appropriate role (here *Strategic Review Board*) instantiating the lead role of the activated process (here *Task Force*). The *Task Force* role is what we called an "abstract" role in chapter 2: it doesn't have permanent instances, in particular such things do not appear on the organisation chart; instances are only created as and when required, and once they have done their work they disappear. When we draw up the RAD for the *Tactical Review* process, we show the "called" role, *Task Force*, and to indicate that it pre-exists – from this perspective – we tick it with a ✓.

Figure 6-14 – Strategic process activates tactical process

Part of Strategic Review process

Strategic Review Board

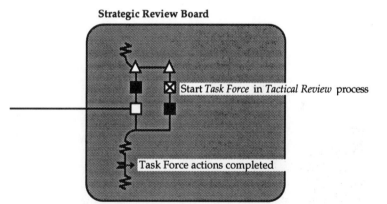

Start *Task Force* in *Tactical Review* process

Task Force actions completed

Part of Tactical Review process

Task Force ✓

Task Force actions completed

Note that we do not need to show in the *Tactical Review* process what makes things start: the ✓ is enough to indicate that we have a role instantiated, so we can simply show what it does when it gets going; that said, we might label the state at the start of the role with a suitable annotation (eg

Task Force started by Strategic Review Board to prepare detailed plans)
simply to make this separate RAD that bit more free-standing, so that it can be
read on its own.

The RAD for the Tactical Review process shows that the role *Task Force*
carries out some activity and then, at some point, is in the state *Task Force
actions complete*. Suppose that this is a state that is important to the *Strategic
Review* process, though they are not interested in how it is reached, only when
it is reached, since the *Strategic Review Board* needs to respond in some way to
the result of the Task Force's work. Figure 6-14 shows how that is represented.
The state *Task Force actions complete* is marked at the appropriate place (or
places in the case of a composite state) in the RAD of the called process, and
the calling process synchronises with that state by waiting on a corresponding
event (*Task Force actions completed*).

Figure 6-15 – Showing how the activation of another process works

Part of Strategic Review process

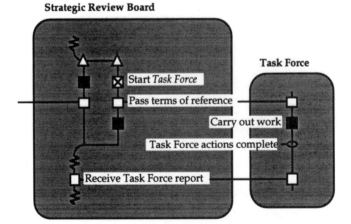

Part of Tactical Review process

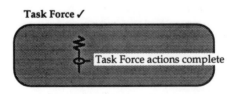

It is important to remember that here we are drawing two independent
processes in separate RADs, each meaningful and readable on its own. By
definition we are not interested in the detail of how the calling of one by the

other takes place, only where it takes place and where there is any subsequent synchronisation. If we were interested in that detail we would draw a different RAD that intentionally records that mechanism. For instance we might want to show the fact that the *Task Force* receives terms of reference when it starts and returns a report at the end of its work. If our strategic RAD perspective was interested in this we would draw the RAD as in figure 6-15.

Now we have included the role *Task Force* in the Strategic Review process RAD in order to show how the interactions work, and, because we are still not interested in how the Task Force does its work we have simply shown that as a black box. As can be seen, now that the activation has all been explicitly moved to the Strategic Review RAD, the Tactical Review RAD only needs to expand the black box *Carry out work* – in other words we use the encapsulation technique described above.

Figure 6-16 – Somewhere between figure 6-14 and figure 6-15

Part of Strategic Review process

Strategic Review Board

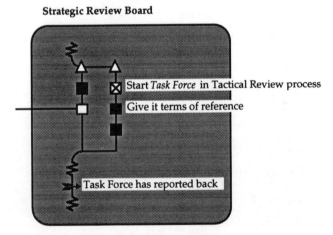

Start *Task Force* in Tactical Review process

Give it terms of reference

Task Force has reported back

Part of Tactical Review process

Task Force ✓

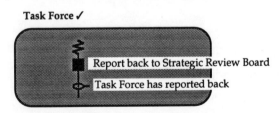

Report back to Strategic Review Board

Task Force has reported back

We might draw a "half-way house" model along the lines of that in figure 6-16. We've kept the two models quite separate as in figure 6-14, but we have transformed the *Pass terms of reference* interaction of figure 6-15 into a corresponding activity *Give it terms of reference* by the *Strategic Review Board,* and we have transformed the *Receive Task Force report* interaction of figure 6-15 into a corresponding activity *Report back* by the *Task Force.* Once again the two models are free-standing but the connections are there.

A final simple example is shown in figure 6-17. In this case *two* roles in the "main" process wait for states to be reached in the activated process.

Figure 6-17 – A process activation

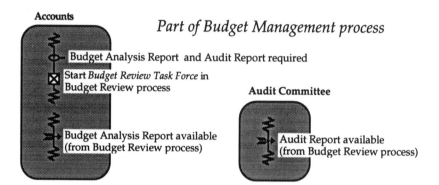

Part of Budget Management process

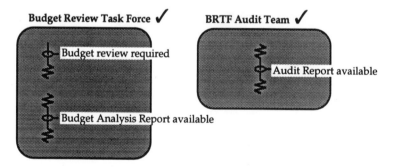

Part of Budget Review process

Summary of process activation

So, the procedure for handling process activation is as follows

1   In the activating process, start an instance of the "lead role" in the activated process.

2   At the appropriate place in the activating process, wait for an event in the activated process with ➤. This event may well import something into the activating process.

3   In the activated process, identify (for information) the start state of the lead role, show that role as having a pre-existing instance, and identify the state whose achievement is equivalent to the awaited event in the activating process. That event might be compound.

COLLAPSING A MODEL

Suppose that we have constructed a RAD which contains many roles, activities and interactions. There are a number of situations where it will be useful to "simplify" it. (Later we shall see how this sort of simplification can also be dangerous.)

Firstly, suppose we have had an interactive session with a set of process owners and actors and interactively modelled their process. We might well have got into considerable detail and now require to remove some of the detail to show the process in a broad-brush way. In this section we look at how a model can be "collapsed" in order to provide a simplified view of a process.

Secondly, if we want to bring people into the thinking about a process, a simplified version can help. Being confronted with a mass of detail can turn people off, but if we walk through a simple version before taking them to the full, unexpurgated version we can help to avoid that.

Thirdly, we may wish at some point to look at the process from a quantitative point of view. In chapter 9, we look at this in detail, but we will see that, for the purposes of modelling, great detail does not contribute anything extra, indeed it can get in the way: we need the bones, enough to attach numerical values for effort or duration to activities and interactions, and probabilities or frequencies to case refinement cases.

We can reduce a model in three ways:

1   by "bundling" process elements into a single activity or interaction

2   by combining related roles

3   by simply ignoring "unimportant" roles or interactions.

The last of these might be used when simplifying for presentation purposes but is not intended for simplification for analysis purposes.

Bundling activities

Suppose we want to simply remove some detail by packaging it up inside a black-box activity or an interaction, not least because it is just "computational detail" that does not affect the process significantly from our current perspective. This is a simple matter of choosing an appropriate label for the new black-box activity – see figure 6-18.

Bundling a convergent case refinement

In some cases we can bundle up the whole of a case refinement into a single activity, perhaps with some suitable choice of name for the resulting single activity, in particular using phrases such as "as appropriate" and "accordingly" (figure 6-19).

Figure 6-18 – Bundling a sequence of activities

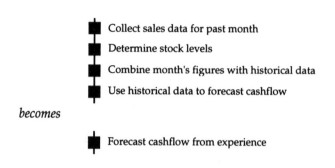

becomes

Figure 6-19 – Bundling a convergent case refinement

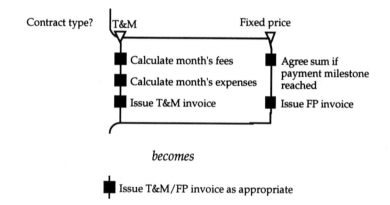

becomes

∎ Issue T&M/FP invoice as appropriate

This only works so easily if the threads converge to a common path. If they diverge we can only really bundle them individually.

Moreover, the bundling only works easily if there are no interactions on the case refinement's threads. The fact that interactions generally cause problems in simplification points to their importance as "irreducible" elements of a process. We can bundle up a set of things that I get on with on my own; but, if we want to show how you and I in our different roles collaborate, the interactions which represent that collaboration remain.

Bundling a convergent part refinement

In a similar way we can bundle up the whole of a part refinement into a single activity, with the name for the resulting single activity including words like "and". We gloss over the fact that we have several concurrent strands of activity by using the word "and" (figure 6-20).

Figure 6-20 – Bundling a convergent part refinement

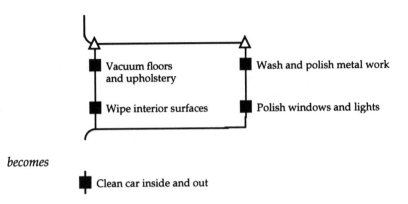

becomes

The same provisos hold about the presence of interactions and the convergence of the threads as for case refinements.

Bundling segments with interactions

Pairs or groups of interactions can be bundled up provided we take care to deal with the passage of grams that might be involved. We should try to preserve the effect of the interactions on *all* parties involved (figure 6-21).

Bundling roles

Some situations might require us to "ignore" entire roles which disappear into a black box. For instance, when *Divisional Directors* send their reports to *The Board* they might go via someone who assembles summary data from a number of such reports and packages that for the Board members, but for our model we might not be concerned with that computational detail: we simply show *Divisional Director* interacting directly with *The Board*.

In other situations we might bundle two or more roles into one larger role which captures that part of the process sufficiently for our purposes; for instance, when drawing a process from the point of view of a company's divisions we might content ourselves with summarising central roles such as *Purchasing, Accounts,* and *Personnel* in one role called *Headquarters* – we are not interested in how "they" split up their work (their part of the process) between themselves, only that it gets done "over there" in Headquarters. Such summarising must be done with care: the resulting "abbreviated" role must be meaningful to the people in the process.

What were potentially concurrent threads in the separate roles now become potentially concurrent threads in the single role and we might choose to put them on a part refinement. We have also to interpret what were interactions between the separate roles as points of synchronisation between the separate threads in the single role – again, the part refinement may be the right notion for modelling this.

Figure 6-21 – Bundling a segment with interactions

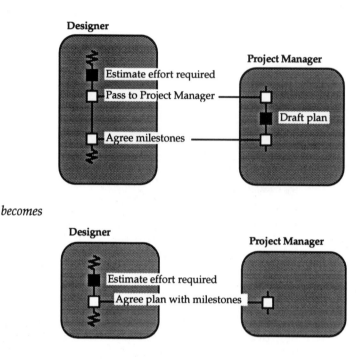

becomes

An example of bundling

If we take the process in figure 6-3 and bundle process elements up, whilst retaining the existing roles, we find we get some simplification: we are getting to the "irreducible" logic of the process, in particular we are getting down to the underlying framework of interactions that binds the roles and forms the underlying infrastructure of the process as a collaborative act (figure 6-22).

HANDLING PERVASIVE FUNCTIONS

Pervasive functions are those which occur throughout a process.

For example, consider an organisation in which the staff make constant use of confidential files that are held in some sort of document registry. Every time a file is required, it is requested from the registry and logged out to the individual. Once it is finished with, the file is returned to the registry. If we were concerned to model the operation of the organisation we might choose not to show the pervasive operation of the registry and the way it controls and records access to files; in other situations this might be precisely the activity that we want to model.

There is a similar example in the software development process where there is very often a need for all products of the development – designs, source code, test suites and so on – to be placed under configuration management.

Whenever a product is produced it is registered; if it is updated, it is checked out to the person changing it and the new version is subsequently booked back in; if people start to base their work on a given version that version must be frozen in some sense.

Figure 6-22 – A "simplified" version of figure 6-3

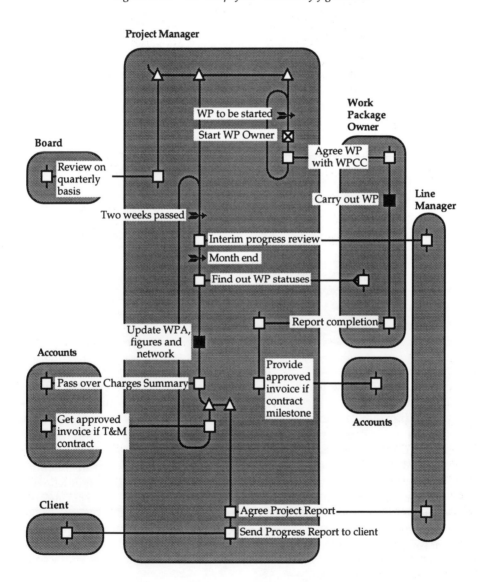

If we try to show the pervasive function in the model at every point that it operates in a process, things can become cluttered with repeated and un-useful detail, and the picture is obscured. However, pervasive functions are frequently essential to the process and do need to be analysed in their own right. This means a separate process model and hence a separate RAD.

What then is the relationship between the roles on the RAD for the "main" functions and the roles on the RAD for a pervasive function? Basically, pervasive roles are shown on their RADs as interacting with abstract roles (ie superclasses of roles). Mainstream roles are not shown on their RADs as interacting with pervasive roles. For instance, within an organisation with a document registry, any role accessing secure materials will in practice go through the registry to get and return necessary materials – in that sense such roles have to interact with the registry role. On the RAD for the mainstream roles this interaction need not be shown, however, provided that the roles/activities that need such access are distinguished in some way as subclasses of abstract roles or activities that do have the interactions defined for them. On the RAD for the registry role(s), the role(s) will be shown interacting with the abstract class of roles/activities requiring access to secure material.

Figure 6-23 – A pervasive process "omitted"

**Communications
Clerk**

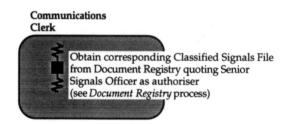

So, in figure 6-23 we show the *Communications Clerk* obtaining a classified file from the Document Registry, representing it with a simple black-box activity. In figure 6-24, which shows a RAD describing the process carried out by the Document Registry, we see the request arriving from an abstract role – *Requesting Classified Document* – and finally being delivered. On the "main" process we did not model the situation where permission to access the document is denied, presumably because it "should not happen". The Document Registry does of course check all requests for approval from the *Named Approval Authority* and has a response to the situation where, for some reason, approval is not granted. As ever, we are separating concerns on the two RADs but showing the connections we want to show.

HANDLING CARRIER FUNCTIONS

We give the name *carrier function* to any function in an organisation that makes interactions happen – they typically "carry" the grams involved. They are the mechanism by which the interaction takes place; in effect they tell us about the concrete interaction. For instance, the interaction between someone sending an order to a mail order company will generally take place via the postal system. The carrier function is the postal company which collects and delivers the paper order. Other carrier functions include electronic mail, fax communication, couriers, a video-conferencing system, and a meeting room.

Figure 6-24 – Part of the Document Registry's process

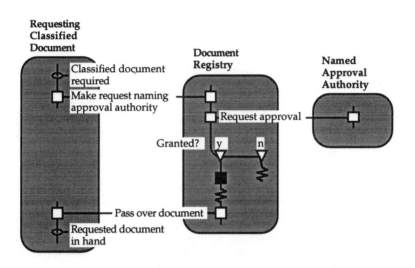

In general, carrier functions can be regarded as "computational detail" rather than "organisational behaviour", so we would not expect to want to represent carrier functions on a RAD unless it was important to the purpose of that RAD. For instance, a carrier function might have an effect on the efficiency of the process: a letter through the postal system might hold up the process for three days if that interaction is on the critical path, whilst a fax could remove that delay almost entirely.

So, carrier functions make the difference between abstract and concrete representations of interactions, and this can lead us to clues to improvements in the efficiency of the organisation.

If an interaction is one way – someone sends someone else something – a carrier function is often involved, and the carrier function (the mail for instance) removes the synchronisation between sender and receiver. Although I might draw my sending my time sheet to Accounts with the RAD fragment in figure 6-25, it's probably not what actually happens, in that I don't wait for Accounts to receive the timesheet (which is what the interaction implies); I just put it in the internal post and forget about it. The internal post then transfers it to Accounts subsequently. Really, there are two sequential interactions with two corresponding synchronisations. But if what I really want to show is the fact that I send my timesheet to Accounts I probably don't want to drag the internal post into the RAD.

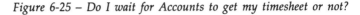

Figure 6-25 – Do I wait for Accounts to get my timesheet or not?

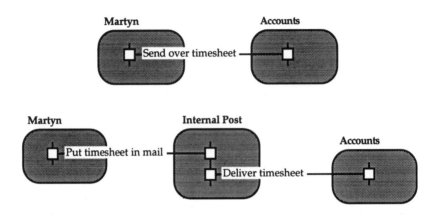

RADs FOR THE "BIG PICTURE"

Because of the constructs involved in a RAD – activity and interaction in particular – it is easy to suppose that a RAD is suitable only at the detailed level, for describing detailed procedures for instance. To show that this is not the case, we finish this chapter with a reminder that a RAD can be used to give the "big picture" of what an organisation does. Figure 6-1 is such a picture. The discussion earlier in this chapter has covered how we can then "drill down" into the detail as and where we wish to.

Even such a big picture RAD preserves a degree of information about the order and concurrency between activities and external events, and it might be that we need a yet more summarised versions of things. In some situations we might consider preparing a "RAD" such as that in figure 6-26 in which all that remain are the roles and the lines between them that convey the fact that the roles interact. Figure 6-26 shows just the bare bones of figure 6-22: the roles and the fact that the *Project Manager* has interactions with the *Board, Accounts,* the *Client, Work Package Owner,* and the *Line Manager.* Nothing else is said about the behaviour of the organisation or what is actually done.

There are moments – most probably for presentational purposes – when such a diagram can help, by providing people with a route into a more complicated RAD that *does* show behaviour.

But, finally, a warning is in order. When we model a process we often get into a lot of detail, sometimes more than we really need, and the issue arises of how we should simplify the diagram. This is a danger area. Our natural inclination is to make the simplification so that the picture becomes neat and tidy. This is all fine and well, but is the process really neat and tidy in that way? And if you show someone that diagram of the process will they say "ah yes, I knew we had a tidy process in place", when in fact the process is a mess but our "simplification" has suggested tidiness and neatness that is not there in reality? Such a simplification can only really be used as a gentle introduction to the process, a way of orienting people and getting them thinking about how their world works. As ever, what has happened is that we have drawn the RAD *for a specific purpose*: namely to get the big picture over to people. Once it has served that purpose we should not expect it to do more for us.

Figure 6-26 – A summary RAD

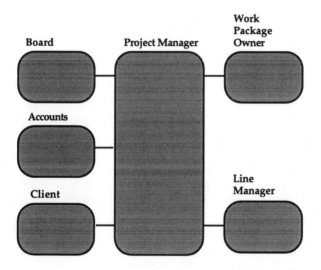

7

PROCESS PATTERNS

INTRODUCTION

We now have in place the machinery for describing processes in the small –
clichés – and for handling large and/or connected processes. In this chapter we
look at the second aspect of modelling-in-the-large: the different large-scale
patterns of organisational behaviour that are frequently encountered. These
patterns will provide us with some important machinery with which to think
about processes.

We start by listing the process patterns that we will examine:

- case processes

- case management processes

- event-driven processes

- cycle-driven processes

- delegation ladders

- contracts

- plans and activities.

Here, we are doing no more than recognising that organisational behaviour
follows certain common patterns – not invariably, but often enough for the
analyst to benefit by being aware of them and of how they look in a process
model. And, of course, we are not saying that the analyst should force an
existing process into the straitjacket of one of these patterns; we are simply
recognising that they can help the modelling and provide alternative views on
a process. The patterns are particularly important because they allow us to ask
certain *organisational* questions in chapter 9 such as:

- What happens at the boundary between these two organisational units?

- Do we have too much or too little control through the management
  hierarchy?

- Do we have too much or too little empowerment?
- Have we defined the responsibilities of the various posts and job titles in a way that minimises the need for materials to be passed between them?
- Does our organisational structure support or hinder the efficient response to a customer request?

And of course, we can expect that any real process will actually be a mixture of these patterns. Nothing is ever simple.

THE CASE PROCESS

In this pattern, the process concentrates on what happens to a single "case", or "unit of work" or "episode".

For instance, consider the part of a life insurance company that deals with new business, and, in particular, applications for new policies; and suppose we look at what happens to an application for a life insurance policy from the point at which it is received by the company to the point where some outcome is reached with the prospective customer. Here, the "case" is the customer application – we want to examine its life history: the process through which it passes.

In Praxis, when we take on a piece of work for a client, we form a "project". That project represents a unit of work that starts with the award of the contract and finishes with acceptance of the software by the client. At any one time we have many projects in progress – many cases active – and all at different stages. The case process is the process that concerns how we deal with that unit of work.

In a pharmaceutical company, suppose we are concerned with what happens to a potential new drug compound from the point where it is determined to have some possible therapeutic effects to the point at which it obtains approval from the regulatory authorities to be put on sale. Here the "case" is the compound – again, we want to examine its life history. The case process is about what the company does to get from "molecule to market" – for a single molecule (ie a single compound).

An organisation that carries out such a case-oriented process will have many such cases at different stages: for example, in a pharmaceutical research company, compound *A* might be in early use with human volunteers, compound *B* might be undergoing major trials with thousands of clinical patients, and compound *C* might be awaiting regulatory approval at the end of its development process. In handling many such cases simultaneously, the organisation needs to have as part of its overall process the *management of many concurrent cases*, concerning itself with issues of planning, scheduling, resource management, task allocation, go/no-go decisions, reporting, and so on. But when we take the case-oriented view, we abstract away all of these "external" concerns and concentrate simply on what happens to a single case.

Figure 7-1 shows a case process. It shows a single instance of a *Post-room* which gets going when a letter arrives from a customer. As necessary, it creates a new *Supervising* role instance for each request, which in turn creates a new

Clerking role instance to handle it. The process is over when the customer has received a reply to their letter.

Figure 7-1 – A case-oriented model of a process

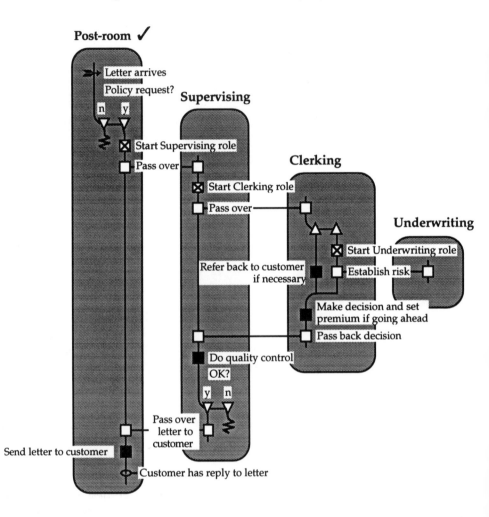

We can see that the process we have drawn shows the processing of one "case", that is, one request-to-response occurrence, here for a single letter. In particular we have not concerned ourselves with the actual number of real people or the scheduling of cases onto people, ie the allocation of actors to role instances. The roles are not people-related, as their names bear witness: *Supervising*, and *Clerking*. But we might guess that in the real world Supervisors do *Supervising* and Clerks do *Clerking*. With such a case-oriented model it is common for the roles to have names which are gerunds; that is, they describe some abstract action (a topic dealt with in detail in chapter 9). Whenever one of these abstract roles is required to perform, an instance is created, passed the work, and waited for. The model does not concern itself with identifying actors, scheduling, waiting for actors to become free from a prior task, queueing, or anything that happens in an organisation *because it is handling more than one case at a time*. The model just looks at the process from the perspective of the single case, rather than the organisation. This can be very important when we are examining where efficiencies can be made in the actual work of an organisation, rather than the *management* of that work, another topic we handle in chapter 9.

Figure 7-2 shows another case process. This time we have kept to "concrete" roles (and there is a pre-existing instance of each but we have not bothered to show this). The case process is kicked off when a *Product Development Team* hears that development of a new product has been approved. They nurse the product through three major phases: development, launch and exploitation, and withdrawal (activities whose names are shown in italics on the RAD). At any time the *Product Strategy Board* may demand the cancellation of the product, but once the product has been developed a *Division* keeps an eye on its performance and might also require withdrawal. Finally the *Product Development Team* reaches the state in which we recognise *Product life over*. The case is quite obviously a single product. The RAD has nothing to say about how, say, the *Product Strategy Board* looks at the entire portfolio of products and decides which ones are for the chop, or any other "supra-case" issues.

Finally, some more examples of case processes:

- the marking of a single examination paper by a university examination authority, starting with the handing in of the completed paper and finishing with the storage of the marks in a central marking system

- the manufacture of a single batch of drug compound in a vessel by a drug manufacturer, starting with the handover of the vessel to the plant operator and finishing with the storage of the drug batch in the pharmacy

- the handling of a single customer enquiry by a telephone hot-line department, starting with the picking up of the initial call and finishing with the customer saying "thanks, you've answered my question".

Note how, in each case process, we recognise some event which tells us that the unit of work has arrived on someone's desk and work is needed to deal with it. When we decide that that is the event that marks the start of the case process, we are making a decision about where we want to start in our description of the process. It is always possible to go back further in time and extend the process backwards, or, contrariwise, pick up the process at some later point. Similarly, we characterise the end of the process in terms of a "target" state, but we could announce completion earlier or later. There are no absolute rules about where processes start or end: we decide those things for each model.

Figure 7-2 – A case process

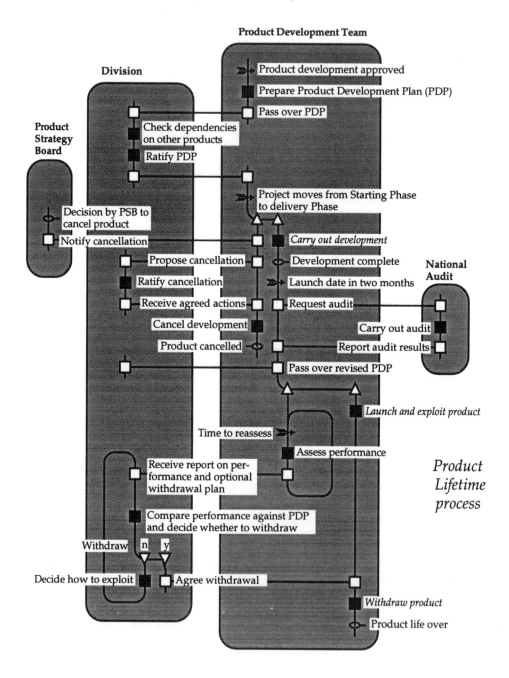

So, to summarise, when we consider a case process we need to identify

1   the "unit of work"

2   the triggering event that tells us we have a unit of work to deal with

3   the state that tells us we have finished this unit of work.

Those three things bound the process; all we have to do is fill in what happens between the triggering event and the final state!

THE CASE MANAGEMENT PROCESS

When we start to model a process it can be very hard to separate in one's mind the underlying, case-oriented, core process ("what happens to a policy request from the point when it arrives to the point when a decision is sent to the prospective customer?") from the way in which the organisation manages the processing of many cases at any one time ("who should deal with this request?" etc).

As an example of this we can look again at the way in which a pharmaceutical development company runs the business of getting new chemical compounds into the drug market. Taking a case-oriented view we can see that each compound will have its own life history: it starts as a candidate drug that has been weeded out from the thousands that have been considered, and it proceeds through a variety of ever larger trials, whilst, at the same time, the process by which it will finally be manufactured is developed in parallel. Assuming the compound is safe and efficacious it will reach the market, and we can construct a model of that whole process. This "molecule-to-market" process will involve many scientific groups involved in dealing with the compound: pharmaceutical sciences, clinical trials, manufacturing process scale-up, analytical chemistry, health and safety, quality assurance, and many, many more.

But the company will, as we have seen, have many such compounds in different parts of the pipeline at any one moment. The organisation is in fact a "case pipeline", designed to get the successful compounds through to the market place in the shortest possible time and to weed out the unsuccessful compounds as soon as possible. There is therefore a separate but related process whereby the company *manages* the pipeline. In particular, if we inspect its operations we will observe it making frequent decisions regarding the priority level each compound should get, the resources it should be allocated, and whether or not it can even proceed to the next stage or must be abandoned. This "pipeline management" process will involve management from the different disciplines, and cross-functional committees formed from the different disciplines, as well as corporate groups such as those dealing with marketing, regulatory and legal issues.

To model the entire organisation we can therefore expect to construct (at least) two process models: one for a case ("molecule-to-market"), and the other for *case management* ("pipeline management"). These two will of course intersect, but separating them is vital for effective analysis.

As a second example, we might consider the way in which a product company operates. Suppose the company is in the business of designing and selling domestic audio products. In modelling its activity we could take a case-oriented view first and model the life-history of a product: how the initial concept is defined by the technology and marketing groups, how initial design is taken to the point where commercial and safety cases can be established, then pushed on into production engineering to establish how the product can be cost-effectively manufactured within the existing range, through to market entry, a period of manufacture and refinement during the product's life-time, finishing with withdrawal from the market place. Such a life history could last many years, and there will be as many active cases as the company has products in R&D or on the market at any one time.

Figure 7-3 – A case management process to accompany figure 7-2

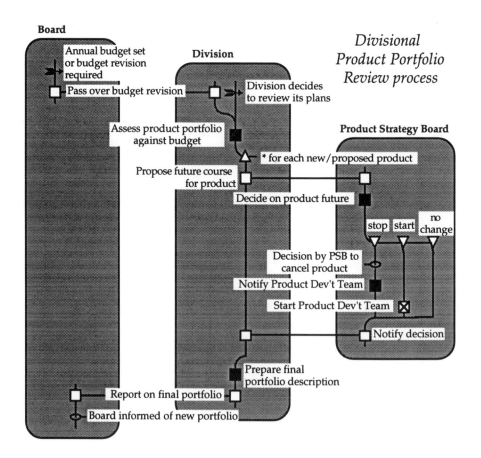

At the same time we might expect the company to carry out some sort of strategic review annually of what products it has in the market place and how its portfolio should change. Such a review will lead to changes in the portfolio: new products will be required, old products will be marked for withdrawal, products currently in R&D will need to be speeded up or slowed down depending on their perceived priorities. This process goes on (say) once a year and would last a matter of months.

So we have one instance of the case management process and many instances of the case process. And clearly the two processes intersect. Typically, the case process needs to interact with the case (product portfolio) management process, telling it each review cycle how it is getting on and receiving instructions on whether it should continue and if so at what rate and at what priority.

Let's look back at figure 7-2, a case process showing the life story of a single product. In figure 7-3 we show what might be the corresponding case management process in that organisation. Note how two events cause the Divisional Product Portfolio Review process to start: *Annual budget set or budget revision required* and *Division decides to review its plans*. The process completes when the Board, in either situation, has been informed of the new state of the portfolio for the Division. This might form part of a larger, company-wide portfolio review process, in which the activity of the Board would concern us.

At one point in the process the *Product Strategy Board* informs the *Product Development Team* (which appears in the case process) that the product is to be cancelled. Note how we tie the case process in figure 7-2 to the case management process in figure 7-3 at this point by identifying the equivalent state – *Decision by PSB to cancel product* – in the shared role – *Product Strategy Board* – in the two RADs.

In another situation the *Product Strategy Board* starts up a new *Product Development Team* for a new product.

In a case management process RAD we will expect to see roles such as

- Boards
- strategy groups
- management teams
- progress chasers
- planning teams
- monitoring groups

and activities to do with

- strategy setting
- planning
- reporting
- policy making
- monitoring
- scheduling
- resourcing

- prioritising
- negotiating
- compromising
- reconciling
- and so on.

EVENT-DRIVEN PROCESSES

Here we are looking at a process which is triggered whenever a certain event occurs. It is a process which represents our response to a certain situation. A case process will generally be an event-driven process.

Figure 7-4 shows the sorts of events that might trigger event-driven processes. *Customer application arrives* and *Sample arrives for analysis* are quite likely the triggers for case processes: we will have a number of customer applications being processed at any one time, and there will be a number of samples at various stages of analysis at any given moment. *Budget change announced*, however, will probably trigger a process that starts and stops ... and maybe is triggered again at some time in the future on the next budget change, but we are not going to be dealing with several simultaneously. In the worst case, we'll abandon our (over-running) attempts to deal with the last one and switch our attention to the one that has just come in.

Figure 7-4 – Typical events at the head of roles in an event-driven process

⇒▮▸ Customer application arrives

⇒▮▸ Budget change announced

⇒▮▸ Sample arrives for analysis

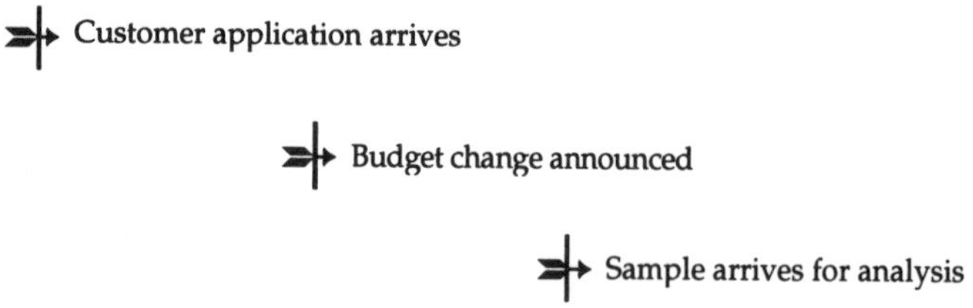

CYCLE-DRIVEN PROCESSES

A cycle-driven process is a particular sort of event-driven process. There is probably only a single instance at any one moment and we fire an instance off at regular intervals, monthly, weekly or whatever. A case management process will generally be cycle-driven: we have a periodic review of things. Figure 7-3 shows a cycle-driven process that, in particular, is fired once a year when the annual budget is set by the Board. In fact it is also an event-driven process: a Division might decide it was appropriate to review its plans for itself suddenly, and the process swings into action to respond to that event, which is not in any way cyclic.

DELEGATION LADDERS

When we model a process with a RAD we seem not to take any explicit notice of one of the most important aspects of an organisation: its reporting hierarchy. Most organisations – even those operating forms of matrix management – use some layering down from the Chief Executive; some *only* operate that way. In fact, in a RAD, although we might not model the hierarchy explicitly, we do model the way it makes itself felt: the business rules that operate in terms of planning, delegating, reporting, authorising and so on. Indeed, it is normal for a RAD that uses functional positions or job-titles as roles to expose the hierarchical aspects of an organisation's behaviour in terms of interactions between "superior" and "inferior" roles. Typically, the hierarchy appears from left to right in the RAD: *The Board* will appear as a role at the extreme left, passing instructions to the next level down, say *Divisional Director*, who in turn pass instructions to their right via interactions with *Project Manager*, and so on further to the right.

Delegation and reporting back are very common process patterns in an organisation and they have a very natural representation in a RAD: they are simply pairs of interactions. If the *Board* asks a *Customer Survey Task Force* to carry out the annual customer survey we will see an interaction between the two roles across which the *Board* gives the *Customer Survey Task Force* its terms of reference. In its turn the *Customer Survey Task Force* delegates parts of that task[1] to other roles: *Pollsters* and *Marketing*, say. See figure 7-5. The task is broken into smaller sub-tasks and delegated out to other roles.

As each role completes its sub-task, it might (or might not) report back to the delegating role to say "I've done what you asked". So we can expect to find a corresponding "closure" interaction for each delegation interaction. Or, at least, it is a useful modelling discipline when you see an interaction that represents delegation to look for a corresponding closure interaction in the real process; if there isn't one there you can question whether there should be; and if there is, you can question that too. Looking back at the sample (and not very sensible) process in figure 3-2, we can see quite readily that the *Divisional Director*, having delegated the execution of the project to the *Project Manager*, apparently never expects to hear about the completion of the project – let's hope that in that model we simply weren't interested in the involvement of the *Divisional Director* after they had started the project off!

In some cases, one role instance might delegate a task to some other role instance which is pre-existent, such as a department or a post in the organisation: each March, the *Board* delegates the annual assessment of effectiveness of the company's IT systems to the *IS Department*; after an accident in the plant, the *Divisional Director* delegates review of plant safety to the *Health and Safety Manager*. In other cases, a role instance might be created for the purpose: we tend to call such roles "task forces" or "project

---

[1] I use the term *task* to mean "responsibility for achieving some outcome", "something one has to do, a piece of work" (OED).

teams". Their job is to carry out the task and then disband. Figure 7-5 shows just such a role: *Customer Survey Task Force.*

Figure 7-5 – A asks B who asks C...

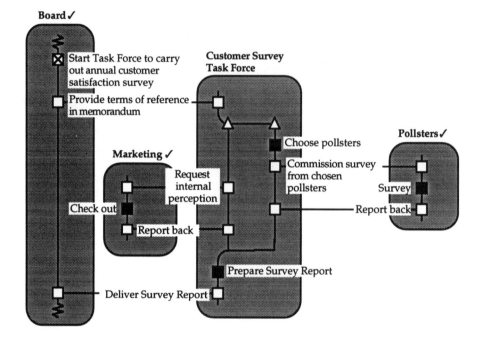

CONTRACTS

Winograd offers a view of organisational behaviour in terms of a four-step cycle between a customer and a supplier[2]:

1   preparation

2   negotiation

3   performance

4   assessment.

In the preparation step, either the customer decides what they want to buy (or, more generally, contract out for), or the supplier makes some offer to a would-be customer; this results in the customer making a request to the supplier. The two parties negotiate the request and two mutual promises result: the supplier

[2] *A language/action perspective on the design of cooperative work*, T Winograd, *Human-Computer Interaction*, **3**, 1987

agrees to provide something in return for something else. The supplier then carries out the performance step which finishes with a declaration that the work is complete, an assertion that the customer tests, finally declaring satisfaction.

Each step can, in its turn, potentially be carried out by a cycle of its own: performance might be broken down into sub-cycles for instance.

In an ideal world, or a new one that we intend to build, we might construct all organisational behaviour out of such cycles. It is doubtful that we can retrospectively *impose* a hierarchical structure of such cycles on an existing process or expect to find one there when we come to model it – we cannot expect that process evolution has preserved such neat conceptual integrity; in fact it would be far more realistic to expect that, as in any other physical system, entropy – the degree of chaos or lack of order in the system – inexorably increases over time unless energy is expended to reverse it (albeit temporarily). We could of course consider BPR as an "entropy-reversal" exercise, one in which the chaos and disorder that has built up over the years is recognised and, through radical change, replaced by a "tidier" and "simpler" system.

Nevertheless, the Flores cycle can be observed, and of course has a natural representation or pattern in a RAD: figures 7-6 and 7-7.

Figure 7-6 – A contractual cycle in a RAD, driven by the Customer

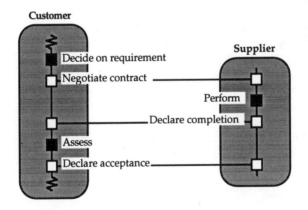

We can elaborate the model at several points to allow for situations where
− there is a breakdown in the negotiation
− the *Supplier* fails to complete the performance.
− the *Customer* is not satisfied with the performance of the *Supplier*
− the various steps are themselves the subject of sub-contracts.

Figure 7-7 – A contractual cycle in a RAD, driven by the Supplier

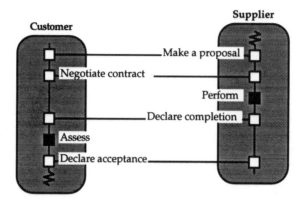

It is a useful modelling discipline to detect interactions which represent acts of negotiation, assessment and so on, in order to see how far the complete cycle is present, and perhaps, if it is not, to ask whether it should be and whether the process can be improved by restructuring it to the "standard" cycle.

PLANS AND ACTIVITIES

The style of working of a process might, in words, look like the following: "I can't describe to you how each project will look precisely; there's no standard process that a project follows in the sense that 'we do A, then B, then C or D, and so on. However each project does carry out a number of well defined things, but in an order that depends on the nature of the individual project. So, we know that a project developing one of our new products will carry out a number of trials with customers and a number of safety trials, but which trials will be carried out and when is very much a matter for the individual project depending on the sort of product. At the outset the project therefore plans the trials it will do and, when the time comes to get a trial under way, it will do whatever is necessary for the trial. We can however define the planning process and we can describe the processes that people follow to carry out the different sorts of trials.".

Figure 7-8 gives an example of this sort of pattern. We show the planning activity, here undertaken by the *Product Planning* role; and we show the activities – customer trials and safety trials – being fired off whenever the plan says it is time, using our ➤ symbol, here detecting an internal event.

Figure 7-8 – A planning activity and its consequent activities

Product Planning

Plan product development (including customer trials and safety trials)

Customer Trials Division

Time to carry out planned customer trial

Product Safety Division

Time to carry out planned safety trial

8

MODELLING THE MATERIALS IN THE PROCESS

INTRODUCTION

In chapters 1 and 2 we looked at the related notions of *information*, *entity* and *essential business entity*. To recap:

- Entities are the subject matter of a process: a paper invoice, a customer, a bank statement, a product line, a drug compound, or a drug trial. They are dealt with or created or consumed by the activities in the process. We saw in chapter 2 how some entities can be the inputs or outputs of an activity, or the grams of an interaction.

- Information tells us about entities, in particular their state. We represent information in the form of data which we conventionally hold in databases or filing systems of some sort. Data consists of neutral text, or bits, or tables, or hypertext structures, or whatever. Information is data with a context which gives it meaning: text which is a name, bits which make up an image, tables that describe company performance, a hypertext structure that provides on-line diagnostic help.

- Essential business entities are just those entities that are the central concern of the business irrespective of how it does its business. A pharmaceutical development company cannot get away from the notion of the *clinical trial* or the *drug compound*. Those are of interest to it, almost no matter how it chooses to organise itself, or what processes it adopts.

In this chapter we look at how "materials" – in particular entities and information – flow around a process and how we can model that flow; and we examine how the *state* of an entity is changed as the process proceeds (its "life history"), and how we can model that too. The complementary nature of RADs, entity model, and entity life history will be more important when computer support is to be designed for a process described in a RAD.

By way of example, let's look at a simple RAD and examine the materials in it. The old favourite from chapter 3 will suffice and is reproduced here as figure 8-1. One change has been made: the names of activities and interactions have been altered slightly to emphasise the materials that are involved in them.

Figure 8-1 – A simple RAD

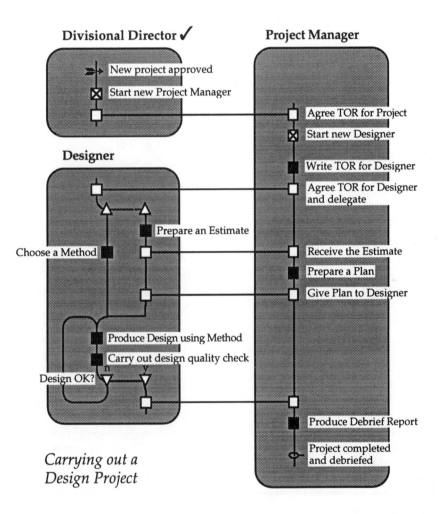

MATERIALS FLOW MODELLING

This is the right moment to revisit the notion of the *role body*. When we look at the part that a role plays in a process, we know that it needs some sort of environment in which to play that part. It needs the materials on which it will work, some resources to use, and maybe also has requirements from the physical surroundings. For example, the *Project Manager* role in figure 8-1 needs

- terms of reference, so that they know what is required of them in detail;
- some means for preparing a plan; this could be a PC-based project planning tool, or a large sheet of paper, for instance;
- a desk and chair at which to work, together with paper, pencils and a PC connected to some useful services;
- some means of communicating with those with whom they have interactions: this could include an in-tray, an e-mail facility, and a telephone.

These things constitute the role body for the project manager. Some are explicitly mentioned on the RAD (because, as ever, we choose to mention them), some are not. For instance, we mention plans because they are our concern in this model; but we do not mention desks as they are not of interest in understanding the business of running a design project. Where do the items in the role body come from? They are either "created" when the role is instantiated and provided to the role, or they are passed into the role instance when it is running. For instance, a Project Manager is given a desk when instantiated ("this is where the project manager of the ABC project sits"), but is given terms of reference by a Divisional Director through an interaction that we decide to model. Whichever is the case, we would like to check that the role body is sufficient and complete at the requisite moments: does each activity and interaction that the role takes part in have the material necessary to carry it out? In other words, is the flow of material around the process coherent?

In processes where activity is strongly linked to documents of various sorts we will want to establish whether the *document flow* through the process, through and between roles, is coherent, ie roles have what they need when they need it, for activities and interactions. The need therefore arises to model the material flow through the process in our process model, and we need to expand on the brief coverage we gave this topic at the end of chapter 5.

The starting point for this is a closer examination of each activity: what materials are its inputs and what are its outputs? Some of those inputs will be abstract, such as the result of a prior decision or some information about the world; some will be concrete ... such as concrete. If we examine the process in figure 8-1 we might come to the following conclusions:

- *Write TOR for Designer*. Inputs: *TOR for Project*; outputs: *TOR for Designer*
- *Prepare an Estimate*. Inputs: *TOR for Designer*; outputs: *Estimate*
- *Choose a Method*. Inputs: *TOR for Designer*; outputs: *Method*
- *Produce Design using Method*. Inputs: *Plan, Method, TOR for Designer*; outputs: *Design*
- *Carry out design quality check*. Inputs: *Design*; outputs: *Design quality check result*
- *Prepare a Plan*. Inputs: *TOR for Project, Estimate*; outputs: *Plan*

- *Produce Debrief Report*. Inputs: none?; outputs: *Debrief Report*.

(Note that I am not assuming that inputs are in anyway consumed, simply that they are used by an activity.) We can do a similar examination of interactions, but we will now need to look at the grams involved and where they go:

- *Agree TOR for Project*. Grams: *TOR for Project* is created during the interaction and goes to both *Divisional Director* and *Project Manager*

- *Agree TOR and delegate*. Grams: *TOR for Designer* is created during the interaction and goes to both *Project Manager* and *Designer*

- *Receive Estimate*. Grams: *Estimate* goes to *Project Manager*

- *Give Plan to Designer*. Grams: *Plan* goes to *Designer*.

There is a final interaction between *Designer* and *Project Manager* which is currently unlabelled. This means it is simply a synchronisation between the two roles: once the *Designer* has reached a certain state, the *Project Manager* can get on with something, in this case producing the *Debrief Report*. A simple check reveals that the right materials are in the role bodies at the time they are needed as inputs to activities or interactions. With one exception. It was not clear what inputs the Project Manager used to compile the project's *Debrief Report*. By inspection, we might find out that such a report covers how long things took in reality against the planned durations, so that future planning estimates can be made more accurate. (One of the goals of the process will probably be to ensure that such information is made available to future projects in a usable form such as a debriefing report.) Clearly, the missing input to *Produce Debrief Report* is something like *Actual Effort Figures*, and this needs to get into the *Project Manager* role body from the *Designer* role body across that final interaction. So we will name the interaction *Pass over Actual Effort Figures*:

- *Pass over Actual Effort Figures*. Grams: *Actual Effort Figures* goes to *Project Manager*.

Where do the *Actual Effort Figures* come from? To be a gram in that interaction, they must already be in the role body of the *Designer*. Clearly we need a new activity at the end of the *Designer* role, just before that final interaction. The RAD now becomes that shown in figure 8-2.

The RAD now has a coherent materials flow, with the needs of interactions and activities satisfied at this level of modelling.

If we inspect the notion of "materials" a little more closely, we can distinguish between information (my age), physical forms of that information (an entry in my personal file), and materials without information content (typically raw materials, such as me). Putting aside raw materials, we will see in chapter 9 how, by looking at a process from an abstract perspective, we can investigate its *intent* or *purpose*; whereas, by taking a concrete perspective, we can investigate its *mechanisms*. Our RAD might mix both. Figure 8-2 contains materials that are information (*Actual Effort Figures, TOR for Project*) and materials that are concrete or physical (*Debrief Report*). The *Debrief Report* might (in a fuller RAD be seen to) be passed to another role which makes use of it in some way. What is happening is of course that the *Debrief Report* is simply the concrete vehicle for the debrief information it contains. Whether we choose to take the concrete or the abstract view depends on why we are modelling – a topic we shall return to in chapter 9.

Figure 8-2 – The sample RAD with coherent materials flow

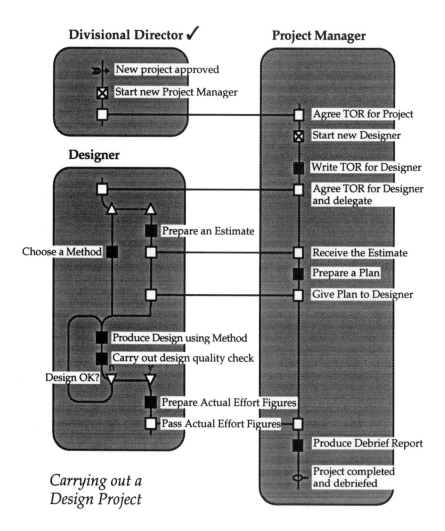

When we examine how materials physically find their way into the role body in practice, we might find a number of different implementation mechanisms, a typical one being that of providing shared access to things. For instance, a document produced by the role *Author* might find its way into some central repository, from which it can be accessed by another role, say *Reader*, apparently without explicit transfer from the role body of *Author* to the role body of *Reader*. We might feel it is sufficient for a given model to simply show the production and use of the document in the respective roles without further comment: there would be an implied transfer from one to the other through the repository – the document would be "shared". Suppose on the other hand we were in a situation where we were trying to establish that the materials flow was coherent, and in particular that there was the correct time ordering so that changes to the document were properly notified to affected parties and that no-one attempted to get access to versions that had not been approved etc. In such cases we would need to be more explicit about the matter, in particular by showing the notification of the document's creation and amendment by the *Author* and its passage to the receiving role body, *Reader* say, via some form of interaction suitably woven into the work of the two roles.

A traditional database-based IT system uses a database as a "subterranean" way of integrating people who produce and consume information – the plumbing is *outside* the plane of the process and allows consumers access down into the database to access the information produced and put there by others. The group is integrated through its use of shared information in the database. In a process support system that uses workflow management, information can also be passed *within* the plane of the process, through the process flow, in some form of "case folder" that is forwarded from role to role by the workflow system using its map of the process. Here the group is integrated through the shared process.

ENTITY MODELLING

The above analysis of the process will easily reveal the materials that are required by the process; as we have seen, they will frequently appear as the grams passing between roles at interactions, for instance.

However, we should note here that *data* that is required purely to record state should not appear on the RAD; for instance, indicators telling us that a plan has been approved, or pointers connecting purchase orders with the goods that satisfy them. Similarly, an entity that is an input to an activity will appear in the definition of an activity; but an entity that is an intermediate result *within* an activity is computational detail and not of concern to the process (this is part of an activity's being a black box).

The traditional entity-relationship modelling technique is a good starting point for an exploration of the entities of the process. The STRIM modelling method therefore includes the optional preparation of an entity model (or ER model) and the derivation from it of formal definitions for the entities. There are plenty of texts[1] on the topic of entity modelling and the interested reader is referred to them; here we are only concerned with how the technique can be usefully combined with role and activity modelling.

---

[1] For example *CASE*Method, Entity Relationship Modelling*, R Barker, Oracle Corporation UK Limited, 1989

So, what are the entities in the process described in figure 8-2? What is the subject matter of the process? As far as entity *flow* is concerned, our analysis has revealed *Design, Debrief Report, Method, Plan, Estimate, TOR for Designer*, and *TOR for Project*. These are things that are explicitly being created, passed around, and used. But a conventional entity analysis would probably suggest others, in particular the three roles involved *Divisional Director, Project Manager*, and *Designer*, and perhaps the most important: the *Design Project*. The RAD as drawn is a RAD of a case process, where the case is a *Design Project*; the clues to this are the title of the RAD – *Carrying out a Design Project* – and the event which starts the activity of the process in the *Divisional Director* role – *New project approved*. The Design Project is in a sense a "key" business entity, and our RAD describes how it is carried out; other entities such as *Design* are supportive entities.

Effectively we are collecting entities from two sources:

– the "internal" subject matter of the activities and interactions, revealed by looking at the materials flow inside the process

– the "external" subject matter of the process seen as a case process: the subject of a case (here a Design Project), and the roles that deal with a case (here the *Divisional Director, Project Manager*, and *Designer*).

With our understanding of processes we can now cast a little light on data and databases. Michael Jackson[2] recognised that a database was simply a collection of what he called "state vectors", one for each of the entity instances known to the system. He viewed a computer system as a mechanism for tracking the state of entities in the outside world and providing reports on them. Ideally, he said, we would dedicate a computer processor to each entity instance and that processor would track the entity instance through its life history (which could be described in terms of its ELH). Unfortunately, we can't build systems consisting of millions of processors dedicated in this way, eg one to each customer of a bank, and, in order to build a system using just the one processor generally at our disposal, we have to make that processor swap its attention between entity instances. When it puts down one instance in favour of another, it remembers the state of that entity as a state vector in the database so that it can pick it up where it left off at some time in the future. A database is therefore created by "inverting the state vectors" as Jackson put it.

STRIM looks at things in exactly the same way, except that we concern ourselves with case process instances rather than business entity instances. A database is simply a way of giving some persistence to the state (data) of a case (process instance). It can thereby act as one means for the roles taking part in that case process to collaborate, by giving them shared access to that state data and hence to the case. So, in processing an application from a customer for a loan in a bank's Administer a Loan process, I, as a Clerk, might assess the credit-worthiness of the applicant by accessing the customer's record in some database and update that record with my assessment. I then pass the name of

---

[2] *System Development*, M Jackson, Prentice Hall, 1983

the applicant to you as Manager, and you access the database, using the name as a key, to see my assessment and other details and authorise the loan or not. We used the database as a communications mechanism through which the case's state passed.

The database can also act as a means of communication between the case process instances and the case management process. In that same bank, you as Manager will have a separate (case management) process concerned with keeping the exposure of the bank to an acceptable level and to do this you will need to know, in summary form, the situation across all the loans outstanding: in STRIM terms you need an overview of the states of all the instances of the Administer a Loan process. Our IT department will typically do this by accessing all the details of the current loans (="states of the current process instances") and calculating some figures that convey the total exposure to you. The single case management process instance is accessing the state of all the case process instances, recorded in the database.

It is our experience that "true" information relevant to a process is readily revealed by examining the process alone. This will generally be information about the entities that are the subject matter of someone's activity, such as a design or a plan, or the subject matter of an interaction between two people. Much data that is seen around organisations either records the state of a process (because people have poor memories like our single processor) or is just a way of implementing interactions. For example, an order-processing system would hold a lot of information about the state of each order; but when we model the order-processing process we do not need to model the process *and* the data that would be necessary to record its state; the latter data is only necessary for an implementation. Similarly, an entity such as an invoice is really only a physical means of making an interaction happen – namely a vendor requesting payment from a purchaser – and of passing information needed to effect the interaction. It might be quite irrelevant to the process whether a paper invoice or EDI or a phone call is used to effect the interaction. The interaction is important; the way data is used to effect it might be incidental.

ENTITY LIFE HISTORY MODELLING

A traditional, complementary view of *entity* used in data-oriented methods is the *entity life history* (ELH). This shows the different states that an entity passes through during its lifetime, ie between its creation and its extinction (if it is indeed made extinct). It is worthwhile looking at how an ELH can be drawn up and related to a RAD.

The ELH standard notation expresses the life history in terms of a simple grammar, most easily explained through a sample *entity life history diagram*, such as that in figure 8-3. (Again, there are plenty of texts on this approach, so I shall not go into detail here except to point out how the method and notation complement STRIM and RADs.)

Figure 8-3 – A simple entity life history diagram

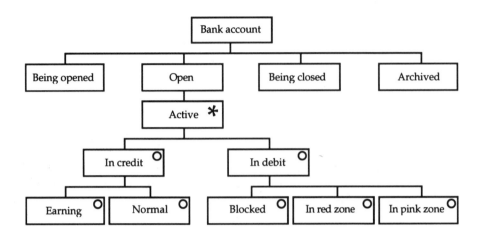

Figure 8-3 describes the life history of the entity called *Bank account*. It says that each Bank account will go through four states in sequence:

- being opened
- open
- being closed
- archived.

Whilst being opened, the account exists and has an initial deposit in it from the account holder but final arrangements have not been made for transactions. It then moves into the state of being open, on into the state of being closed where new transactions on it are blocked except total withdrawal or repayment, and thence into the archived state where it is dormant but recorded. Whilst in the open state, the diagram tells us that it passes through the state *Active* many times, the "many times" being indicated by the star in the box, and each repetition of the state *Active* is either *In credit* or *In debit*, the "either-or" being represented by the circles in the boxes. Similarly, while in the in-debit state, an account can be in one of

- *In the pink zone*, where it is overdrawn and charges are made for transactions.
- *In the red zone*, where charges are made for transactions and interest is payable on the amount of the debt.
- *Blocked*, where no further withdrawals are allowed, charges are made for other transactions, and interest is payable.

So, as an example, a short-lived bank account might go through the following sequence of states:

1   being opened

2   open, in credit, interest earning

3   open, in credit, normal

4   open, in debit, in the red zone

5   open, in debit, blocked

6   open, in debit, in the red zone

7   open, in credit, interest earning

8   being closed

9   archived.

Various things in the process cause the state changes, always according to the "allowable" changes indicated in the ELH. The question we can ask is "what things in the process model correspond to (or cause) changes in state of the entity?". In general those "things" will either be activities or interactions. A withdrawal by the account holder will move the account between the different states under *Active* or leave it at the same active state, depending on the size of the withdrawal, the funds in the account before the withdrawal, and perhaps the limits agreed between the account holder and the bank.

As a further simple example, we could consider the entity *Design* in the RAD in figure 8-2. Once a design has been created it is subjected to quality control checks and reworking until it is satisfactory. We might draw the ELH shown in figure 8-4.

Figure 8-4 – ELH for the entity Design *in figure 8-3*

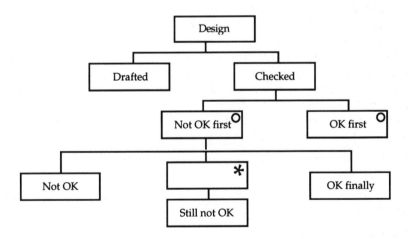

The design starts off in a drafted (but unchecked state), and then becomes checked. In the checked state it is either OK on the first check (*OK first*) or not (*Not OK first*). In the latter case it goes through a sequence of three states: starting in *Not OK*, moving on to a state which might be repeated an indefinite (but hopefully finite) number of times – *Still not OK* – finally moving to *OK finally*.

We can trace these state changes through the RAD. *Produce Design using Method* will, in the first instance, produce as an output a design in the state *Drafted*. The activity *Carry out design quality check* moves the design to the *Checked* state where it will be *OK first* or *Not OK* (under *Not OK first*). On subsequent *Produce Design using Method* "runs" (which we assume rework the existing design), the design will remain *Checked* but subsequent design quality checks will either move it on to or leave it in the state *Still not OK*, or finally on to *OK finally*. The case refinement *Design OK?* essentially uses the state of the design (which is part of the state of the process) to determine how the role should proceed, whether to have another go at the design or to complete its work.

Our RAD effectively contains a state diagram for the design showing what activities in the process change its state.

Returning to our ER model, we could add the attributes to the entities that record their state: eg checked status and quality status. We then have a three-way view of state across our analysis:

1   The flow of an entity through the activities and interactions will be shown on the RAD; the activities and interactions will change the entity's state.

2   The attributes of the entity, as shown in the ER model, might cover its state.

3   The state changes caused by the process will be shown on the ELH.

We return to the possibilities that this three-way representation offers in chapter 9 where we examine ways of analysing a model.

9

ANALYSING A PROCESS MODEL

INTRODUCTION

If our aim in drawing some models of a business process is to re-engineer the process or the organisation or to improve the process, we need to know what sorts of questions we can ask of the model that will tell us interesting things about our process. This chapter looks at how we can use a STRIM process model for re-engineering and improvement. It is now that we shall start using the machinery that we have been building up over the preceding chapters, and we shall also add one final piece of machinery: the notion of concrete and abstract models.

Let's start by looking at why change is needed.

PROCESS SPRING-CLEANING – WHY IT BECOMES NECESSARY

Over time, an organisation and its processes become convoluted. A process that started out simple and clean has, somehow, become complex and messy. The business itself has changed, or the business environment has changed around it and it has changed its process in response. It is worth a little time looking at how such complexities can arise.

"We won't let that happen again!"

Bad experiences can lead to extra twists being added to a process. A change might be made to plug a loophole, particularly if a mistake has at some time caused trouble, such as financial loss. Suppose that one day, a manufacturer ships some equipment to a customer but the spares arrive late. Perhaps, in the past that has happened before but without any major repercussion – the spares have caught up a little bit later. But this time, the equipment failed soon after arrival and the spares were quickly needed, and weren't there. The customer sustained a significant loss of business and sued the equipment manufacturer. "We're not going to let that happen again" vows senior management, and extra steps and checks are added to the process to plug that possible loophole. Of course, on average each shipment is now probably held up that bit longer, just to ensure that the earlier mistake is never repeated.

"We won't give them another chance to mess us up!"

Separate functional units can become self-protective. Suppose group *B* gets materials from group *A*. And suppose *B* starts to get trouble with poor quality arriving from *A* and as a result and, too often, has to return material for reworking, having wasted their own materials and resources working on poor inputs. Group *B* is very likely to institute checking procedures at the interface with group *A*, and perhaps to put in place elaborate hand-over and fault-reporting procedures, in order to protect themselves in the future.

Now everything is checked, everything is signed for, faults are recorded and reported formally and there are procedures for tracking faults and cross-charging for the costs of faulty work. More complications for what should be a simple hand-over process. All that new activity adds no value, only cost.

"We're in another world!"

The nature of the business can change. A process that was adequate under one set of market conditions can become quite ineffective when those conditions change, and, if the change occurs slowly, work-arounds will be added bit by bit to try to overcome the increasing inadequacy of the old process.

As an example, consider a company in the business of making fitted kitchen furniture. Some years back when life was slower and customers relatively undemanding, the order-filling process relied on a simple flow of manufacture, with orders and changes to orders being dealt with on a cyclic basis: on the first Monday of each month, the recent orders would be looked at and the production schedules adjusted for the coming month. The whole thing satisfactorily revolved around that monthly cycle.

But customers started demanding quicker delivery, and some stores started promising faster delivery to certain customers. Some orders couldn't wait for the monthly production meeting and so had to be handled as exceptions: "short-circuits" and "fast tracks" were added to the simple monthly cycle to handle the exceptions. But as time has passed and things have become more hectic, more and more such work-arounds have been added to the main cycle, and the work-arounds have become institutionalised and the norm, with the result that that monthly meeting is now more about finding out what is happening and handling the big bush fires, rather than planning. Planning is effectively being done out in the work-arounds.

Essentially, what must happen is that the old cycle-driven process, which is now unwieldy and unresponsive, needs to be replaced by an event-driven process, one which is clean and responsive. Instead of piling things up to be handled, they need to be dealt with as they come in and changes need to be made to production schedules on the spot. The current role structure and the interactions in it, as defined by the monthly cycle, could continue to exist in order to monitor the process from a managerial standpoint, but the day-to-day control of the process needs to be made the focus.

ASKING THE RIGHT QUESTIONS

Once the RADs and ER model have been prepared, a number of questions can be asked of the resulting model and the process it describes (if we have not already started asking them!). Our aim is to look for features in the model which might help us to further understand or improve or re-engineer the process or indeed the organisation.

No process model can of itself provide the answer to a process problem: it can only act as a sort of searchlight on the process. If a process is in trouble or inefficient, the symptoms will often be recognised and understood by people to some degree. The purpose of the process model must be to *reveal*: to reveal the process, the roots of its problems, and potential ways of attacking the trouble. Sometimes a RAD can reveal the nature of the problem and suggest a solution very quickly; something in the RAD is like a flashing light saying "here's your problem". In other situations, revelation comes more slowly, perhaps as the right – revealing – perspective is homed in on.

This is not a book on BPR or TQM, both huge topics that certainly raise a requirement for process modelling and analysis, but which also contain many soft (but difficult) issues such as the management of change, visioning, motivation, culture, and ethics.

My sole purpose in this chapter is to explain how, in a variety of improvement situations, STRIM can be used to find and explore opportunities for both radical and incremental improvement of a process. If you intend to carry out a BPR or TQM programme, you should look to other sources for guidance on the soft issues, but you will see from this chapter how STRIM can be a powerful tool when, during that programme, you look at your processes and re-engineer them.

We will want to analyse the process from two points of view: *qualitative* and *quantitative*. To set the scene for a description of the sorts of quantitative and qualitative analysis that are possible on a RAD, let's first look at the different styles of process improvement that are possible.

There are four ways in which we can improve matters:

1 by "point-wise" improvements to individual activities or interactions in a process

2 by "flow-wise" improvements to a process

3 by restructuring roles in a process

4 by realigning the organisational structure and the process structure.

In any given BPR or TQM programme, some mixture of these will be used. Levels 1, 2, and 3 are generally the domain of the TQM disciplines, concentrating on incremental change and incremental improvement; levels 3 and (particularly) 4 are where BPR looks for radical change.

We take these in turn before considering the sorts of analysis of a RAD that would lead us to answers at these four different levels. It is also worth reminding ourselves once again that which of these levels we want to consider will very much determine the perspectives – and hence the RADs – we elicit and draw.

SOME STARTING POINTS

As an item of work passes through the process our expectation is that each stage – activity or interaction or decision – adds value in some way. It might add direct value to the customer of the process by bringing us a little closer to the desired end result, or it might add value to the organisation by providing it with something that it needs to ensure efficient and effective operation of this or another process. By looking at a RAD and following the path of the work item we can identify the *value chain*. It might not be a single path through the RAD: it could be a network of paths branching out from the initial trigger and coming together at the final goal, or it could appear more like a fishbone with side chains coming in and adding their contribution (figure 9-1). A simple value chain indicates a simple production line flow from role to role. The network shows a set of roles responding in turn to the trigger and providing their contribution. The fishbone shows separate roles feeding into the main value chain that originated with the customer request. (We have not shown the feedback loops and corrective loops back.)

Figure 9-1 – Value chains

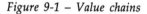

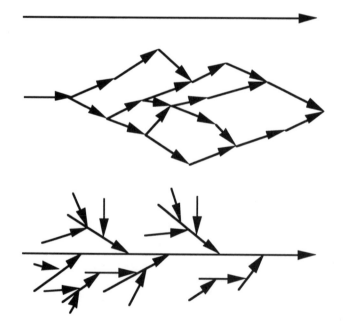

These will be familiar to anyone who has worked with activity networks for planning purposes. One of the important ideas when working with such networks is the *critical path*: that sequence of activities whose total duration is the duration of the process. If an activity on the critical path takes ten days longer then the whole process takes ten days longer. The critical path determines the overall duration of the process. We saw in chapter 5 that the RAD can be annotated with the duration of each activity and interaction. It can be a simple manual activity to find the critical path. The possible presence of loops in our process makes the situation a little more complicated of course, but the principles remain. In complex cases, assuming the loops can be compressed or ignored and all but the longest thread on each case refinement discarded, the (cut-down) RAD can be transferred to a traditional project planning tool which will find the critical path automatically.

Finally, it is essential that the goals of the process are clearly spelt out somewhere. We can then ask the questions:

- Are the completion states of roles the same as the stated objectives for the roles? ie do the roles have clearly stated objectives that are identifiable in the RAD? Where in the RAD is the point where we can say "when we get to this state we have finished and the goal of the process has been achieved?". The process's goal(s) might of course correspond to a number of states in different roles.

- Where a role operates on a continuous basis, can its "steady-state" objective be identified as an invariant of the process?

- Where a role operates cyclically, can some "periodic" objective be identified as an intermediate state at some point in the process?

POINT-WISE IMPROVEMENTS

Here we are concerned with increasing the efficiency (use of resources) or effectiveness (reliability and quality of result) of individual activities in the process.

A common way of achieving point-wise improvements is to help the individual carry out an individual activity; we give people tools to do their work. In the office environment, helping the individual to do their work increasingly means using IT through personal computers: personal productivity tools such as spreadsheets, organisers, and word processors for example. We might improve the way that interactions are carried out by providing e-mail, better-equipped meeting rooms, video-conferencing facilities, or even an arbitration service. Which activities and interactions we choose to concentrate on when searching for point-wise improvements depends on where we are seeking the benefits of improvement.

This is not a book on TQM, but we can ask the question "How can we use a RAD to look for the right activities and interactions to improve?".

Reducing overall cost

Any activity will take time and resources for its completion. If our concern is to optimise our process in its use of resources and hence its cost, we shall look for ways of speeding it up so that an actor can get through more cases in a day. Our aim is to reduce the overall cost of the process, in particular the cost to process a single work item in a case process. As we saw in chapter 5, the RAD can be very simply annotated with the resource usage of each activity and interaction. Now is the time to look it over:

– Every activity and interaction must be a candidate, so look at each in turn to see which have the largest resource usage and which therefore might yield the biggest savings.

– Look for case refinements concerned with checking for poor quality. Look at the frequency with which the thread that deals with faulty material or errors in previous work is followed. Trace back through the process and identify where that fault was introduced. What can be done in that activity to reduce the likelihood of poor quality? And can the fault be detected earlier in the process, so that the cost of rework is reduced? These are all traditional TQM-style questions which the RAD can help you answer.

Shortening cycle time

We might be seeking a reduced time-to-process for an individual case: we want to get the result – the service or the product – to the customer as quickly as possible (this might be different from optimising the throughput of an individual worker). A key tool here will of course be critical path analysis (CPA):

– Look at each activity and interaction on the critical path. If we can reduce the duration of any of those, we shall, by definition, reduce the duration of the whole project (up to the point, of course, where another path through the process becomes the critical path).

– Look for the activities and interactions on the critical path whose duration has the greatest variation. In some situations, the perceived quality of a service can be increased as much by making the service *reliably* of a certain duration as by making it shorter in most cases. "I don't mind if it takes three days, providing I can be sure it doesn't take any more".

This works quite well except for situations where the process has loops, or repeated activity in it, or threads that are only traversed under some circumstances, for instance for rework. In RAD terms, we have to deal with (ie remove) loops and case refinements, neither of which can be represented using everyday network planning tools, and which therefore make critical path analysis (CPA) difficult. We can do that in one of two ways:

– By adding some "overhead" to the part of the process that, on occasions, needs to be redone. Suppose we have a reviewing cycle that is repeated until the thing being reviewed – a document say – is deemed acceptable. We might, for the purposes of CPA, simply assume that the reviewing cycle is always done twice, and thereby remove the loop.

–   By treating alternative paths in some proportional way. Suppose we are processing forms, and suppose type A forms take six days while type B forms take twelve days. About two-thirds of the forms are type A. We might say that the processing of type A and B form takes eight days, thereby removing the case refinement.

This is not very satisfactory. We would prefer to leave the full process structure in place and deal with it intact with loops and alternative threads. The approach of *System Dynamics* can help here. In System Dynamics[1], a process is seen as a set of "flows" of material between "stocks". The flows form a network which can include feedback loops and alternative paths for materials. PC-based tools for animating such models allow the flow rates to be specified as formulae and in particular to be made dependent on each other, on stock levels, and on external variables, on the passage of time, and on the date or time; those relationships can involve statistical probabilities, so we end up with a model that can be animated allowing us to determine the cycle time as a probability distribution itself: a much richer representation, especially if we are trying to understand the variability of the time a process takes. Such a model also allows the process's long-term behaviour to be explored: "Is the process stable over time?", "What happens to the throughput and cycle time over the seasonal rush?".

A RAD can be converted into a System Dynamics model by turning states into stocks, and activities and interactions into flows. Case refinements become split flows whose rates sum to one, whilst part refinements become joint flows in which the material is replicated on each flow. In practice, the RAD must be greatly simplified first as it contains a great deal of detail that does not need to be carried into the quantitative model; it was for just this reason that we looked at "collapsing a model" in chapter 6.

Discrete models permit similar quantitative representation of a process in terms of flows of "stuff" from one activity to another, but that stuff now takes the form of discrete objects with attached properties which can be handled differently by an activity according to their attributes: green widgets are packaged in tens, red widgets in twenties.

To complete a quantitative model we will generally need to collect information about other "influencing factors" that affect the quantitative behaviour of the process:

–   the rate at which cases arrive for processing

–   the time of year (the rate at which work arrives might be seasonal)

–   staff morale, which in turn might affect ...

–   staff productivity

---

[1]   *An introduction to computer simulation: a system dynamics approach*, N Roberts, D Anderson, R Deal, M Garet, W Shaffer, Addison-Wesley, 1983

- the numbers of staff available to carry out different activities
- the availability of tools, machinery, and other resources needed in the role body
- consumer confidence
- interest rates
- weather patterns
- population movements
- and many more.

We can start to see that a quantitative model deals with factors which are strictly outside the sort of model we have prepared with STRIM. Moreover, experience has shown that a quantitative model is most often beneficial if it is kept at a fairly high level. This leads us to the conclusion that we should not expect to find quantitative solutions from a qualitative model, nor qualitative solutions from a quantitative model. Whilst there is some overlap between, say, a RAD and a System Dynamics model, we are better thinking of them as complementary tools for the analyst, each with its own things to tell us.

FLOW-WISE IMPROVEMENTS

Given a set of roles and responsibilities, how can we improve the flow through the process? What changes can we make to the ordering of activities and interactions within a role in order to reduce the overall case processing time, or reduce resource requirements?

Increasing parallelism

One approach to reducing the overall elapsed time that it takes a case to be processed through a process is to increase the overlap between activities, especially where this reduces the length of the critical path. This is an approach well known to those who plan projects using activity networks.

Figure 9-2 – Increasing parallelism in a role's activities

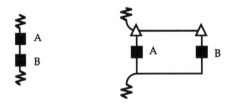

To reduce the overall elapsed time of a project, the planner looks for the critical path through the project and looks for ways in which the amount of concurrent activity can be increased so that activities that were once done sequentially are now done in parallel. The RAD equivalent is to move from the process fragment on the left-hand side of figure 9-2 to that on the right-hand side. (The assumption is of course that *B* does not depend on *A* and that there are actors available to do *A* and *B* concurrently.)

The effect of this is to change the elapsed time of this fragment from the sum of the time it takes to do activities *A* and *B* to the maximum of those two times.

Our inspection of the critical path might suggest that there is no need for activity *B* to be on the critical path at all and moving it off will be our immediate response.

Applying the 80:20 rule – from generalists to specialists

Does every case that goes through a process need to go through the same process? Does every purchase order need to be seen by the Finance Director? Could we limit the ones needing the FD's approval to those over a certain value? If we can do this, we can reduce the average time it takes for a case to be processed.

Figure 9-3 – Complicating a process for improved average speed

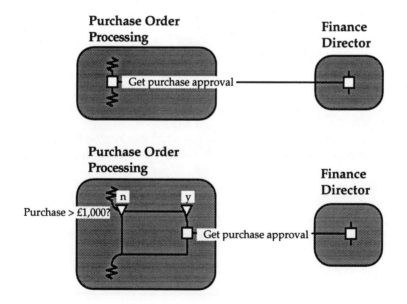

It might look as though we are complicating the process, and indeed we are, but the effect can be positive, assuming that the extra decision making and iteration require very little time. We might replace the top process fragment in figure 9-3 by the bottom fragment.

This can be extended further. Rather than routing simple and complex cases through the same people, thereby requiring them all to have the same high level of skill so that they are able to handle any case of any degree of difficulty, we can consider filtering out difficult cases either at the beginning of their processing or at some intermediate point and passing their processing to a smaller number of expert personnel. The personnel who handle the run-of-the-mill cases no longer have to have the same degree of skill and could therefore be a less expensive resource. Once again the process becomes slightly more complex to incorporate the filtering, but the benefits could outweigh the costs. The equivalent in RAD terms is shown in figure 9-4.

Figure 9-4 – Splitting cases by difficulty

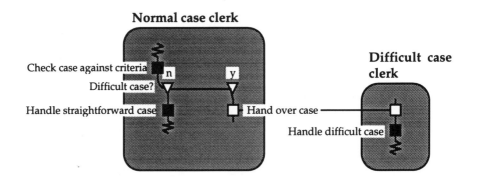

Planning for success

"Planning for success" is a technique that is used where shortening elapsed time is of paramount importance and where wasted resource can be countenanced if the potential time gains are great enough. A product development process is a typical example. Getting to the market place earlier can mean increased product life and earlier revenue flow. A business might consider the possibility of doing work that has to be thrown away if development is abandoned if it gets the product to the market place earlier in the cases where development is successful.

The approach goes as follows. Suppose that the "sensible" way of doing things is

1   do activity *A*

2   decide whether it is worth continuing this thread/product/route

3   if it is, do activity *B*.

If the decision at step 2 is that it is not worth continuing with the product, we have not wasted effort doing activity *B* to no avail. The time it takes to get through this is of course the sum of the time to do activity *A*, the time to make the decision (typically small in comparison), and the time to do activity *B*.

If we plan for success, we start activities *A* and *B* at the same time. When *A* finishes we make the decision and, if the decision is "go" we let activity *B* continue; otherwise we chop *B*. This is equivalent to replacing the left-hand fragment in figure 9-5 by the right-hand fragment. (Remember that an activity can be terminated for a number of reasons: in this case either *B* finishes naturally because it was allowed to run to completion, or it was aborted. How we proceed at the end of the part refinement depends on whether *B* was aborted or not.)

Figure 9-5 – Planning for success

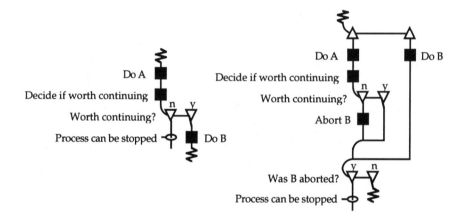

The upside of this change is that, whenever the decision is "go", we save the elapsed time of doing activity *A* – we get to market that much faster. The downside is of course that, whenever the decision is "no go", we have wasted whatever has by that time been spent doing *B* to no avail. Whether the upside is considered bigger than the downside is clearly going to change from one situation to the next, but the RAD provides a way of exploring the possibility.

The pharmaceutical industry offers many examples of the potential benefits of planning for success. Each extra day that a successful drug is on the market can mean a considerable amount on the bottom line; this can justify risking wasted effort on activities that prove to be unnecessary.

Checking for coherent information flow

We saw in chapters 3 and 8 how we could annotate the activities in a process model with the information they need and the information they produce, and how we could similarly annotate interactions with the information flow (if any) that occurred between the collaborating roles. Given that annotation, we can check that the information flow through the process is *coherent*, ie that information gets around the process in one way or another from the roles that produce it to the roles that use it. It is not unusual for the work-arounds that we find in a process to be there simply to cope with the inadequacies of the formal process when it comes to moving information between the roles. "Why is that interaction there? Well, I normally end up going back to the originator because, for some reason, the information asked for in section 5 of the report is rarely enough for me to do my bit". Those work-arounds, as is often the case, provide clues for improvement of the process.

We can finally ask such questions as:

- Is all information generated needed?
- Is all information generated before it is needed?
- Are all grams used by the receiving role?

Checking the state changes of entities

If we have prepared an entity life history (ELH) for one or more entities in the process, we have an opportunity for some cross-checking, given the three-way view of entity state across our analysis:

1 The flow of an entity through the activities and interactions will be shown on the RAD; the activities and interactions through which it flows will change its state.

2 The state changes caused by the process will be shown on the ELH. We can check where in the process those state changes occur, and ensure that the ELH and the RAD tell a consistent story.

3 The attributes of the entity, as listed in the ER model, should cover its state. We can check that the attributes are sufficient to describe the entity's different states.

Checking for customer focus

Activities – especially those on the critical path – can be externally focused, ie focused on the customer of the process; or they can be internally focused, ie supporting some internal function that is not directly relevant to delivery to the customer.

A useful approach is to classify each process element (activity or interaction) under one of three headings:

1 it delivers value directly to the client of the process (mark these in green)

2 it delivers value only to the organisation (mark these in blue)

3 it represents waste in some form: quality control, handling exceptions, correcting mistakes, apologising etc (mark these in red).

Ideally only type 1 process elements should be on the critical path or the main value chain. Type 2 elements should be moved off the critical path or main value chain if necessary. Type 3 elements need to be eliminated of course, though this will require change to the other parts of the process to make it right-first-time.

Catching faults earlier

If someone makes a mistake somewhere in the process, it might not be found until later on, and then correcting can involve unwinding things, and tracing back to the source to get the fault corrected – complications in the process and delays in the processing.

Earlier fault detection can reduce the likelihood of faults getting through to later stages and can reduce the cost of correcting them. Check the RAD for places where faults are detected and see if the detection can be moved to an earlier point, nearer the source.

IMPROVEMENT BY RESTRUCTURING ROLES

As we map the process we reveal a structure that is the result of possibly decades of change in people's job descriptions, in the way the organisation is structured, in the business of the organisation, in the use of technology, in unionisation, ... a host of factors for change. The precise content of each role – particularly where it is defined as a job title – will not be wholly rational if viewed dispassionately. But from our role-centred RADs we can look for ways of rationalising the structure of roles, in particular by moving activities between roles, combining roles and so on. We might try explicitly to reduce the number of interactions that are necessary to make a process work, and this would typically mean restructuring the roles and what they do.

We are now at the level where we are considering more radical change than tinkering with an activity here or a procedure there. We are starting to look at the relationship between the roles and the organisation. To do this we need to step back and take a closer look at what we mean by a "role" and also at two different sorts of process model that we have hinted at but not fully addressed: *concrete models* and *abstract models*. This is a major part of the machinery we need in a re-engineering or improvement situation.

What is a role?

Once modelling has started it is not long before the question arises of "just what is a role?". In STRIM we use the word "role" in a very general way. In chapter 2 I described a number of different types of role:

- a unique functional group
- a unique functional position or post
- a rank or job title
- a replicated functional group
- a replicated functional position or post
- a class of person
- an abstraction
- a computer system.

I shall characterise a role as follows:

A role is an area of responsibility for some contribution to a process, carried out through a set of partially ordered activities which share a single *role body* or set of resources.

The resources that a role uses can include its physical environment, materials, and tools.

Roles and functions

It is very easy to assume that a STRIM role is a function, ie that it can be equated to a job title or post (*Chief Machinist, Managing Director, Test Supervisor*) or to a part of the organisation (*Goods Inward, Main Board of Directors, Programme Scheduling Department, Salaries Section*). It might in some cases be appropriate to have a strong or even one-to-one mapping between the two. But in other cases it can be a very poor way of modelling, particularly if the ultimate aim is process improvement or re-engineering. Once again our motives for modelling will determine whether we want to associate roles and job titles strongly. Some examples will serve to illustrate this point of judgement.

If we model the Purchasing process within an organisation our first instinct when looking for the roles will be to write down job titles – *Purchasing Manager, Line Manager, Goods Inward Clerk*, etc – and we can start to identify the activities they carry out and the interactions they have. But once the RAD is complete for our purposes, the role box for *Line Manager* will contain only a fraction of the activities carried out by a line manager, albeit that fraction to do with purchasing. To get a real understanding of the process, an alternative is to see that fraction as a role that we might call *Authorising*. This is one of possibly many roles that are acted by someone carrying the job title *Line Manager*. If we want to re-engineer or improve a process, perhaps by mapping it anew onto the organisation, or conversely by adjusting the organisation and allocation of responsibilities to align them more closely to processes, then seeing the role in this rather more abstract light can be rewarding.

By way of example, let us revisit Reception at Praxis' Bath office. It might be tempting to regard the work of the staff in Reception as a process in itself: there are clearly some people there doing things during the day, the same people in the same area of the building. But of course Reception staff undertake a variety of roles that contribute to a variety of processes in the company. For example, they contribute to our purchasing process by acting as Goods Inwards, receiving deliveries, signing for them, determining who in the company the delivery was for, notifying them, matching delivery with purchase order and so on. They also contribute to our marketing process insofar as they greet visitors and operate the telephone switchboard. Moreover, they contribute to the training process in the company by gathering the names of those wishing to attend internal seminars, arranging food, AV equipment, and rooms, etc. We might label these roles as *Goods Receiving, Visitor Greeting, Telephone Answering*, and *Seminar Logistics Handling*. Doing this makes it easier for us to see how our mapping of such roles onto job functions – Reception – can be analysed and perhaps changed.

If we are trying to design a new or improved process, we can take a leaf from the book of structured software system design and talk about the *cohesion* and *coupling* of a set of roles. A role should have high cohesion, that is the activities that form it should be closely related and collectively have a single purpose. As a set, the roles should be loosely coupled, ie we should expect few interactions between them.

The process as pizza

If we could design our process without worrying about who was to do what, or how the process would work with our particular organisational structure, we can imagine coming up with the perfect process in the form of a nice circular pizza. It would be a tidy, simple structure with only the essentials there. But in real life we have to take that nice circular pizza and cut it up between the different people we employ in the different parts of the organisation, each of which needs to be managed. When we take the cutter to the pizza and pull the sections apart we find we have a mess of strands of mozzarella on our hands. The more pieces we cut, the more the strands.

Each strand is an interface: an interaction. It does not add value. It is only there because we have cut the pizza that way. And the obvious observation is that by cutting the pizza another way – by changing our organisation so that the pizza pieces are fewer when the pizza is cut over it – we can simplify things and have less of a mess on our hands.

To understand that key relationship between the process and the organisation – hierarchies, management structures, job titles, etc – we need one more piece of machinery: concrete and abstract process models.

Concrete and abstract models

A RAD concentrates on the "organisational behaviour" of the process being modelled and does not consider the "computational detail"; for instance, the need for two people to agree on terms of reference is part of the organisational process, whilst the tool that is used to write the terms of reference might be considered "computational detail". Of course, one person's organisational behaviour is another's computational detail, and it is important to understand that what is or is not computational detail will be determined by the reasons we are modelling.

If we are modelling how a process operates *now*, we might wish to capture, for instance, the division of labour between what is done by people and what is done by computer systems, if it is important to us. Alternatively, we might decide that it is not important initially whether an activity involves people or machines, and decide instead to capture the "essential" content of the process, not worrying how it is manifested physically. Yet again, we might decide that in future we want a particular activity to be done by a person, or automated and given to a machine to do, or done by a person with the aid of a machine (such as a computer database system accessed through forms), and we might choose to model this. As ever, our reasons for modelling will affect our model.

We can take this notion a step further. We can think of both *abstract* models and *concrete* models (much as we do with entity models in data modelling). If we model an existing process, we might find ourselves describing things that are actually ways that the "real" process is implemented. In other words, we might be modelling mechanisms – the concrete process. For example, we might model how you get a purchase order form from someone who keeps a stock of blanks, fill it in with the details of something you want to buy, pass it to me, get me to authorise the purchase by signing the form, and return it to you. We might represent this process fragment as some activities in our respective roles and two interactions between them. Those interactions have a purchase order form as the gram passing between us.

Here, we are modelling the concrete process. The abstract process might simply be "I ask you to authorise a purchase": a single interaction without any gram. What we capture is not the mechanism but the intent. As with entity models, whether we choose to model a process concretely or abstractly depends on what we are trying to achieve by modelling. For process improvement or re-engineering we should consider

1   drawing up the current concrete process model

2   "abstracting" it: the current abstract model

3   finding a better way of implementing it: the new concrete process model.

(Remember that we are not thinking here of preparing detailed as-is concrete models, and then deriving complete abstract models, and then complete new concrete models. The suggestion is only that by "moving" in some sense from the concrete to the abstract and back to the concrete we will gain insights. That could mean simply thinking it through in rough sketches or on white-boards. Masses of complete models rarely serve any purpose.)

This route also makes sense when we are process modelling as a prelude to providing computer support to some or all of it.

Comparison of a concrete model and its abstract counterpart can reveal two sorts of "sub-culture" in the organisation that we have looked at before:

–   those functions within the organisation that act as mechanisms for interactions (eg the mail room, secretaries, an e-mail system): *carrier functions*

–   those functions that operate throughout the organisation (eg a change control function, a document registry, a time recording function): *pervasive functions.*

The key to this lies in the fact that in a concrete model we look at *mechanisms*, in other words *how* things are done; in an abstract model we look at *intent* or *purpose*, in other words *what* things are done. Let's pull these notions together by looking at concrete and abstract versions of activities, interactions, events and roles.

Concrete vs abstract activities

When we draw an activity on a concrete RAD we will want to show how the activity is done; we will want to talk about the mechanism. In an abstract RAD we will talk about the intent or purpose of an activity. So, in figure 9-6, we see a very concrete activity – *Complete form 21B* – whose name is explicit enough to be a work instruction, but gives us little idea as to the outcome of this activity except that a form has been filled in. The figure also shows the activity expressed in abstract terms – *Prepare sales analysis for the month* – which tells us what we want to achieve but not how we do it.

Of course, we are quite at liberty in our models to give activities names that tell us both things – *Prepare sales analysis for the month by completing form 21B* – but it is as well to be aware of the two contrasting styles.

Figure 9-6 – A concrete activity and a possible abstract counterpart

Complete Form 21B

Prepare sales analysis for the month

Concrete vs abstract interactions

Precisely the same applies naturally to interactions, as illustrated in figure 9-7 (which we saw earlier in chapter 3).

Figure 9-7 – A concrete interaction and a possible abstract counterpart

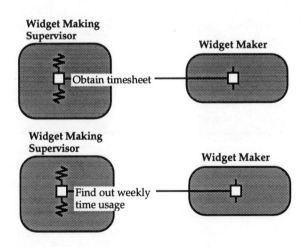

Let's take some more examples of concrete interactions. Note how the verbs that we see are words like "send", "receive", "get", and "copy" – mechanisms.

- A Staff Member *passes a Dependency Allowance form 21A to* a Personnel Clerk
- A Benefits Clerk *receives claim verification documents from* a Staff Member
- A Manager *returns a signed expenses application to* a Staff Member
- A Project Manager *passes a budget report to* the Line Manager.

The abstract versions might be

- A Staff Member *requests dependency allowance from* the Organisation
- A Staff Member *proves entitlement to* the Benefits Clerk
- A Manager *authorises an expenses application from* a Staff Member
- A Project Manager *reports on the budget to* the Line Manager.

Note how the verbs that we see now are words like "request", "delegate", "authorise", "approve", "report" and "agree" – intents.

Concrete vs abstract events

The differentiation between mechanism and intent carries naturally into events. We might label an event as *Form 21b received from customer* or as *Customer makes a claim*.

Figure 9-8 – Concrete roles and possible abstract counterparts

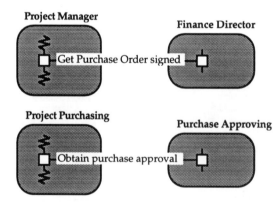

Concrete vs abstract roles

Finally, we can do the same thing for roles, something we have discussed a lot before in earlier chapters. When we take a concrete view of a process we will be very likely to choose as our roles things recognisable in the organisation: posts, departments, job titles and computer systems. When we take an abstract view we will be more likely to choose "areas of responsibility" without reference to the way they are mapped onto organisational entities.

So, in the top part of figure 9-8, our concrete model shows the job title of *Project Manager* and the post of *Finance Director*. In the bottom part, where we are taking a more abstract view, we talk in terms of areas of responsibility called *Project Purchasing* and *Purchase Approving* (abstract role sorts – see chapter 2).

An example

In figure 9-9 we have a very concretely expressed RAD. Real posts and job titles and departments appear as roles; activities appear that are involved in scheduling the case between those concrete roles; interactions are expressed in terms of the paperwork involved; and there is even a computer system taking part as a role.

Suppose now that we rework this model, trying to move towards a more abstract representation of this process. We might draw something similar to figure 9-10. Note how much simpler it looks – we have removed a lot of stuff that is really only there in figure 9-9 because of the way we have chosen to implement the process: job titles, posts, computer systems, communications mechanisms, paper flow etc. Figure 9-10 is getting at the *essence* of the process, at what we are trying to do.

Note though that abstraction should not be seen as some sort of summarising. Our aim is to model the process in terms of intent or purpose, rather than mechanism. A *side-effect* might well be that the model is simpler, because we will ignore "implementation detail". (True summarising is what encapsulation was all about – see chapter 6.)

The moment that we draw the abstract version of the model, ideas will present themselves. We might consider for instance

- collapsing whole areas into single roles
- using technology to speed interactions and remove the need for paperwork
- removing buffers or batching.

Moving responsibilities between roles

One of the times we might want to consider moving to abstract roles is when we are looking for ways of restructuring roles, in particular of transferring responsibility for certain parts of a process between roles. Take as an example the process of Purchasing Capital Equipment which will be present in many organisations. At some point we could expect to see, say, the *Managing Director* role contribute to the process by approving purchases costing over £10,000. To label the role "Managing Director" as shown in figure 9-11 would be a strictly correct model of the concrete process, of the ways things are actually done.

Figure 9-9 – A very concrete process model

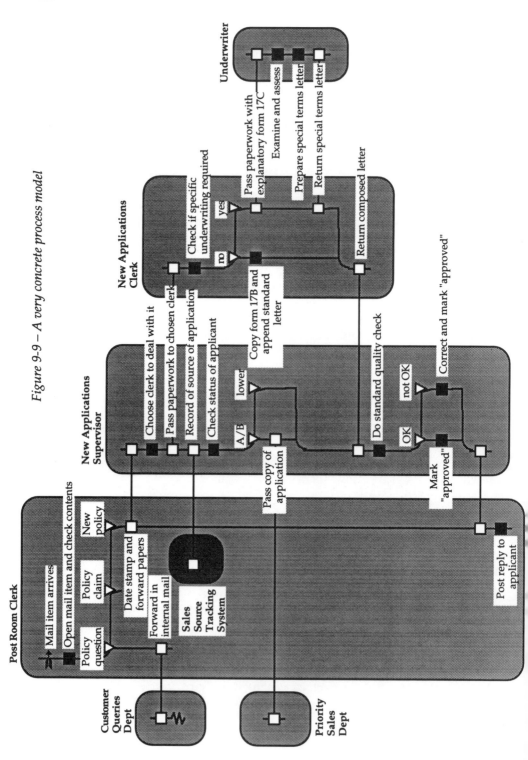

Figure 9-10 – A more abstract model for the process in figure 9-9

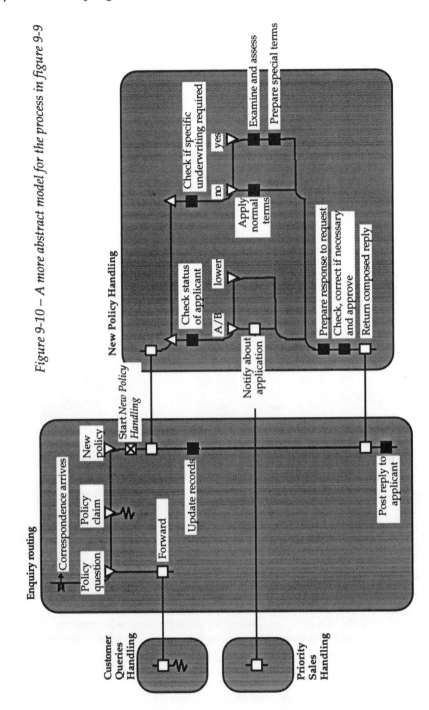

But of course the box on the RAD does not capture everything done by the MD, only the degree to which the MD contributes to the process under consideration. We might then look at that contribution and try to characterise it in some way. We might decide that what the MD is actually doing is giving approval on behalf of the Board, taking into account the cash position of the company and the priorities for contending calls on that cash; the MD has access to the knowledge of what else is going on in the company and the priorities necessary to make the decision. It just so happens that the MD is the person/role designated currently to make that decision, but in our desire to speed up decision making we might be prepared to move that responsibility around.

Figure 9-11 – Is this all the MD does in life?

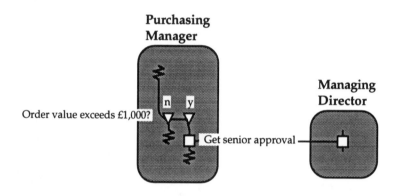

Suppose we relabel the role *Approving Large Cash Outflow* as in figure 9-12. By separating it from the current holder of that responsibility we allow ourselves to think more radically about whether, for instance, *any* Director could undertake the decision if the necessary background information were available to them too; or we might empower Divisional Directors to authorise expenditure up to a larger amount than currently, if they had access to the necessary information.

Approving Large Cash Outflow becomes in essence an abstract role in the sense described above: it is a role that someone "slips into" at some point in order to contribute to a process. This makes it a candidate for restructuring.

Let us generalise this sort of thinking. There are basically four steps:

1   Draw up the as-is process showing the actual, concrete roles.

   We make the roles match the actual posts or job titles or functional units that exist in the organisation. We are going to assume that the organisation will remain the same – the same posts, job titles and functional units – but that we want to explore how we can divide the activities of the process over them in a way that, for instance, reduces the number of interactions that are necessary. Remember that every interaction is a potential waste of resource, a potential delay and a potential buffer and conflict point.

Figure 9-12 – Abstracting a role

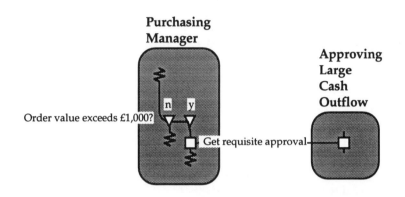

2   Identify the abstract roles.

Once we have the as-is concrete model we look for the abstract roles within the process. We mark them on the as-is RAD simply by drawing lines around activities and decisions, grouping them into abstract roles. The activities and decisions have, over time and for a variety of reasons, ended up being the responsibility of the various posts and functional units shown.

3   Identify ways of re-allocating activities and decisions in the abstract roles to the concrete roles.

We decide where activities and decisions could be moved between roles in order to reduce the number of interactions necessary. This is not a mechanical process: it requires experimentation, and it can also require the organisation to rethink some of its policies, particularly in areas to do with delegation. There might be many alternatives to consider.

4   Redefine the concrete roles.

Depending on the criteria we are using to choose the "best" re-allocation of activities and decisions, we leave ourselves with a new, restructured process in which we might still have the same roles as we started out with, but now with their responsibilities changed.

The key to all this is that the concrete and abstract models are helping us to look at the relationship between the process and the organisation.

Relaxing/strengthening approval and authorisation

A RAD is excellent for revealing the approval and authorisation mechanisms that the organisation has put in place. They can all be questioned, with a view either to strengthening the mechanism or relaxing it. "Does the Finance Director have to see all purchase requisitions?", "Would it be better to introduce the requirement for senior management approval at this point, rather than waiting till further down the process?", "Should this sort of situation be escalated to a higher management level than it is now?".

Specialists to generalists – the "case worker"

When we divide a single task over two people we generate a need for interaction between them, across which the task will flow. When a case or gram moves from one role to another via that interaction, we will often find a *buffer*. If the respective roles process their own cases – units of work – according to their own cycles, some way is needed of "decoupling" the cycles at the point where they intersect. That's a buffer. Concretely, it can be folders accumulating in an in-tray, unread messages in someone's electronic mailbox, or all the other ways we have of piling up work to be done. Buffers introduce delays, break the flow of processing and make tracking and monitoring difficult.

The flow of work for a single case can appear very simple, perhaps of the kind shown in the left hand-process fragment in figure 9-13. Apparently each role makes its contribution to the processing of a case and passes it on to the next role down the production line – rather like a bucket chain at a fire: each person in the chain turns to their left, grabs the bucket and swings it to their right. Provided everyone is synchronised it works fine. The bucket (ie the case) moves smoothly down the chain. Most case processes are not like this; the roles take different amounts of time with their contribution and different numbers of people are put in to deal with each stage accordingly to even the flow. In other words we introduce case management. And the normal mechanism for smoothing the flow down such a chain is to introduce buffers at the interactions: buckets pile up between certain individuals and some people then hand on three buckets at a time.

Figure 9-13 – From specialist stream to case worker

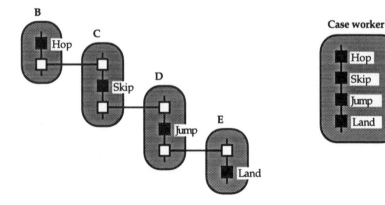

In fact it can be more revealing to look at the case management process which is where we will see the mechanisms that get put in place to handle the flow.

As each role (work area, processing step, department) tries to optimise its performance, so the overall flow can start to become uneven as the compartmentalisation works against optimisation of the overall process. Many traditional production line industries have, for many reasons including the motivational, moved away from the bucket chain approach and introduced "case workers" who take responsibility for the entire handling of a case, as suggested by the right-hand side of figure 9-13. In automobile manufacture for instance, a production "cell" might take a car through from chassis to final inspection, working with it right down the line.

Is the case structure adequately managed?

If a process is concerned with handling cases – customer requests, orders, expense claims, new products, etc – it is worth asking whether there is also somewhere a corresponding case management process. The case process itself might run more or less well, but if the case management process is ineffective or even totally absent then individual cases can conflict with each other, priorities can be poorly understood and ineffective, and people might have to make do to get by. One would expect to see ways of resourcing individual cases, managing changes in the case load, handling sudden changes in the priority of individual cases and changes in the nature or content of individual cases. If these are not adequately dealt with there could be trouble.

That said, the word "adequately" is an important one: it can also be the situation that a case management process is *too* cumbersome and is unnecessarily bureaucratic. The modelling will help the analyst to decide whether things are under- or over-managed.

Is everyone doing something useful?

Are there roles which have few or no activities of their own, and which seem to be only third-parties in other people's interactions? These may be redundant, adding no value, and only slowing things up. I have seen a role which seemed to sit between two organisational units and passed stuff between them. It was quite hard to see what value was added en route, and some hard questions could be asked about that role. Figure 9-14 suggests the sort of thing we might see.

REALIGNING THE ORGANISATION TO THE PROCESS

So far we have looked at changing the process in three ways:

1   by making point-wise improvements, without changing the flow of activity within roles

2   by improving the activity flow, keeping the existing responsibilities of the given roles

3   by moving responsibilities between existing roles, leaving those roles in
     place.

Figure 9-14 – Is this intermediary role adding anything?

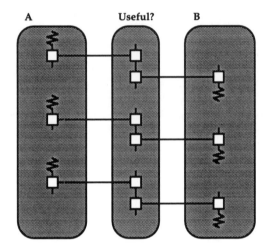

The fourth and most radical change we might consider is changing the
organisational structure itself – the posts, the job titles, the functional units –
in order to make that structure more closely aligned to the process. In RAD
terms this will mean restructuring the roles themselves: adding new ones,
deleting existing ones, merging and splitting them.

Our aim in doing this will principally be to reduce the amount of cross-
functional flow, those strings of mozzarella. We know that when the flow
crosses a boundary between two functions, there is often delay. In particular,
there may be buffers intended to handle the different rates at which the
functions handle their work. And there may be conflicts in priorities between
functions. All this deserves closer analysis.

Case-case clashes

Within an organisation there will be many case processes. At the outermost
level, the obvious choice of case for a pharmaceutical company is the
candidate compound and so, in the list of core processes for such a company, we
would expect to see a process corresponding to the life history of a candidate
compound. But as soon as we look inside this we will see new cases, depending
on the perspective we are taking. For instance, each candidate compound will
go through a number of clinical trials, and each clinical trial will be a single
case as far as the clinicians are concerned; the clinical department essentially
deals with a pipeline of trials. To support the clinical trials, other groups will
be making batches of the compound in a pilot plant; they deal with a pipeline

of batches going through the pilot plant. Meanwhile, at many points in the process, analytical chemists will be called on to carry out analyses of samples of compound to establish its purity; they deal with a pipeline of samples to be tested.

So we find that there are (at least) four case viewpoints: the compound, the trial, the batch, the sample. And, as is so often the situation, there is no simple relationship between them. For each of these viewpoints there is a process model that can be drawn, and we will need to show the intersections between these.

Figure 9-15 shows this *case structure* of the organisation diagrammatically. Each ellipse represents a case (eg *Sample*) and is tagged with the name of the group for whom it is the unit of work (eg *Analysts*). The arrows show how cases are related. For instance, a batch of compound *involves the testing of one or more* samples; in other words we can expect that for each case corresponding to a batch there will be one or more cases corresponding to samples to be handled by the analysts. The cases are in fact very likely to correspond to the essential business entities we described in chapter 8.

If we look a little more carefully we will see that in a "conventional" organisation, the different units of work are the domain of different organisational units (known pejoratively as "functional silos" – see figure 6-1 for instance):

- the Analytical Chemistry department deals with all analytical samples

- the Pharmacy is responsible for the preparation of the dosages ("patient packs") for each clinical trial

- the Process Chemistry department is responsible for making batches of compound.

We organise things this way as an expedient: to concentrate the skills and expertise necessary to deal with those units of work in a specialist area. And each specialist group organises itself and its working practices to optimise the throughput of its case load; it might even be incentivised and targeted on achieving certain throughputs. But we know that there are complicated relationships between "neighbouring" cases: to deal with one of my cases I have to ask for a service from you; in other words I have to generate a case for you, and that case will go into your system for dealing with your work. My case gets transformed in one of yours when it crosses the boundary between us, and, unfortunately, my priorities can be lost in the transfer.

How do these case-case interfaces appear on a RAD? If we draw a RAD showing the two case processes *A* and *B* interacting we will see an interaction from one case structure to another, the interaction taking the form of a request for service in some shape ("please analyse this sample"). If we are interested in the *management* of the interface it is more likely that we will show *A* interacting with the case management process of *B*, since it will be *B*'s case management process that will concern itself with the scheduling and prioritising of that work within the group that does process *B*. *B*'s case management process will in turn pass the case onto *B* to deal with and perhaps will also return the results of the service to *A*.

Figure 9-15 – The case structure of a pharmaceutical development company

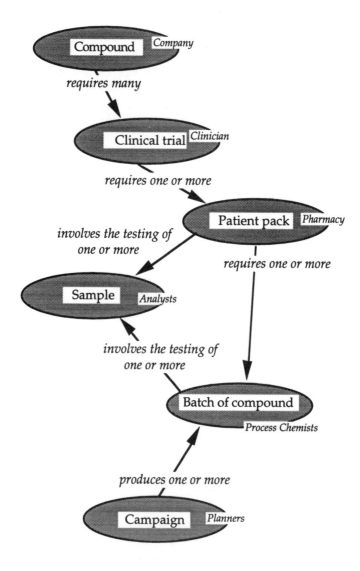

If we are analysing an organisation to look for a structural change that will align it more closely to the core processes and their ancillary support processes – which will typically be case processes – then mapping that case structure is an important first step.

Analysing interactions

The interactions in the process are there because our roles – organisational units – need to collaborate, and the way we define our organisation determines the way the collaboration works. By looking at the interactions we can therefore get some clues as to how the organisation might or might not be getting in the way of the process.

Auramaki[2] examines office communications using discourse analysis, and its analysis of "illocutionary acts" is useful as a way of examining interactions in RADs (the following is due to Tim Huckvale).

Offices can be seen as communication networks which create, maintain and fulfil commitments. In a RAD, commitments are represented by interactions and it is useful to analyse these to see what sorts of commitments are being made. (An interaction might involve several separate commitments.) If we refer to the role that initiates the interaction as the "speaker" and the other roles as the "hearers", we can identify five types of commitment (following Auramaki):

1 *assertive*: the speaker is noting an actual state of affairs

2 *directive*: the speaker is asking the hearer to do something

3 *commissive*: the speaker is committing to do something

4 *declarative*: the speaker is bringing about a new state of affairs

5 *expressive*: the speaker is expressing attitudes or feelings about the state of affairs.

Some of this clearly echoes our examination of process patterns in chapter 7, so let us look at each in more detail.

An interaction carrying *assertive* commitment would be one in which roles are being informed about the completion of some activity. We can ask "do the hearer roles really need to know?". It is not unusual for the modelling activity to reveal that A always copies a certain document to B who has never known what to do with it and has always binned it.

When the commitment is *directive* we would expect to see each of the hearer roles doing something as a result (or else why are they being told?), and at some later point reporting back in an assertive commitment to the speaker role, to confirm completion. We can check this. We can also check that each hearer is able to carry out the requested action (ie has the authority and resources, knows what is to be done, and is willing to accept instruction from the speaker). And finally we can check that the speaker has the authority to give these instructions.

When a speaker makes a *commissive* commitment (ie promises to do something), there should be a later interaction in which the speaker makes an assertive commitment to the same set of hearers, confirming completion of the promise. We can check that this interaction occurs, for all the original hearers,

---

[2] *Modelling offices through discourse analysis: the SAMPO approach*, Auramaki, Hirscheim & Lyytinen, *Computer Journal*, **35**, 4, August 1992

and that the speaker has the authority to make the commitment in the first place.

An interaction carrying a *declarative* commitment might be hard to distinguish from one carrying assertive commitment, but one would expect in the declarative case that all roles involved would see this interaction as a trigger to get on with some new activity (they already know *what* to do; this interaction is giving them permission to proceed). We can check whether all roles know what to do.

(*Expressive* commitments are outside the sort of modelling we undertake with RADs, so I shall not examine them further.)

We can also make the following checks:

– Is there a pair of roles with a mass of fine interaction? This might indicate a poor division of activity between the roles or a confusion over objectives.

– Are there roles which have the same type of interaction with many other roles? This might reveal a pervasive function that should be dealt with separately.

– Is the concrete form taken by an interaction "long" in some sense? Slow interactions might be inefficient.

– Does an interaction have a buffer in its concrete form? Buffers slow up interactions. The existence of buffers might reveal a carrier mechanism that could be automated or removed. A carrier mechanism might also prove to be pervasive and hence needing separate modelling and analysis as a process in its own right.

– Does each activity and interaction on the chain from initial event to achieved objective add value in some way?

– Does all the checking, authorisation, referring back, copying for comment, input, or approval, etc help in the achievement of goals?

DEMING'S TESTS FOR FLOWCHARTS OF PROCESSES

Deming identifies a number of ways in which a flowchart description of a process can be analysed to check for potential improvements in the process. There are straightforward corresponding analyses that can be carried out on a RAD to check for the following in a manner that should by now be clear:

– duplication

– unnecessary tasks

– illogical or insufficient sequencing

– complexity

– unclear lines of responsibility

– opportunities for error

– impact of supplier inputs

– inconsistencies

–   disconnects.

HAMMER'S "PRINCIPLES OF REENGINEERING"

In his article *Reengineering Work: Don't automate, Obliterate*[3], Michael Hammer lists some principles for restructuring processes. It is instructive to see how RADs can help the Hammerite to apply some of these principles.

–   "Organize around outcomes, not tasks".

An "outcome" in our terms is a "goal", a desired state of the process. Hammer proposes that case managers perform the entire process, so that one person/group/department performs all the steps in the process. Rather than having an "assembly line" of roles taking the case through the case process, consider whether the activities and decisions necessary can be carried out by a single (concrete) role.

–   "Have those who use the output of a process perform the process".

"Now that computer-based data and expertise are more readily available, departments, units, and individuals can do more for themselves. Opportunities exist to re-engineer processes so that the individuals who need the result of a process can do it themselves". The aim is to reduce interfaces and hand-overs. Look for parts of the process where a service is requested from a service group and consider whether that part of the process can be pulled back if the information needs of the service requester can be met in some new way, perhaps through IT.

–   "Subsume information-processing work into the real work that produces the information".

Separate roles might produce information and process it. Do they need to be separate? Can we remove the interaction that becomes necessary because the production is separated from the processing?

–   "Link parallel activities instead of integrating their results".

Suppose we can see two strands of a process proceeding separately and then coming together to integrate their work, with all the problems that invariably occur because of the separate worlds the two parties have moved in so far. What opportunities are there for earlier collaboration (interaction) to ensure that the integration will go smoothly? What information can be exchanged, and what decisions can be jointly made, during their separate development?

–   "Put the decision point where the work is performed, and build control into the process".

In Hammer's words, this principle "suggests that the people who do the work should make the decisions and that the process itself can have built-

---

[3] *Reengineering Work: Don't Automate, Obliterate*, M Hammer, *Harvard Business Review*, pp104-112, July-August 1990

in controls. Pyramidal layers can therefore be compressed and the organization flattened". In RAD terms, he is suggesting that the case management process should be *moved into* the case process, not just woven in by adding the managerial roles to the case process, but by moving the management activities and decisions themselves into the roles that carry out the case process.

A related phenomenon in a dysfunctional organisation is that of "having responsibility without accountability". For instance, the Personnel department might be responsible for handing out training grants to those who are eligible, while Finance is held accountable for the expenditure. The result is that Finance protect themselves by duplicating the checks made by Personnel.

A CASE STUDY

In one organisation I worked with, a sizable mechanism had evolved over the years to deal with requests made to the service part of the organisation. Dealing with these requests – which involved making and delivering specialist goods to a hard and fast timescale and specification – was a top priority for the organisation and hence for the service group. When the requesters said "get these supplies to this location on this date" it had to happen. To make life that little bit more interesting the requesters were, for perfectly valid reasons, in the habit of changing the details of their orders at any time, and making new requests at short notice. Arms and legs were broken by the service group to make sure the requests were correctly satisfied, and invariably they were. But the stress was increasing and it was not clear that the mechanism or the people could stand the projected increase in work load and hence in the rate at which requests would arrive. What was to be done to reduce the stress? Point-wise improvement – increasing the productivity of the activities required to make the supplies – was not the issue. Some other solution had to be found.

We modelled both the case process – how an individual request or request change was satisfied – and the case management process – how the stream of requests were handled, prioritised and so forth.

The main issue for the management of the whole affair was the fact that satisfying a request required contributions from four main teams, each struggling to solve difficult technical problems to fulfil their contribution. Each new request or change to a request meant getting all four teams to rejig their schedules whilst keeping all previous requesters happy.

In the old days, when life was slower, this "negotiation" of changed schedules could be dealt with by one of the regular meetings held by different committees – there were four altogether, dealing with the management of the process from the day-to-day tactical level to the long term strategic level. But as time pressures had increased, people had found that the formal process was too slow, and during the modelling we found the many work-arounds where people would try to sort out a solution and then get it signed off at the next appropriate meeting. This became evident from the RAD which showed, buried in a mass of work-arounds, the original four time-driven cycles. What the RADs also revealed was a mass of bilateral interactions by which the four teams attempted to negotiate changes to their separate schedules.

These insights into what was happening led the service group to look for a new way of running things. What was needed first of all was an *event-driven* process rather than a cycle-driven process: things could no longer be held up until the next cycle but had to be dealt with as and when they came in. The need for a quick solution was now the norm not the exception. Moreover, the negotiation of schedules between the four teams needed to be made the responsibility of a single new body (role) that would replace all those bilateral interactions with a single negotiation, recognising that many bilateral negotiations lead invariably to whirling around in circles ... and stress.

The change of process pattern and the introduction of a new role simplified the management of the business considerably, offering less stress and continued satisfaction of the requesters. In essence the case management process was discarded entirely and replaced by the new role that effectively led the case process.

Conclusion

We have now brought together all the machinery for thinking about business processes, especially for re-engineering and improvement.

We have ways of looking for improvements at the activity level, in the flow of the process through the roles, in the role structures, and finally in the structure of the organisation itself.

The case structure of the organisation, derived from an understanding of the essential business entities, tells us where to look amongst the core, support and management processes for the case processes and their corresponding case management processes. This will direct us towards the points where the functional silos make us cut the pizza in a messy way and will suggest how the organisation could be better aligned along process lines, rather than against them. By working with the abstract model of a process, derived perhaps from a concrete model of the as-is process, we can look for better alignments.

10

MANAGING THE MODELLING

THE PROCESS MODELLING PROCESS

So far we have looked at the business of modelling a process from the "technical" point of view. But the modelling activity itself needs to be managed if it is to be successful. This chapter provides some guidance on running the modelling work to ensure that it gets at the facts in as efficient a manner as possible. We look at the modelling activity from a procedural point of view (ie as a process itself), and, to a lesser extent, from the "soft" point of view (the sociological and political and people issues). The chapter is structured around a basic process modelling procedure, with the soft issues being addressed as we go through.

There can be no hard and fast rules for the procedure that the modeller and analyst should follow. This can be affected as much by political and logistical issues as by technical modelling issues. However, if we had to recommend one route it would run as follows:

1 Decide on the objectives of the modelling.

2 Start by getting an overall picture, no matter how coarse or inaccurate, decide on the appropriate perspectives, and draw up one or a small number of RADs that capture the overall process from those perspectives.

3 Interview senior people, eg department heads.

4 Interview groups about how they collaborate in the process, to build the models.

5 Interview individuals about their individual role in the process, to refine the models.

6 Review, revise, and validate the models.

7 Analyse the process.

8 Respond to the analysis (radical or incremental change, application of technology, etc).

We now look at each of these steps in detail, but remember that there is nothing sacrosanct about this ordering: it is just a starting point. In particular, step 7 – the analysis step – really starts as soon as the modelling starts: invariably, the act of modelling brings to the surface the problems and potential solutions.

STEP 1: DECIDING ON THE OBJECTIVES OF THE MODELLING

If you do not know why you are modelling and do not have a clear idea of the outcome you are looking for or what you want to be able to do with the model, the modelling activity will be slow and undirected at best and at worst will fail. We have already seen that there is no single model of a process, so when we start to model we need to know what perspectives we should be taking. In chapter 1 we identified three broad reasons for modelling: to describe, to analyse and to enact. So in step 1 we must decide which sort of process we are modelling and why we are modelling it. Do we want to understand it, communicate it, change it a bit, change it radically, or find ways of doing it more effectively or efficiently by applying some technology to it?

Write down your answer to the question "what do we want this model to do for us?".

STEP 2: GETTING AN OVERALL PICTURE

The aim in the second step is to map out the ground, in particular to identify the boundaries of the process (or rather to decide where the boundaries to the modelling project are to be drawn), and to identify the perspective or perspectives that will be of interest. Our aim is to get ourselves briefed before the group workshops and individual interviews, so that we have a good idea of what we can expect to hear: the roles we can expect to hear about, where difficulties and tensions lie, where the process starts and finishes, and so on.

We have found that this can be done efficiently by interviewing someone who has a good grasp of the whole process even though they might only operate a part of it. They might not be a senior person in terms of rank, but they might well be senior in experience in that organisation, having worked in many parts of it, for instance. The essential thing is that they should have a high-level perspective. This approach is vital if the organisation or process that you are modelling is large and the group interviewing approach described below cannot be used. If an organisation has previously done some sort of investigation into how things work (or don't work), the person who led that could be a useful starting point.

This work can take a couple of days of intensive discussion, using lots of pictures and some early RADs.

At some point there will be enough information about the process to take a first cut at a RAD. This can be the hardest part. The question arises "what should our initial perspective(s) be?". There are a number of considerations here:

- Are we looking at a core process, a support process or a management process?
- Which process patterns should we consider as the basis for our perspective(s)?
- What is the case structure of the organisation (or at least of the part we are looking at)?
- Are we looking for a perspective that gives us the right view for describing, analysing, or enacting?

Let's take these in turn.

Perspectives for core, support and management processes

Our starting point is figure 10-1, from chapter 1. In it we saw *core* business processes, *support* processes and *management* processes. We can use the ideas developed in recent chapters to get guidance on how we should model these. (How you decide on those processes in the first place is part of a larger issue which is outside the scope of his book. The reader is recommended to refer to texts about business strategy for guidance.)

Figure 10-1 – The three sorts of process

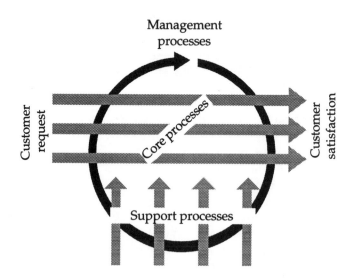

With this picture in mind, we can use the following guidelines to help us look for processes of the right sort in the right place (but remember that there are no hard and fast rules here):

- Core processes concentrate on satisfying external customers (or "stakeholders"), and in general they will be case processes: they are about how the organisation responds to a customer request, about what happens between customer request and customer satisfaction. As we saw in chapter 1, a "customer" can be an individual with money in their hand or the market place in general. Examples might be "Fulfil Equipment Order", "Answer Customer Enquiry", and "Launch New Product".

- Support processes concentrate on satisfying internal customers, and will most likely be case processes, with the unit of work representing some service to a core process or the business at large. Examples might be "Procure Raw Materials Requested", "Set up New Project Area", "Set up New User on Computer Network", and "Provide Requested Information". They may be activities carried out on a continuing basis, providing an environment to the business: "Provide 24-hour E-mail Service" and "Keep Building Warm and Clean". It is worth looking inside such continuous processes, however, and looking for the events that trigger activity: "someone reports a lost file", "someone reports a cold office", "the weekly maintenance schedule is due", and so on.

- Management processes that concern themselves with managing the flow of cases through the core processes or the support processes will of course be case management processes. Management processes that concern themselves with planning at the business level will probably be cycle-driven or event-driven processes.

An important clue in identifying and bounding any case process is understanding who the *customer* for the process is – who is it that gets a service or a product through the satisfactory processing of a case, a unit of work?

Looking for process patterns

In fact, in general, the main process patterns described in chapter 7 should be considered as potential perspectives for the modelling:

- case processes
- case management processes
- event-driven processes
- cycle-driven processes.

These patterns will suggest the overall perspective and structure of the models that we draw. The most important of these is the case process. It should be the first thing you look for.

When we look at an organisation, we can find the case process(es) by asking questions like "what are the units of work?", "what things appear in people's in-trays that start things off?", and "what sorts of requests can a customer make?". When we see a unit of work or a request we might have the basis for a case process. As we look across the organisation we will probably see – in different functional areas and different departments – different case structures. A department might well be structured around dealing with one or more different types of units of work. In figure 9-15, we can see that units of work can often correspond to essential business entities: the *compound* and the *batch*. Moreover, those units of work are the day-to-day business of separate organisational units: the Company as a whole, the Pharmacy, and the Pilot Plant. At this point we can build the case structure of the organisation along the lines of figure 9-15.

So if we look at a pharmaceutical company as a whole we can see the *compound* as a unit of work. Each compound has a "life history" during which it is developed to the point where either it is abandoned as being un-promising or it reaches the market place. That life history forms the case process. If we look at what happens inside the Analytical Department we will see the sample as the unit of work. Again, each has a life history from the point where it arrives from a chemist, to the point where an analysis against a specification is returned to the chemist. Its life history forms a case process. These and other case processes are connected in different ways (see chapter 6).

Figure 10-2 – Different perspectives for different aims

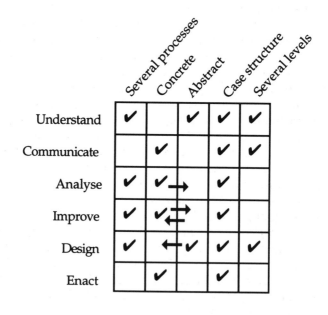

✔ = consider this perspective for this aim

→ = then consider this perspective

Perspectives for different purposes

Figure 10-2 provides guidance on the sorts of perspectives that should be considered for different modelling purposes. We've divided our earlier categories of *description, analysis* and *enactment* from chapter 1 and opened them up slightly: *description* is divided into understanding and communication, and *analysis* is extended with design.

It is noticeable that an understanding of the case structure of the organisation is important to all six reasons for modelling. Drawing out and modelling the case processes is likely to feature in any modelling activity.

If our aim is improvement we will probably start with a concrete model, move to an abstract model, and then back to a new concrete model. If we are designing a new process from scratch we will start with a nice clean abstract model and then decide how we want to implement it, in terms of real roles, real mechanisms for interactions and so on; in going from the abstract to the concrete (ie when we cut up the pizza) we will find ourselves creating new interactions between the concrete roles.

Choosing perspectives for communication

If you are modelling to communicate, the scope and perspective of your model needs to be chosen so that the model tells people what they need or want to know, and omits everything else, or perhaps relegates it to "the edges" of the model. A strength of RADs is that we can decide at each point of the boundary how we want to "summarise" it: with a black-box activity, with an external event or with an interaction, as we saw in chapter 5.

At each point in the modelling we ask "is it important to us to know this, or to know beyond this point?", or "does it help our understanding to get into this area?". In some instances we might say "definitely not" and simply terminate that "thread"; in other instances we might say "we don't need to know the detail but it would be useful to have some context" in which case we might "summarise" the process beyond the area we are interested in. Again, on a RAD it is quite simple and natural to mix the level of coverage to suit your purpose.

For such informal communication, say as part of an exercise leading to shared understanding of a process by a large group, we might choose to describe the process at a "high" level, and perhaps from a couple of different perspectives for different subgroups: for instance, one model emphasising the quality assurance content of the process, another showing the view from the manager's desk, and another from the customer's. There are few rules here: the RAD is very much an *exploratory tool* and it should be used as such. Draw whatever is interesting and helpful.

Choosing perspectives for prescription

Suppose now that our model is required as a *formal* description. Perhaps we plan to use a model as some sort of work instruction, eg in a Quality Manual; perhaps it is to be used as the keystone of a Process Standard or a Standard Operating Procedure. We want to *prescribe* how a process is to be carried out –

"this is how we do things around here". Let's look at the features we will expect of our model:

- Our model will need to be sufficiently precise and detailed for us to be able to "dictate" what we expect of people where we want to dictate to them, and to leave room for discretion to people where we want discretion to be used.

- Our RAD might need to be precise[1] and testable enough to allow third-party auditing of the way the process is actually being carried out in order to check for conformance. In this situation we can expect to draw a single RAD, drawn from the point(s) of view of the user(s) of that Standard.

- It is likely that we will model in terms of the appropriate case process. How is a single unit of work to be dealt with? What is the process for dealing with a customer complaint? How is a module of source code to be tested? What is the procedure for formulating and packing the dosage forms for a clinical trial?

- The roles that appear on such RAD will probably be *concrete* roles – either posts or job titles – and the descriptions of activities and interactions will involve concrete mechanisms. Conformance is easier to establish if definitions are precise and close to the real world.

- In an ISO 9001 context we will expect to see an emphasis on the control of the process, especially quality control and corrective action, in other words answers to questions such as: "at what points in the process are checks on quality carried out?", and "if a fault is discovered in the product or service what action is taken to (a) correct it, and (b) ensure it does not happen again?".

- Independent verification or validation plays an important part in highly regulated industries, and in a RAD we have the mechanism – through roles – for showing this explicitly. We will expect to see the roles that have responsibility for authorising actions, approving actions, and signing things off, and we will expect to see the interactions that express the execution of that responsibility.

- To provide context we can expect to provide a process model at perhaps one level above the work instruction level.

Choosing perspectives for process analysis and process improvement

We saw in chapter 9 that there are a number of different sorts of analysis we might be interested in for the different types of improvement that we might be looking for in the process. It's possible that we will have one or more in mind when the modelling activity has started, perhaps from some other analysis of what is happening in the organisation, from anecdote, or from hard facts.

By taking a concrete perspective and then developing from that an abstract perspective of the process, we get important information: the abstract model

---

[1] "Precise" does not mean "excessively detailed"

tells us what the process is about in essence; whilst the concrete model exposes how the way that we have chosen to "cut" the process over the organisation we have in place (through choice or history) affects the process. To improve the process we can design a new process by going from the abstract model to a new concrete process design.

We will certainly want to look at the case structure of the business. Each case process – our response to one sort of customer request – needs investigation in our search for improved response time and reduced resource usage. We will also want to look at how closely related processes interact – in particular at the point where case processes mesh.

Choosing a perspective for later enactment

Developing a model for use in process enactment is a large topic which is itself the subject of the larger method *Basyl*. Suffice it to say here that the case process notion of STRIM clearly ties in closely with the "case" or "work item" notion of most workflow management products, and that any workflow system will also have built into it those aspects of the corresponding case management process which can usefully be put within the process support system, typically prioritisation of work items, allocation of work items between a number of process actors, and so on.

For this reason, the perspectives that should be chosen are the case process for the work item whose processing is to be supported and its corresponding case management process. An abstract perspective should be taken at some point in order to ensure that the new process support system does not simply mimic the existing paper-based system, but instead takes advantage of the potential of a fully electronic environment: document management, document imaging, smart telephony, EDI, network communications, group support products, etc.

Drafting a first list of roles

As we home in on our initial ideas about where the boundaries of the process(es) are and what perspectives we want to take, we can start to list the roles that we are likely to come across as we get into the group interviewing and modelling sessions. Natural sources are

- posts from the organisation chart
- job titles
- departments, branches, etc
- roles identified in existing written procedures
- committees, task forces, working groups, etc
- the customer(s) of the process, and perhaps their customers
- suppliers to the process
- regular meetings.

Maintaining a glossary

Now is the right time to start a glossary of terms. If, as analyst, you are new to the business you are modelling, you have what is both an advantage and a disadvantage: you don't know the terminology of that business. This is a disadvantage because at first you will find it slow to understand what people are saying when they use terms that have a special meaning for them. This is an advantage too because, in trying to find out exactly what they mean by those terms, you will start to uncover ambiguities in the organisation's views about its own terminology; two groups will use the same word but with slightly different meanings. Such ambiguities can be indicators of misunderstandings or even conflicts.

Such a glossary can be based on a simple conceptual model with each concept/term sitting in a bubble and connected by arrows to related concepts. Figure 9-15 gave an example drawn from the pharmaceutical industry.

STEP 3: INTERVIEWING SENIOR PEOPLE

Working your way down through the organisation chart will generally be the politically correct approach: involve department heads early on. Find out whom they regard as authoritative about what goes on in their groups, get their commitment to the use of their staff's time, engineer their expectations about possible outcomes, etc. Precisely what is politically correct and what is desirable to get the facts you want about the process will determine what order you speak to whom. This is all bound up with the way in which the larger project – for radical change, or incremental change, or the introduction of a Quality Management System, or whatever – is itself being handled. Most such initiatives require senior level backing and sponsorship for success, a topic that is adequately covered in the literature on these larger topics and one which I do not address here. But you should be aware of that problem.

STEP 4: INTERVIEWING GROUPS

Having been briefed in the processes we're interested in and having cleared the way with the senior people involved, we now reach perhaps the most important step in the process modelling project. We aim to get in one room a representative from each of the roles that we have previously established, during our briefing, play a part in the process we are looking at. It may be the first time those people have been in a room together, so ingrained might be the functional divisions of the organisation. For the first time they might be seeing how their work fits with the work of others, and facing for the first time, from a general point of view, the areas of conflict or stress between groups in the process. Because of this, the group session might not just be a group *modelling* session; it can also be a group discussion session.

The aim is to flush out the roles, activities, entities, and role interactions that together make up the organisation's process. We are essentially asking people "what do you do?" and "who do you do it with and for?".

The first step is to introduce members of the group to the notation that will be used: RADs. This takes no more than perhaps fifteen minutes. We talk through each of the symbols in turn perhaps using figure 3-1 (though possibly leaving out the role instantiation symbol until we need it), carefully ensuring the group's understanding of each. We then walk through a simple example: figure 3-2 can serve for this purpose, but ideally one should have a simple example from their everyday life pre-prepared, even if it is only the procedure they use for claiming expenses or getting their timesheet agreed!

Once these preparatory remarks have been gone through, we find that there is then little or no need for the analyst to interpret the model for the actors as it is drawn. The notation is intuitively straightforward and we find that a group readily models in it, provided that the analyst actually does the drafting for them. The notation is sufficiently transparent for people to work on their *process* during a modelling session, rather than to work on (struggle with) the notation.

Before getting into the model itself, it is useful to spend some moments agreeing the bounds of the process to be modelled. Questions that help this exploration include

- What's the unit of work?
- What makes the process start? What events trigger action?
- How do we know when the process finishes (if it ever does)? What are the goals of the process?
- Who are the people or groups involved? What posts, job titles, and functional groups will we expect to see appearing in the model?
- What areas do we want to ignore today? What areas are definitely in the discussion?

Our prior briefing has told us what to expect to hear and where to probe. Getting the answers to the questions onto flipcharts and thence onto the walls helps bound the discussion for the rest of the session but also gets people thinking about the process. The flipchart sheets can stay on the walls as reminders whilst the process itself is modelled.

For the actual modelling, we find a large whiteboard essential. You need a large area to work in and you will be drafting, correcting, changing, and rubbing out a great deal – space and flexibility are key. I heard of one group who lined the walls with large sheets of brown paper and then constructed the RAD by sticking onto it differently coloured Post-It™ notes and, for interactions, lengths of string with Blu-tack™ at the ends. Apparently they didn't like the symbols used in this book and had invented their own variations. Good for them.

Then there comes the moment when the modelling has to start.

If the process has a natural start-to-end flow about it – perhaps it is a case process – the modelling can take advantage of this: the analyst draws in the triggering event that starts the case starts at the top left-hand corner of the white-board and puts it into the role where the process starts ("who detects this trigger?", "who first gets to hear that something is needed?"). The goal of the process is drawn as a state description somewhere in some role at the bottom right of the whiteboard. The rest of the workshop is now about filling in the process between these two points. Roles appear as they enter the process.

If the process does not have a neat timeline, the procedure is less easy, and it becomes necessary to do the same thing for each of the threads that exist, and the analyst has the task of tying the threads together on the fly.

Either way, as the RAD develops, it will be drawn and redrawn many times as the group explores the process. Few will have thought about their daily lives in this way, so there is an (enjoyable) element of exploration for them. There will be problems that the analyst has to solve as the modelling proceeds. Just how much detail do we want to get into? Shall we ignore that role's contribution at this stage? Is it sufficient to summarise that set of interactions as just one for now? Do we want to separate those two roles or treat them as one at the moment? Shall we collapse all that activity into just one black box? Should we regard the work going on in that other process as outside our boundary and simply capture it as an external event or two? There are, as ever, no stock answers to these questions. It all depends why you are modelling. That said, there is virtue in being able to get the model on the available whiteboard, and it is important to get to the end of the process in the available time. Going away with at least a rounded – if not "complete" – model has a value, since further detail can always be explored in later sessions either with the same group or with smaller groups and individuals.

Given that a process will generally have many threads and that they cannot all be explored simultaneously, the analyst needs to be careful to note where threads still have to be closed off. And it is useful for the group to know that this care is needed so that it can be encouraged to point out unfinished threads that will have to be returned to at some time. Simply drawing a "spring" on the RAD at the appropriate point is usually enough to indicate "unfinished business" on the RAD.

Another question is whether the modelling should look at the "normal" situation first and then come back and add the exception condition handling and abnormal situations later, or should try and deal with them all on a single sweep. There is some virtue in the first approach in order to build a framework on which everything can be hung. The danger is of course that exception and abnormal situation handling can easily be forgotten if put off "until later", and it is often those parts of the process that reveal areas for improvement or suggest the possible use of computer systems to reduce the likelihood of error. Work-arounds – additions to the "approved" process in order to make it work – are a fruitful source of ideas about what is going wrong and what could be done to remedy things. It is not unusual to hear something like "then I go and get approval from the monthly Management Meeting ... well, I say that, in fact sometimes I can't wait that long so I check it out with so-and-so and then get it rubber-stamped at the next Management Meeting, otherwise nothing would get done". That work-around is a clue. Indeed, the analyst will need to probe for the existence of such work-arounds: "what do you do if you don't get the stuff in time?", "do you ever get on with that even though you haven't had authorisation?".

Identifying all the roles is not always as easy as it might seem. People think naturally in terms of departments and named individuals and this is a perfectly good starting point. In his work with a leasing company, my colleague Tim Huckvale worked with a group who identified Kate as the person who did such and such – Kate had always done that. As the modelling proceeds people will start to abstract away from named individuals – "well, Arthur does do that, but he's signing it off in his capacity as Site Safety Officer" – and the roles appear. Quite often roles that are not on the "main" stream of the process can be missed initially. They might "only" be involved for a single interaction but of course it can be that interaction that frequently holds things up, simply because it is some form of approval that is required from the "outside" role: "Get Health & Safety to sign off the risk management plan", "Get the plan signed off by QA", "Get Finance to agree to the budget". Equally, the modeller should be prepared to strip out roles that don't materially contribute to the process or its understanding as the modelling proceeds.

This is part of the trick of knowing what to put in and what not to put in – it's a dynamic decision. The boundary needs constant validation:

–   "we've got this role in here – do we care for now?"

–   "is it worth looking at what happens before this trigger or not?"

–   "is this really the goal, or is there actually something earlier/later that we are really interested in?"

and so on.

The analyst at the whiteboard has an important task: eliciting the process from the group, getting it onto the whiteboard, allowing the group to own what is drawn and to buy into what is drawn, steering the modelling, and bringing it to a conclusion. The result of their work is that RAD on the whiteboard. But many other important items of information and clues will have cropped up during the discussion and debate, things that are spoken or just hinted at, and for this reason we find it essential to have another person simply keeping a record of things like

–   avenues explored but backtracked from

–   decisions that detail would be ignored for now but would need to be picked up later

–   concerns about the way the process works or doesn't work currently

–   suggestions as to how it could be improved

–   situations where errors frequently occur

–   points of stress in the process

–   judgements about the relationship with other processes/departments and their effect on the process under discussion.

Much will be said by people in the group during the modelling that could act as pointers to inefficiencies, problems and solutions. They all need to be recorded for later analysis. The note-taker, perhaps more than the analyst at the whiteboard, has to be sensitive to what is said: "when these forms arrive, the applicant's policy number is rarely filled in and we end up having to go back to the originator to get the information", "we rarely have enough time to handle that fully and we generally go back to it when we get a quiet period", "couldn't that be sorted out at the weekly meeting rather than waiting for the next management review?". All these signals need to be noted for future use if they are not explored there and then.

A group session can last for several hours, or even a day, but if possible we like to get through the process in two hours since concentration can flag after that. The group activity allows individuals to relax now and then while others take up the strain. The situation is quite different when we see a single interviewee, as we shall see below.

As the modelling proceeds we can ask a host of questions under a number of general headings:

–   What are the overall structures and their business goals? We elicit the overall command structure of the major functions in terms of the relevant business rules: objectives, targets, goals, plans, etc.

–   What are the roles and what are their business goals? We start the process of eliciting the roles that are present in the organisation.

–   How do the roles interact? We explore the interactions between roles and the organisational motivation for those interactions.

–   How does a role work? We look at the activities of a role that are "private" to that role.

–   What entities are essential to the process? Data that records state is not important for this modelling. For instance, a written instruction by a customer to open a savings account is essential data in that it causes further activities (ie changes state rather than recording it), and it plays an essential part in a transaction between two roles. On the other hand, the account record itself is not essential data: it simply records the state of the customer-bank part of the process, in particular the history of previous interactions.

–   How long does this activity/interaction take? How much of people's time does it take? We will be asking these sorts of questions if we intend doing some quantitative modelling at some stage. We simply annotate the relevant process elements with the information we get.

As might be expected, many of the traditional analysis issues are relevant – listening, feedback, group dynamics etc – but I shall not go into them here. The aim is that, by the end of the session, the process on the whiteboard is their process, and the model is their model – they have after all drawn it, albeit with the help of the analyst who held the pen. This element of ownership is as ever vital for subsequent work.

At the close of the workshop, the analysts have more material than they can deal with and they now have to organise what they have heard. We tend to go away for at least the rest of the day (see the end of this chapter) and draw up the RADs "properly". This inevitably reveals unfinished threads, missing detail, doubts, misgivings, questions about terminology, and so on. These are all collated for the individual interviews to come, as are all the signals and messages the note-taker heard during the discussions.

To summarise, a good procedure for a group modelling workshop is

1   Arrange to involve representatives from all the likely roles.

2   Ensure the workshop room has whiteboards and flipcharts.

3   Introduce the group to the notation.

4   Agree initial definitions of the trigger and end goal of the process. Write them at the corners of the whiteboard.

5   Put up an initial list of roles involved.

6   Walk through the process from start to end.

7   Revisit the trigger, the end goal, the boundaries in general constantly.

8   Record separately all issues and concerns as they are raised.

STEP 5: INTERVIEWING AN INDIVIDUAL

The group session can then be followed up as necessary by sessions with individual representatives of the separate roles, for detailed definition of the process where detail is necessary. If an individual was present at the drafting and hence has seen the notation before, then walking them through the diagram seems to work well. If they have not seen a process model before, then the analyst must decide whether introducing the notation and then walking them through the model is the best way of doing things, as opposed to a simple question and answer session. We never feel obliged to show the RAD to the interviewee.

Once again, we prefer to have two analysts carry out an interview of an individual: one questions while the other records. It can be beneficial to hold the interview at the interviewee's normal place of work. Very often, in order to explain something to us, the interviewee will say "let me show you an example ...", reach into their filing cabinet and produce an illuminating document. This has to be balanced with the usual problem of interruptions to the interview and hence everyone's concentration, but on balance interviewing people on their home territory seems most effective.

We normally estimate that a two-hour interview is about the most that both sides can take. The interviewee becomes drained, and the interviewers overloaded with information. We normally budget about half a day for the two analysts then to go over the information gleaned, in particular working it back into the RADs, recording new questions and issues that will need to be referred back to the interviewee or on to subsequent interviewees.

Setting the scene at the interview is key. Time is limited and there is much to cover, and so we like to spend a few minutes covering a number of points with the interviewee. They go roughly as follows:

1 *Thank the interviewee* for their time.

2 *Ask how long we have actually got* for the interview. Although we might have asked for a two-hour interview, we are probably starting late, and the interviewee will have subsequently agreed to give someone else the second of our two hours! Agreeing at the outset how long the session will last means that we can pace our questioning and ensure that we cover the key points rather than wasting all the precious time on smaller issues; and the interviewee makes some sort of commitment to the time that's agreed.

3 *Outline the purpose* of the project. The interviewee might well have heard of the project and have some idea of what is going on. We like to describe the project overall, and then place our activity in that framework. Being open about our motivations (generally neutral, ideally positive and career-enhancing for the interviewee) helps the interview along. It is generally the case – and we like to stress it – that our work is non-judgemental: we are not there to observe and then say : "aha, there's wastage, that's inefficient, why on earth are you doing it that way?". The role of the facilitator is to bring the organisation to these sorts of statements from its own observations and judgement.

4 *Describe how we are doing our work.* We want to position this interview in the larger scheme of things. Why are we interviewing people, and this person in particular?

5 *Say whom we have already spoken to.* This helps to prevent repetition and to make it clear either that this person is very important and is being seen first, or that we have already spoken to this person's boss and hence are here with some authority. There are of course sensitivities here and dangers too: repetition can be a good thing if it reveals differences of opinion about a process, and a different viewpoint often provides new detail or insights. Also we don't necessarily want subordinates to feel that they have to toe the party line and say what their superiors would want them to say.

6 *Explain how far we have got.* How much have we found out so far? What areas do we think we have some grasp of, and which do we think we are struggling with? People generally like to tell you what they know, so admitting ignorance at this point encourages them to tell.

7 *Describe what we are doing now.* Are we trying to establish the ground? Or do we have a good model already and are we trying to flesh out detail and cover minutiae?

8 *Tell the interviewee how they can help* us now in this interview.

9 If we plan to use a RAD with the interviewee, *describe the notation* to them, probably by providing them with a quick walk-through of a RAD of

a part of the process that they are familiar with or that we want to talk through with them.

This leaves us ready to get to the core of the interview.

Other sources of facts

The STRIM analyst gathers facts principally from interviewing, an approach which has obvious drawbacks: interviewees can tell us untruths, they can forget to tell us about interesting things, they can tell us what they think we want to hear, they might conceal things they don't want us to hear, and so on. The techniques of ethnographic fieldwork could in time be used to overcome these shortcomings, though they currently have shortcomings of their own: the time they can take to perform (consider an ethnographic study of the drug development process which can take ten years) and the concomitant cost. But they and a number of other sources are worth considering.

Examining existing documents

A document almost invariably gives solid form to an interaction. There are four groups of people involved with a document, and they represent roles interacting for some reason:

- The author(s). They have some reason for producing it: to communicate, to inform, to instruct, to report, etc.

- The reviewer(s). They provide quality control on the document and its contents.

- The authoriser(s). They are approving or authorising the publication of the document for some reason: they are the budget holder, the information is being released in their name, they are responsible for public statements, etc.

- The recipient(s). They are presumably expected to act on the document. The recipient might receive the document "for information only" and not act on it, but each "copied to" represents a potential interaction, whether or not it serves a useful purpose. When we look at the "copied to" list we might see a list of job functions or positions – "Finance Director", "Marketing", "QA" – or a list of names. In the latter case we have the task of determining which role the recipient is acting when they receive the document concerned.

Examining existing documented procedures

These can take a number of forms including manuals, work instructions, Quality Manuals, etc. Where these exist they will clearly be an important source for the analyst, in that, in theory at least, they should describe the process in some fashion. The procedures might even be described diagrammatically, making transformation into a RAD that much easier. But there is a danger here too: written procedures and practices are not always followed scrupulously, especially if they can only be made usable and efficient by "adapting" them. In modelling sessions people often ask "do you want us to tell you how we actually do this, or how we're supposed to do it?".

Examining existing terms of reference, personal objectives, etc

The objectives of a role are often communicated to the incumbent in writing as written terms of reference or objectives. These can give us clues as to the desired outcome of the work of a role.

Identifying regular meetings and their purpose

Boards and committees frequently have regular meetings and they are worth some investigation.

We can represent a meeting as an interaction between the roles that are represented at the meeting, or we can regard the group that meets as a role in itself. Which view we take depends on whether the group that meets has some identifiable responsibility in the process or is simply a way for separate roles to "get together".

We have modelled a process in which the *Weekly Development Meeting* was shown as a role. The meeting was really just an interaction between the four development departments who sent representatives but, because it had responsibility for making a joint decision in the process (in theory at least), we decided to emphasise it as a role. In practice, the meeting was often unable to make decisions, as we discovered when we attended one, because representatives were not always empowered to make decisions on behalf of their departments. As a result the meeting became more of an updating session – an interaction that could be carried out in many simpler, less expensive ways.

When we look at meetings we should ask questions such as

- Who attends?
- What roles are they playing when they attend?
- Why do they attend?
- Are they there for reporting, receiving information, authorising, or taking decisions on behalf of themselves or the group they represent?
- Or does the group that meets play a role itself?
- How does the outcome of the meeting get propagated?
- How does it cause subsequent action in the process?
- By which roles?
- Does the meeting report its outcome to other roles who did not attend?
- How are they supposed to react?

One way of answering these questions is to actually attend the meetings and observe what happens.

Watching the informal as well as the formal communications

Interactions – even quite formal ones – can take place by telephone, unscheduled meeting, or scribbled note. Some organisations eschew paper and believe only in personal communication.

STEP 6: REVIEW, REVISE, VALIDATE THE MODELS

Throughout the modelling activity, the RADs will be under constant change as more information is obtained, other information is discarded, the perspective is altered, and so on. The nature of the activity is one of following leads, following our noses, chasing things to ground, following leads and backing off them. There is no simple procedure for successful process modelling. Like any fact-finding and analytical activity, the skill of analysis is with the analyst and not with the method.

However, constantly taking the RADs back to the process actors and replaying new versions is clearly a major part of the analyst's work. A feedback session is one way of doing this. It naturally involves a group of people who have some stake in the process. It is not unlike the group modelling session, except that the model is now being replayed to the people who originally had a hand in producing it or who, though not originally involved, play a part in the process.

Such a session can serve several purposes:

– It is a way of validating the models that have been constructed.

– It provides a way of letting the process actors work through and explore potential improvements for themselves.

– It can be an important part of change management in a radical or incremental change programme, by providing a communications channel from the change management team back to the organisation.

The RAD provides a vehicle for description, discussion, and decision in all situations.

We aim to keep old versions of our RADs as they develop. Small changes can be made to the current version ad lib, as the process is clarified or the perspective is clarified. But when a major change is made – a major realignment of perspective or a major restructuring when a new pattern is found – we tend to store the current version (call it version N) and to copy it to a new one ($N+1$) on which the major change is made. This saving of versions serves two purposes. The first is the pragmatic one that, even though a major change feels right today, in the cold light of tomorrow it might not seem such a good idea and it is nice to be able to return to a previous version without pain. The second purpose is that the record of how the RADs changes itself forms a useful teaching tool: you can see how the analysis went, went wrong, was put back on the right tracks, diverged, returned, and so on; all this information will help you to understand the modelling process itself and do it better next time.

Quality control of a RAD

As the modelling proceeds, we like to maintain tight quality control over the RAD: being tidy helps enormously, especially since you are showing the RADs to people constantly and there is great value in their seeing a consistent notation and usage in what you show them.

As in any language, good style helps communication. The following rules should be used from the beginning; it is better to get into the habit of using them even when sketching a RAD, rather than trying to "correct" the RAD once it has been captured.

– Label activities in verb-object format.

   For instance, *Prepare the monthly report, Classify client request,* or *Assemble business case for approval.*

– Identify the nature of an interaction by an appropriate verb.

   For instance, *Agree ..., Approve ...,* or *Delegate ...*

– Label interactions against the initiating role and word them from the point of view of that role.

   For instance, *Hand over monthly report, Receive classified client request,* or *Approve business case.*

   If an interaction has no initiating role put the label in the middle of the horizontal line.

– Label important states so that just the interesting part of the state is briefly described. Describe the state with a sentence in the present tense.

   For instance, *The monthly report has now been prepared, The client request is new and exceeds £10,000,* or *There is no approved business case.*

– Use the adverbs "optionally" or "possibly" in the name of an interaction or activity to avoid a simple but unimportant case refinement. Or include the condition under which the interaction or activity takes place in its name.

   For instance, *Optionally order new stock,* or *Optionally use the standby equipment.* Or *Order new stock if volume is less than agreed minimum.*

– Annotate the RAD with an italicised text block when you need to make a meta-comment about the accuracy of the RAD.

   For instance, *What happens now if the application is refused?, What happens to the documentation of a refused proposal?,* or *Regional Manager step omitted for simplicity.*

STEP 7: ANALYSE THE PROCESS

As I said at the start of this chapter, analysis is really not a step, more a continuous activity throughout the modelling. The very act of modelling a project will itself throw up all sorts of observations and ideas about the process: where it is going wrong, why it is going wrong, what has changed to make it ineffective, and how it could be improved. That said, there will be a point in the exercise where we will want to ask "what is this telling us?", and it is here that we can ask the sorts of questions covered in chapter 9.

STEP 8: RESPOND TO THE ANALYSIS

Our response to the modelling will if course depend on our aims of the modelling exercise:

- *Understanding.* It is generally enough that the group has modelled its process; understanding comes from the modelling work itself.
- *Communication.* The model can be drawn up as a work instruction in a Quality Manual or Procedures Manual as appropriate. A RAD can be accessed on-line by process actors given appropriate workstations and computing facilities.
- *Analysis for improvement and design.* The model can be used as a starting point for change, either radical or incremental, to the organisation or to the process
- *Enactment.* The model can be used as a starting point for the development of a computer-based infrastructure to support the process. This is a large topic that forms the development method *Basyl*. It is outside the immediate scope of this book, but deserves some coverage, which follows.

Process enactment

One of the reasons that we might be modelling a process is that we intend to support that process with some form of computer system, in particular one that explicitly supports workflow. Such a "process support system" will be built with some mix of three technologies:

- *workflow management* (WFM)
- *workgroup computing* (WGC)
- *traditional information systems* (IT).

In crude terms we can characterise the parts that each technology might play as follows. The overall process and the flow of activity is managed by the workflow system; the "hard" flows are computer supported. Within that framework, "softer", complex interaction are supported with workgroup computing facilities. And finally, the information needs of the individual are supported through traditional information systems and personal productivity tools, many of the former possibly being existing systems that are now to be integrated into the larger whole.

Life used to be rather simpler. There were databases and there were tools that we could use to give people access to the data in them. Our methods – SSADM, IE, Yourdon, whatever – were correspondingly simple. We would look at the entities, study their relationships, look at the data structures and the data flows, design the database and satisfy the information needs of the individual through forms and reports off the database.

Life is no longer so simple. We still have databases. We still have our data-oriented methods and database products. But there are now those two whole new types of product at our disposal – workflow management and workgroup computing – and a process support system may need to integrate all three types of product within the same architecture: workflow, workgroup, and database. This is a major technical challenge, and one in which our users will need to be even more heavily involved than before, because the two new technologies (what together we refer to as *Process Technology* or *PT*) are much more about supporting the way that people work, and work as a group, than we have ever been forced to consider.

Supporting future processes with a combination of PT and IT

Take the RAD in figure 10-3 as an example. It is the sort of RAD that might result from work to analyse and design a process that we want to support through some combination of Process and Information Technology (P+IT). We have taken it more or less to the point where we can start to decide which areas of the process can be supported with some sort of computer system, and – importantly – which areas are amenable to which sort of technology.

The RAD shows a simple process for handling a job application, and, in particular, it is a case process: the individual application forms a case which traverses the process.

Every applicant gets an acknowledgement in the form of a standard letter (a P11), some are turned down on the basis of the application form and receive a P12 letter, others get an interview but are turned down with a P33 letter, and successful applicants get a job offer in a P47 letter. The *Personnel Manager* handles all interactions with the *Job Applicant* except for the interview which is done by the *Requesting Manager*. If a job offer is to be made, the *Requesting Manager* and the *Finance Director* need to negotiate between them the terms of the offer, in particular the salary.

When the *Personnel Manager* receives an application from the *Job Applicant*, they put together a "case file" for this application. In a manual system that file could be a manilla envelope which is then passed round by hand from person to person with the case. In a "pure" IT system it could be a new record on a central database which can be accessed by anyone involved in handling the case. In a "pure" PT system it could be an electronic case folder which the underlying workflow management system could convey with the case on its travels round the workflow. We can suppose for now that we have chosen to use an underlying workflow management system to deal with the "hard" workflow, and that there is therefore such an "e-folder".

Before processing the application further, the *Personnel Manager* needs to check whether the *Job Applicant* has ever applied for a job with the company before, and, if they have, attaches the details of the previous application to the case folder. Here is a situation where we need to decide how to support the information needs of this role in this activity. It might well be that there is an existing database which holds such details and which therefore the *Personnel Manager* needs to interrogate through an existing legacy system. We can therefore expect them to use some standard forms to get at that database, and to transfer the results into the e-folder for the case.

The e-folder can now be forwarded to the *Requesting Manager* for further work. That interaction is a "hard" interaction and could be simply supported within the workflow management part of the system.

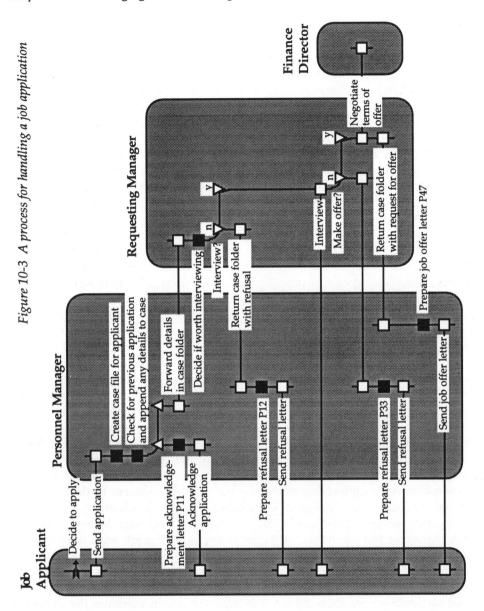

Figure 10-3 A process for handling a job application

Subsequently the *Personnel Manager* will interact with the *Job Applicant* in various ways: acknowledging the application, turning down on paperwork, getting in for interview, turning down after interview, and making a job offer. Each of these involves preparing a standard letter. Here is an opportunity for traditional IT personal productivity tools: in particular a word processor, perhaps used in conjunction with the e-folder to get applicant-related details automatically into the letter. In fact we can imagine an implementation of this system which does not require the intervention of the actual *Personnel Manager* at all: the system could prepare and despatch the letters automatically on their behalf.

If the *Requesting Manager* decides to make a job offer, the negotiation with the *Finance Director* needs to take place. One can imagine a whole range of ways in which the negotiation could be mediated. The two might get together every Monday morning and go through the current list of offers to be made, haggling over each. The *Requesting Manager* could call the *Finance Director* every time there is a job offer to be made to haggle there and then on the phone. Or there could be a system-mediated interaction supported with a workgroup computing style of solution – a "soft" interaction where something between free form and strong control is necessary; where the order in which things happens is not pre-determined, but where the parties need to be able to keep tabs on what is happening and work together with the support of the system.

The need for PT and IT integration

What have we seen with this simple example?

1   Some activities require the individual to have access to the right information at the right time and perhaps to update that information. Such information needs are traditionally supported by plumbing people into corporate or function-related databases – the domain of traditional database products.

2   Other activities require the individual to prepare material, perhaps drawing information from a variety of sources. Here we might integrate databases with personal productivity tools such as word processors and spreadsheets.

3   Some interactions and workflows are "hard", that is they are pre-defined and straightforward in nature, involving the transfer of materials. They are precisely the sort of thing that workflow management products are designed to support.

4   Other interaction are "soft"; that is, they cannot be pre-defined in detail but can still be mediated by workgroup computing products.

5   Other interactions still will remain the province of the face-to-face meeting and the phone call.

Building a system to support any business process is always going to mean more than just installing some workflow management product licences. The question is "what can be done and how can it be done?". What we have seen above shows that, in the general case, the developer needs to consider an *integrated* system pulling together traditional IT solutions, perhaps in the form of legacy systems, and the new PT solutions in some mix of workflow management and workgroup computing.

The question then becomes one of how to make the right mix.

The starting point for this must be some form of model that highlights the information needs of the individual *and* the process needs of the group: the flows and the interactions. STRIM provides that model in the form of a Role Activity Diagram.

Where do the poor old users come into this?

In the world of IT, we have relied to a large extent on the fact that the subject matter of a business – its *entities* – tend to remain pretty fixed. This was the basis for JSD's[2] initial real-world entity modelling phase and for SSADM's[3] concern with entities. And even the sorts of information we might want to hold about those entities remains reasonably constant over time. This is not to say that IT systems have always been a good fit to the business. But where they have been a poor fit, we might well suspect that it is more to do with the degree to which the IT system assumed (implicitly or explicitly) a business process that was different from the one that was actually there; as a result, people trying to do their jobs with the IT system found a clash between the way they wanted to work or were used to working and the way of working imposed/assumed by the IT system.

The problem can only get worse when we start to use PT. Whilst the business entities remain reasonably fixed, an organisation's process is much more liable to change: people change the way they do things quite often, either informally or formally. And this raises two important issues for anyone contemplating a process support system: how can we ensure we get the system to support the *right* process in the first place, and how will we make it responsive to changes in that process over time?

Getting the right model in the first place is clearly an important step. And getting the users involved in that step is going to be vital. This is a lesson we have learnt in IT; we must not forget it in PT, which is why user involvement in both process modelling and process design is a key feature of STRIM as we have seen in this chapter. A feature of workflow management and workgroup computing products is that they can make prototyping a reasonably affordable option, but that prototyping needs to be done against a well worked out and evolving process model – it cannot be left to chance and random experimentation.

The overall shape of Basyl

In broad terms we can expect the following simple translations of a RAD:

- Some black-box activities are potentially automatable in their entirety, for instance the archiving of a document.
- Some black-box activities will be carried out by human agents but with computer support. This could range from using a word processor to prepare a document which is to be the output of the activity, to using a management information system with its attendant databases, forms, window interfaces

---

[2] *System development*, M Jackson, Prentice Hall, Englewood Cliffs, 1983

[3] *SSADM version 4 manual*, NCC Blackwell, 1990

etc to determine which of two courses of action should be taken next in the process.

– Some interactions are potentially directly supportable by a workflow management system, with grams being documents or forms being sent to the following activity(s), for instance the transfer of a case folder from a Supervisor to a Clerk.

– Other interactions are potentially supportable by a workgroup computing system, for instance refinement of a business plan over a period of time between a group of managers.

To achieve this, the Basyl development approach involves, in general terms,

1   the preparation of a concrete RAD of each case process and each case management process

2   the preparation of abstract versions of these RADs

3   any necessary restructuring of roles in the case processes, resulting in RADs that have (new) concrete roles but retain the abstract interactions

4   any necessary restructuring of roles in the case management processes taking into account decisions about the concrete roles in the case processes from step 3, again resulting in RADs that have (new) concrete roles but retain the abstract interactions

5   the recombination of the RADs for the case and case management processes

6   examination of the information requirements of the (abstract) activities and interactions

7   reduction of the abstract interactions into concrete interactions that can make use of the facilities of the chosen workflow management product

8   restructuring of the (now concrete) workflows for efficiency

9   decisions about provision of information needs via transmission through the chosen workflow management product (via folders for instance), through plumbing into legacy or new information systems, and through non-computer-supported means such as paper, telephone, meetings etc.

A key point to note is that the approach starts from an analysis of the *process* flows. Once these have been established and any necessary re-engineering done, the *information* needs of the players can be looked at. Then and only then do we examine how the available technologies – process and information – can be brought in to satisfy them. Process precedes data.

From STRIM to traditional IT

Because STRIM gets to the heart of what is going on in a business, the models it produces are ideal starting points for the development of traditional IT systems. Each such development starts (hopefully) with some sort of analysis of the business and, thereby, where and how an IT system can help. But traditional approaches have not looked seriously at the *process*, something that we now have the machinery to do.

Traditional methods concentrate on the information needs of the individual and the way that information finds its way between individuals through "plumbing" between them and some database. To do that it uses techniques such as the entity model, the data flow model, and the entity life history model. The information collected during a STRIM analysis connects tidily into those needs:

- When we looked at the essential business entities in order to get at the case structure of a business, and modelled their relationships as a step to understanding the likely relationships between case processes, we had a sound starting point for the traditional entity or ER model.

- When we examined the inputs and outputs of activities and the flow of grams in interactions, we were building the basis for a data flow model of the process.

- When we follow the history of an entity (typically through the case process that deals with it), we can map out its state history – a RAD is a state machine with the state of entities forming part of the state.

In short, a RAD, having done its job in helping us understand, analyse, and re-design a process, also provides us with a starting point for the development of an information system to support aspects of that process.

From STRIM to object-oriented systemdevelopment

One of the central notions in STRIM, whose roots are in the formal object-oriented language SPML, is that of the *type* (or *class*) and the *instance*. We saw how everything on a RAD is actually a type, and that we can "run" a RAD by looking at how, when and what instances of types of roles, activities and interactions are created as the process runs.

It is not difficult to see then that there is likely to be a very strong link between a STRIM model of a business process and the sort of object-oriented analysis that starts the development of an object-oriented computer system to support that process. That link can be seen by, for instance, taking the concepts in James Martin's approach[4] and comparing them with those of SPML as outlined in the paper[5] published from the IPSE 2.5 project.

SPML exactly mirrors the object-oriented notions in Martin's book:

- "B is a component of A" (Martin) = "B is part of A" (SPML)
- "B is a subtype of A" (Martin) = "B *isa* A" (SPML)
- cardinality rules on types (Martin) = invariants of types (SPML)
- object states (Martin) = assertions about instances (SPML)
- events correspond to state changes in objects (Martin) = the same in SPML

---

[4] *Principles of object-oriented analysis and design*, J Martin, P T R Prentice Hall, Englewood Cliffs, 1993

[5] *Defining formal models of the software development process*, M A Ould & C Roberts, in *Software Engineering Environments*, ed P Brereton, Ellis Horwood, 1987

- events and triggers (Martin) = the same in SPML
- events invoke operations (Martin) = assertion instances trigger activities (SPML)
- operations change object states (Martin) = activities have post-conditions (SPML)
- operations are isolated from cause and effect considerations (Martin) = activities are isolated from their triggering conditions and post-conditions (SPML)
- one trigger can fire a number of operations (Martin) = the same in SPML
- hierarchical schemas of the form trigger–operation–event (Martin) = encapsulation in STRIM (with a corresponding representation in SPML)
- and so on.

The combination of STRIM and an object-oriented development approach therefore has great potential, as it marries the business emphasis of STRIM with the strong engineering emphasis of object-oriented design methods.

ESTIMATING A MODELLING PROJECT

How long will will a modelling project corresponding to steps 1 to 6 take? The answer is of course "it's as long as a piece of string". But we can parameterise an answer from our own experience:

- We will take about two days on the initial briefing, a sizeable proportion being spent with the process expert. In that time we will start to build up the sketch RADs and role lists as input to the group session in particular and the individual interviews in general.
- Each interview of a senior person will take one to two hours and will require the rest of the day to absorb, derive questions from and so on.
- At least one group modelling session should be planned. Half a day should be assumed. The rest of that day and perhaps the next will be needed to absorb what has been heard and to refine the model, the glossary and the list of issues.
- Further group modelling sessions might be needed, though they might take less time.
- Expect to do an individual interview of at least one representative from each role. More than half of those interviewed will be interviewed twice. Each interview will take up to two hours and will require the rest of the day for absorption.
- Feedback of the "final" models can be good for the group and preparation for this and the event itself can consume a further day. Overall, preparing and giving feedback across the organisation can add 20% to the overall project effort.

A constant problem throughout the project and one which can radically affect the effort that goes in and the benefit obtained is knowing when to stop. We saw in chapter 1 that there is no limit to our model: there is always more detail downwards, more process before where we have started and after where we have finished, and more to the sides of what we have drawn. The rule of thumb is "stop when you are not revealing anything useful". When the model isn't telling you any more, back off or up. But remember, high-level models often need understanding of the lower levels first, and can take longer to produce ("I'm sorry this letter is so long; I didn't have time to write a shorter one"). And *starting* at the top with a "high level" model and the "decomposing" the process into smaller and smaller pieces is, I believe, a dangerous approach since it encourages the idea that the process is itself neatly structured in this hierarchical way – when it probably isn't. Allow yourself to draw the overview model ... *last.*

And what elapsed period should be allowed for the modelling work? When you have added up the elapsed time on the above basis, be prepared to double it to allow for the difficulty of getting interviews and group sessions when you want them. As the model is being built, the analyst will often want to get to see someone at short notice to clarify an area before progress can be made and there can be a major problem in getting interviews scheduled into busy diaries. This will stretch the elapsed period, but is no bad thing. A bigger danger is a helter-skelter programme of interviews, so tightly packed that there is no time for the analyst to absorb, review, rework, and validate the model and their understanding before the next interview; useful input can be lost or forgotten unless they take out a suitable period for digestion.

Remember also when estimating that wherever possible two people should be involved in the interviewing of both individuals and groups.

The following are figures from our own experience. In one case, two analysts carried out 20 interviews producing ten RADs in 40 days of effort over a three-month period. In another, two analysts did 30 interviews producing seven RADs and 40-page report in 70 days of effort over a five-month period. In all cases a single RAD fitted onto an A3 sheet, albeit reduced to fit and remain legible. In a further case, three consultants carried out 30 interviews and prepared 90 RADs in 180 days of effort over a three month period. The variation in the figures is invariably due to differing degrees of complexity, and, perhaps most importantly, differing degrees to which the process has already been mapped and understood.

11

EPILOGUE

I have tried to present STRIM in a manner that will suggest to the analyst ways in which business processes can be pictured so that things are revealed, situations are understood, improvements can be seen, and work instructions drawn up. In developing STRIM we have aimed to provide not just a way of drawing pictures, but also some "machinery" which the analyst can use to do these things.

Pictures on their own can certainly help understanding, simply because they can be perceived in one glance. Their two-dimensionality, together with the structuring concepts that they use (the "role" in the case of STRIM), present information more immediately than text which must be read serially. But we should expect more from our modelling methods than just a way of drawing easily readable pictures. We want ways of *thinking about* processes. In STRIM they include

- the ability to distinguish case processes, case management processes, event-driven processes and so on
- the ability to build a case structure for the organisation
- the ability to model a process in both concrete and abstract terms and to move between the two
- the ability to model the complex relationships between separate processes
- the ability to model from different "heights" and to connect those models accurately
- the ability to model at different levels of detail and to move between them.

At the risk of repetition, let me say again that many models can be drawn of a process, all will be wrong, but some will be useful. There are models for all reasons. If you know the reason you have for process modelling, STRIM will provide you with the machinery to select an appropriate set of models and the expressiveness to construct them. In particular, it will help you understand that relationship between the process and the organisation which is central to re-engineering and improvement.

INDEX

abstract event, 166
abstract interaction, 165
abstract model, 164
abstract role, 166, 171
activation of processes, 110
activity, 37, 43, 165, 194
activity as a boundary, 88
activity type, 48
actor, 31
analysing a process, 8
area of responsibility, 14
as-is process, 170
Basyl, 12, 189
boundary of a process, 61, 74, 88, 124, 193
bundling, 115
Business Process Re-engineering (BPR), 3, 5
business rule, 13
calendar time, 62
carrier function, 120, 164
case management process, 129, 173, 189
case process, 125, 173, 189
case refinement, 49, 92
case structure, 175, 185, 189, 207
case worker, 172
case-case clashes, 174
cliché, 75
clock time, 62
cohesion of processes, 163
collapsing a model, 115, 155

combining threads, 59
commitment, 177
composition of processes, 97
concrete interaction, 121
concrete model, 164
concrete role, 170
concurrent threads, 56
conditional interactions, 82
conditional iteration, 51
core process, 2, 185
corrective action, 188
coupling of processes, 163
critical path, 153
critical path analysis, 154
customer of a process, 160, 185
cycle-driven process, 132, 185
data flow model, 207
database, 138, 144, 201
delegation ladder, 133
Deming, 178
discrete model, 155
document flow, 140
duration of an activity, 92
enacting a process, 9, 189, 201
encapsulating a process, 102
entity, 7, 16, 41, 138, 145, 194
entity life history, 145, 160, 207
entity model, 7, 143, 207
episode, 125
essence of a process, 167
essential business entity, 17, 138, 207
event-driven process, 132, 185
event, 61
external event, 62
external event as a boundary, 89
flow-wise improvement, 156
function, 162
functional group, 32
generalist, 157, 172
glossary of terms, 190
goal, 12, 39, 194
gram, 38, 45, 117, 120, 143
group modelling session, 190
Hammer, 179
incremental improvement, 4
information, 6, 16, 138

information flow, 159
information system, 201
input, 38
instance (of a type/class), 30, 69
interacting with systems, 84
interaction, 38, 45, 75, 109, 177, 194
interaction as a boundary, 89
internal event, 65
interviewing, 190, 195
IPSE 2.5, 10
ISO 9001, 8, 188
job title, 33
management hierarchy, 124
management process, 2, 185
materials flow, 139
meetings and their purpose, 198
object-oriented system, 207
organisational structure, 174
output, 38
parallelism, 156
part refinement, 56
part-interaction, 45
passage of time, 62
personal objective, 198
perspective (of a model), 187
pervasive function, 118, 164
Petri Net, 69
planning for success, 158
plan, 136
point-wise goal, 13
point-wise improvement, 153
post, 33
post-condition, 37, 48
pre-condition, 37
procedure, 197
process, 1, 3, 26, 68
process analysis, 188
process improvement, 188
process model, 3
process pattern, 93, 124
process support system, 189, 201
process technology, 3, 10, 201
quality control, 188
quality control of a RAD, 199
Quality Management System, 3, 4, 8
Quality Manual, 8, 93, 187, 197, 201

quantitative modelling, 194
radical change, 5
replicated part refinement, 58
resource consumption, 92
resources (of a role), 15, 91
responsibility, 167
restructuring roles, 161
RML, 11
role, 14, 29, 43, 161, 166, 194
Role Activity Diagram, 7, 42
role body, 15, 139
role forms, 35
role instance, 35
role instantiation, 45
role type, 48
Soft Systems, 18
specialist, 157, 172
SPML, 7, 11, 30
Standard Operating Procedure, 187
state, 39, 40, 47, 69
state diagram, 148
steady-state goal, 13
stopping condition, 37
STRIM, 6
sub-culture, 164
sub-state, 69
summary RAD, 123
support process, 2, 185
synchronisation, 45
System Dynamics, 155
terms of reference, 198
token, 48
TQM, 3, 4, 9
triggering condition, 37, 45, 48
type, 30, 69
understanding a process, 201
unit of work, 125
value chain, 152
Winograd, 134
workflow management, 3, 6, 10, 201
workgroup computing, 3, 10, 201

Postscript: Stykkisholmur is a beautiful village in the north-western fjord area of Iceland. It has a sense of humour: when I was there, in the shop you could buy car-stickers reading

London   Paris   New York   Stykkisholmur